THE
GHOSTS
OF
CHICAGO

JEN HATHY

About the Author

Adam Selzer is the author of *Your Neighborhood Gives Me the Creeps*, as well as the author of books and e-book shorts about haunted Chicago. He has also written several critically acclaimed novels, including *I Kissed a Zombie and I Liked It* and *How to Get Suspended and Influence People*. By night, he works as a historian specializing in places around Chicago that are supposed to be haunted. He runs approximately three hundred ghost tours per year.

Follow his research and podcasts at http://www .chicagounbelievable.com.

THE
GHOSTS
OF
CHICAGO

The Windy City's Most Famous Haunts

ADAM SELZER

Llewellyn Publications
Woodbury, Minnesota

FIRST EDITION
First Printing, 2013

Book design by Donna Burch
Cover art: iStockphoto.com/441164/Ken Babione, 11433755/Agnieszka Gaul
Cover design by Lisa Novak
Map of Chicago provided by the author

For a complete list of photograph credits, see page 337.

Llewellyn Publications is a registered trademark of Llewellyn Worldwide Ltd.

Library of Congress Cataloging-in-Publication Data
Selzer, Adam.
  The ghosts of Chicago : the windy city's most famous haunts / Adam Selzer. —
First edition.
      pages   cm
  Includes bibliographical references.
  ISBN 978-0-7387-3611-2
1. Ghosts—Illinois—Chicago. 2. Haunted places—Illinois—Chicago. I. Title.
  BF1472.U6S44 2013
  133.109773'11—dc23
                    2013014006

Llewellyn Worldwide Ltd. does not participate in, endorse, or have any authority or responsibility concerning private business transactions between our authors and the public.
  All mail addressed to the author is forwarded, but the publisher cannot, unless specifically instructed by the author, give out an address or phone number.
  Any Internet references contained in this work are current at publication time, but the publisher cannot guarantee that a specific location will continue to be maintained. Please refer to the publisher's website for links to authors' websites and other sources.

Llewellyn Publications
A Division of Llewellyn Worldwide Ltd.
2143 Wooddale Drive
Woodbury, MN 55125-2989
www.llewellyn.com

Printed in the United States of America

Other books and e-books by Adam Selzer

Sparks (writing as S. J. Adams)

Speaking Ill of the Dead: Jerks in Chicago History

Weird Chicago (co-author)

Your Neighborhood Gives Me the Creeps

The Curse of H. H. Holmes

Devil Babies

Inside the Murder Castle

The Resurrection Mary Files

Three Terrifying Tales from Chicago

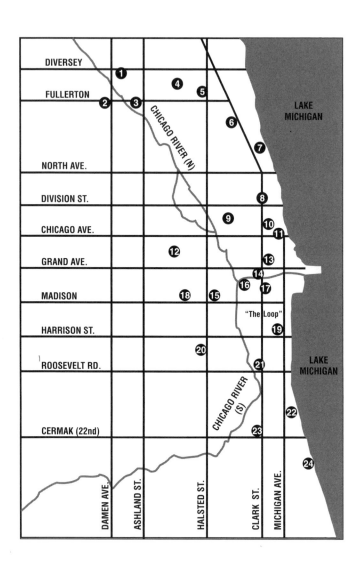

DIVERSEY

FULLERTON

CHICAGO RIVER (N)

LAKE
MICHIGAN

NORTH AVE.

DIVISION ST.

CHICAGO AVE.

GRAND AVE.

MADISON

"The Loop"

HARRISON ST.

ROOSEVELT RD.

LAKE
MICHIGAN

CERMAK (22nd)

CHICAGO RIVER (S)

DAMEN AVE.

ASHLAND ST.

HALSTED ST.

CLARK ST.

MICHIGAN AVE.

1. Luetgert Sausage Factory
2. Sobieski Street "body dump"
3. Liar's Club / Vampire of 1888
4. H. H. Holmes's North Side apartment site
5. Biograph Theater / Dillinger's Alley
6. St. Valentine's Day Massacre site
7. Tomb of Ira Couch
8. Site of tavern owned by widower of the "Italian Bride"
9. "Death Corner" in "Little Hell"
10. Bughouse Square
11. Early cemetery site
12. Adam's neighborhood
13. Gallows site
14. *Eastland* disaster site
15. Haymarket rally
16. Republican "Wigwam" / Mary Bregovy death site
17. Iroquois Theatre
18. Harpo Studios
19. Congress Hotel
20. Hull House
21. Dybbuk of Bunker Street
22. Battle of Fort Dearborn
23. Sam Cardinella's pool hall
24. Early cemetery site

Contents

Introduction

Everywhere you go in Chicago, history peeks through the cracks in the pavement, through the spaces in the crumbling mortar between the old bricks, and from old painted signs now buried behind a maze of pipes and cables.

Let's say you're walking west on Chicago Avenue from the Old Water Tower, and you decide to turn south on Clark Street to get to the Loop, the downtown area. You've just gone right through an area that was a graveyard in the 1830s, and in less than a block you'll see a neon sign that says "STOP AND DRINK," a relic of the days when Clark Street was one of the city's many "skid row" districts. Go another block and you'll be passing an upscale restaurant that inhabits the site of the McGovern Brothers' tavern, where mob boss Dean O'Banion got his start as a singing waiter in the 1910s, and which was a notoriously rough jazz bar in the 1950s.

Continue a couple of blocks beyond that, past the "Rock 'n' Roll McDonald's" (where you just might see a ghost-tours bus parked), and you'll pass the site where Tillie Wolf was stabbed in the face with a sharpened umbrella stick in 1898. Cross Grand Avenue, and you'll be passing the site of the C and O restaurant, where gangsters shot "Hoops-a-Daisy" Connors through the eye and the groin in 1929.

Look to your left as you cross Illinois Street and you'll see the fire station that was built over the site of the old prison. Near the site where Garage #3 sits now, around ninety men were hanged by the neck until dead between 1872 and 1927.

These same sort of stories could continue all the way to the Loop, and well beyond. Sometimes these stories have been lost to history, buried in microfilm reels in a newspaper archive and waiting for someone like me to dig them up and blog about them or talk about them between stops on ghost tours. Sometimes an old building survives, and sometimes you can even see a faded old sign on the side of it that has survived dozens of Chicago winters. Sometimes you can see old streetcar tracks in the potholes, or old bricks peeking out through the blacktop.

And sometimes, even if the building is gone and the story is forgotten, perhaps the ghosts are still there.

I've spent the last several years working as a ghost-tour guide in Chicago; in 2012 I ran just under three hundred of them. When people ask how I got interested in ghosts, they usually expect me to follow the formula common on ghost-hunting TV shows and say, "I never believed in any of this stuff, until one day ..."

However, for me, my interest in ghostlore probably just came from *Scooby-Doo* on Channel 9 when I was a kid, and getting the idea that driving around in a van solving mysteries was the *way to live*. Even now I'm quite skeptical about the paranormal and supernatural; I've only occasionally come across a ghost that turned out to be a guy in a mask, but I'd say that I can explain away most of what I've seen and heard on ghost investigations and tours.

Still, I'm not so skeptical that I don't allow myself to have fun with ghost investigations, and "most of" is not "all of." Now and then I'll see, hear, or even record something that forces me to take pause. And, anyway, tromping around in old buildings looking for ghosts is great fun, and now and then I even get to solve a mystery.

Though many of the ghost stories in this volume have been told before, sometimes again and again and again, I've tried to trace stories back to their roots, finding as many primary sources as possible, to determine what we *really* know and how we know it. Sometimes I've found that common ghost stories and legends have no basis in fact, and other times I'll find new bits of information, like the address where a famous ghost actually died or the name of some previously nameless murder victim whose ghost is said to haunt an old tavern. I've always been a stickler for getting at least the historical parts of my stories right—after all, this is the Internet age. People can fact-check me on their phones in the middle of tours!

Of course, finding firsthand sightings of even the most famous ghosts can be notoriously difficult. Sometimes we can get photos or equipment readings at local "hot spots," but it's hard to know whether those things in the pictures are truly ghosts or just optical illusions; I always tell people that there's no such thing as "good" ghost evidence—only "cool" ghost evidence. But I'm always surprised by just how many witnesses can be found if you look enough.

This book is essentially one of my tours in book form—with all the information and footnotes I don't have time to work into stories that I have to tell before the bus makes it to the next stop, and including a lot of places that I can hardly ever take a tour group because they're simply too far away. It's hardly intended to be the last word on the "true" story of any location, or whether any given place is truly haunted. We're finding out new stuff all the time.

There are a lot of mysteries still out there, waiting to be solved.

Adam Selzer
chicagounbelievable.com

Glossary and Tips

Here are some terms that will come up in this book. I make it a point not to get too into paranormal jargon, but there's no getting around these ghost-hunting terms (and names of my various tour bus drivers).

Abandoned graveyard: can refer to a graveyard that is no longer officially maintained (such as Bachelor's Grove) or a space that *used* to be a graveyard, but from which the bodies and tombstones have been removed. Examples include Lincoln Park and the area around the Water Tower on Chicago Avenue. They seldom, if ever, actually move *all* of the bodies.

Apparition: a ghost that looks like a person. This is the kind of ghost you normally see in movies, but actual sightings of these are rare.

Black Hand: a Chicago gang that specialized in extortion via the mail in the early 20th century (before Prohibition and laws that made extortion through the mail a federal crime).

Cold spot: a little localized area that's several degrees colder than it ought to be. These are sometimes said to be the result of a ghost.

EMF: electromagnetic field. Some believe that when a ghost is present, a jump will be detected on an EMF meter. Such meters have gotten ubiquitous on ghost hunts, but in a big city there's so much EMF going around in the environment to begin with that they're pretty much useless. Even in more lab-like conditions, I find the theory that EMF can indicate a ghost to be lacking. Like just about every other ghost-hunting gadget on the market, these meters best used when you consider them to be "for entertainment purposes only."

Era cues: the practice of playing music from the era in which a ghost lived in order to induce it to come out. I'm not sure it's totally effective, but it's more fun to try.

EVP: "electronic voice phenomena"—voices that aren't heard by the naked ear, but can show up in audio recordings. On the TV shows that really ham it up, the EVP guy is usually the one saying, "Are there any spirits who have a message for me?" I keep waiting for an episode where a spirit says, "Yes, I do! Your wife wants you to pick up milk on the way home." I joke about this sort of thing a lot, but now and then I do pick up a recording that knocks my socks off.

Fire insurance maps: detailed maps showing what kind of buildings were in which location. They can be very useful, though they were seldom drawn in the right year for any given area; for instance, the map of Sobieski Street, where H. H. Holmes may have had a body dump (see chapter 5), wasn't drawn until nearly twenty years after his death. Still, they're among the most reliable sources out there for the locations and addresses of historical buildings.

Flophouse: a place where drunks could sleep on the floor for a low price. Such places were once numerous in Chicago.

"Haunted feeling": the creeped-out feeling you sometimes get at "haunted" locations. Sort of like a ghostly "Spidey sense" or a "psychic intuition" felt even by those of us who have things growing in our fridge that are probably more psychic than we are. Of course, one has to keep in mind that many "natural" environmental factors can cause this feeling, such as low-frequency noise or a lot of electromagnetic activity—those things can mess with your head. However, I get this feeling on certain nights at my regular tour stops, but not on others.

Hector: the bus driver for many of my first tours and co-host of the Chicago Unbelievable podcast.

Intelligent haunting: the kind of ghost that seems to be aware that it's there and able to communicate, respond to stimuli, and so on.

Ken: one of my two usual drivers today. Ken is the only driver I've actually seen threaten an aggressive panhandler with a baseball bat.

Matrixing: a term used to describe our brain's tendency to see faces in random visual noise (such as when one sees a facelike shape in foliage or smoke).

Olfactory apparition: the kind of ghost you smell, as when people say they can still smell Grandpa's pipe tobacco or that specific mix of perfume and vodka that Grandma always smelled like.

Orb: a little ball of light that shows up in photos (through rarely seen with the naked eye). There is almost *always* a logical explanation for them, and few ghost hunters take them seriously anymore; in fact, making a big deal about them can cost you a lot of credibility among ghost hunters these days. Hector once aptly described them as a "parlor trick." If you tell a group of people that ghosts appear as little white balls before they get out and take pictures of a dark outdoor area, then there's about an 80 percent chance at least one person will get pictures of them. It's a great way to get tour groups excited, but I almost never mention them on tours anymore. I do, however, try not to get too adamant about them when people on the tours are having fun with them. It just doesn't seem polite to spoil their fun. However, I sure don't want people going online and saying, "Adam Selzer says these are ghosts."

Poltergeist: a mischief-making ghost. These ghosts aren't usually seen or heard directly but make their presence known by having objects fly across the room, making lights flicker, etc. Some researchers have noted that houses with such activity are often inhabited by adolescent girls and speculate that the activity is really a result of some sort of unconscious telekinesis on their part.

Portal: an invisible gateway to another realm. Some are said to exist in various locations around Chicago, but I've never been sucked into the netherworld even once myself.

Like "Indian burial grounds," portals are usually a story people use to explain a place that seems to be haunted, but for which no historical story can be found. The garden next to Hull House is said to be both a portal *and* an Indian burial ground. What kind of realm they're portals *to* (the netherworld? Another dimension? Toledo?) is seldom part of the story.

Psychic imprint: mental energy that can theoretically be left behind in an area following feelings of intense emotion (e.g., sudden, traumatic death). The term is a bit "new agey" for my taste, but it's a simple phrase that people can easily understand. The idea that leftover "energy" is perceived by the living as ghosts has been going around for over a century. It's still considered pseudo-science, but it might not be forever; I know of one guy who says we could reproduce the effect using a volunteer murder victim and a particle accelerator.

The term *energy* gets thrown around a lot in ghost-hunting circles, but it's probably not the best term to use, since "energy" isn't the kind of object you can capture in a jar. I've been using "brainwaves" instead, lately. I'd go with "vibrations," but using that word tends to make people start singing Bob Marley songs.

Residual ghost: a ghost that is not so much a conscious entity as an echo—a video recording of an event playing over and over, and that in some cases we might be able to perceive. To some ghost hunters, these don't count. Others think that these sorts of ghosts account for *all* hauntings.

Richard Crowe: Chicago's original professional ghost hunter, and basically the inventor of the modern ghost tour;

he ran the first such tours in the city in the early 1970s and was quoted in pretty much every article about ghosts in the Chicago press for years. He largely stopped doing any investigations decades ago, but many notable ghost stories in town survive largely because he continued promoting them through tours and media appearances. We saved him a seat on our bus for several weeks after his death in 2012, and even now I keep expecting to see him on the route one night.

Shadow person: a rather cartoonish name for ghosts that appear as vague shadows, often seen moving quickly through a location. One guy on my team prefers the term *soft shapes*, which is a better description of them, if a bit less dramatic. The term *shadow person* also suggests a dark personality that's hard to assign to something you normally just see for a split second out of the corner of your eye or in a photo.

Simulacra: Something that looks like something else—such as when a cloud looks like Van Gogh playing a banjo, or when a reflection of one's ear in a window looks like a guy in a hooded robe. Similar to matrixing.

Spirit box: a device that scans radio frequencies and picks up random pieces of sound. Some say that "spirits" can use these to communicate with us. They're fun to play with, but, to me, saying that ghosts use radio sounds to communicate is about the same as saying they appear by making smears in windows look humanesque. Like many ghost-hunting gadgets, I find them fun to play with, but you have to take everything you get on them with a grain of salt.

Ursula: my boss in the ghost tour biz, Ursula Bielski, whose
Chicago Haunts books are probably the best works on the
ghostlore and mythology of the city.

Wendy: one of my current drivers. Tough enough that I
sometimes joke that she got the job by killing the previous
driver.

Willy: my other original driver. Willy was employee of the
month every month for three solid years at a company I
used to own.

A Few Things Every Ghost Hunter Should Know

Most ghost-hunting gear is for entertainment purposes only.
No one has yet developed a gadget that will actually tell you
if there's a ghost in the room. There are gadgets that will tell
you if there's a change in the electromagnetic field, the ion
count, the temperature, or what-have-you, but there's really
no way to tell what's *causing* that change in most cases. With
almost all equipment readings, including audio and photo
evidence, you have to use your imagination a bit to make
yourself think it's a ghost. I tend to prefer sightings that can
be made with the naked eye or ear. As I often say, there is no
"good" ghost evidence, only "cool" ghost evidence.

No one has this all figured out yet.
There are no real rules here—there's no one theory that
would explain every ghost. Often you'll hear guys like me
going on about ghosts being "spirits" of people calling out
to be remembered or coming back to take care of unfinished business, or of souls in purgatory, or of leftover mental energy. This is really just us talking out of our asses. No

one theory covers every kind of ghost, and ghosts never seem to sit around discussing physics.

On a similar note, there are no real "rules" for how to look for ghosts. Some people insist on using only film cameras and analog audio recording, but, again, I've seen cool pictures taken with all kinds of gear.

It usually turns out to be something else.

You can't get all upset when it turns out that the story you've heard behind a supposedly haunted place turns out not to be true, or if the photo that appears to show a ghostly form turns out to be a smear on the window or an outright hoax. This is *usually* what these things turn out to be. Not always, but usually. Sometimes I'm almost loath to analyze things too closely—when you get a really cool shot, why ruin it?

Of course, there *are* people out there who say that ghosts let us know they're here by making dust particles appear in photos, or by making smears on the window or shapes in foliage look like faces. And how can I argue with it? Now and then I do see a "face in waves" shot that looks so detailed that it's hard to brush it off as an optical illusion.

A Few Things That Every Chicago Researcher Should Know

Most buildings were renumbered and given new addresses in 1909.

Any time you see an address published for a building in the 1800s (such as H. H. Holmes's "Murder Castle"), you'll be going to the wrong place if you go to that address now. Many street names have changed as well. There's a renumbering guide that was printed in 1909 that can be very helpful, but it's not 100 percent reliable either. Cross-checking with fire insurance maps, when possible, is usually a wise idea.

Be careful with neighborhood names.

One enduring source of confusion for researchers is that neighborhood names change now and then, and sometimes the same name comes up more than once. There were a couple of places called Smoky Hollow, for instance. Even today, what neighborhood a building is said to be in can depend on how much a landlord wants to charge for rent.

"Indian burial ground" stories are probably false, but ...

As one of my colleagues once put it, "Try finding a place where a Pottawatomie Indian *wasn't* buried around here." Indeed, there are dozens of abandoned or "lost" cemeteries around town, and bodies are buried all over the place. City workers run across them occasionally while digging.

Official records won't always answer all the questions.

When we dig up records on properties, they tend to make the story even *more* confusing. Fudged and incomplete records are very common. This is no excuse not to look them up, though.

Basements may not have always been basements.

The street grade in the city has been raised a couple of times over the years. Often, the level that is now the basement (or "garden level") was originally the first floor.

Variant last-name spellings are common.

Looking up census records, military records, and the like can give you a lot of a good clues, but many names were spelled a variety of ways. For instance, whether gang leader/gallows victim Sam Cardinella's last name was Cardinella or Cardinelli or Cardinale varies from record to record. Many families slowly "Americanized" their last names over the course of a few generations.

Surviving relatives are not always reliable sources.

It's great when you can find a descendant of someone you're researching, but after a few generations they rarely have much more reliable information than anyone else, particularly if they were born a few decades after the person in question or only would have known them as toddlers.

Newspapers aren't always reliable sources either—but they're often the only *source for stories.*

Many of the stories of murders, hangings, and other events were only ever told in newspapers. Reporters, however, were not shy about printing hearsay or exaggeration in the old days, and some entire papers are totally unreliable. With stories that were published in multiple local papers, you can sort of triangulate between the various accounts and figure out which parts were true reasonably well.

CHAPTER 1

The Iroquois Theatre

On this site—the current location of the Oriental The-
atre, at 24 W. Randolph Street—one of the deadliest fires
in United States history occurred. The "Alley of Death
and Mutilation" is the alley between Dearborn and State
Streets, half a block below Lake Street.

Just east of Randolph Street, between State and Dearborn, stretches Couch Place, which is more of an alley than a street, used primarily for stagehands to load equipment into the Oriental Theatre, and for students at nearby Columbia College to smoke. It's a nice place, particularly following a recent renovation that added lighting. But in one of their *very* classiest moves, the *Chicago Tribune* once called it "the Alley of Death and Mutilation." It's usually the first stop on my tours.

I'll start the story when the bus reaches State Street, pointing out that while State is now one of the nicer destinations in town, it wasn't always that way. A few generations ago, the stretch of State a few blocks south of Lake was known as "Whiskey Row," and the next mile south was known as "Satan's Mile." At the end of Satan's Mile was the levee district, where things got *really* rough. The bars there were known by such colorful names as the Bucket of Blood and Bed Bug Row. People who were robbed on State would seldom report it, since that would involve admitting that they'd been on State Street in the first place. On at least one occasion, a judge dismissed a man's case on the grounds that he got what he deserved for being there.

As of the turn of the 20th century, even after the triumph we'd enjoyed with the World's Fair in 1893, that was still pretty much the way Chicago was thought of by much of the country (and it's still how many suburbanites think of downtown). But the city's cultural profile was certainly rising; a number of new theaters were built in the early 1900s, perhaps most notably the ill-fated Iroquois, which stood on Randolph between State and Dearborn in the exact footprint where the Oriental Theatre now stands.

Ground for the Iroquois was broken in July of 1903, and it was open in time for the holiday season in November. As anyone who lives in the city will tell you, it normally takes at least a year and a half to get a pothole filled around here, so it's hard to imagine that they could get a gorgeous, elaborately designed theater built in only three and a half months without cutting an awful lot of corners.

And cut they were. Even though the law already required that all exit doors open out toward the street, it was easier and cheaper to have them open in toward the lobby (so the hinges would be on the inside and wouldn't be exposed to would-be burglars who could easily unscrew the doors if they were accessible from the street). A sprinkler system was never installed. Lots of things that were *supposed* to be fireproof weren't. Exit signs were not lit.

The Iroquois Theatre as it was shown in the souvenir programs.

But according to the paperwork, the building was up to code. Most likely, the man in charge of building it had gone to City Hall with a stack of fifty-dollar bills and collected all the signatures he needed, which was how most buildings in Chicago were built in those days. The theater may have been a death trap, but it wasn't *more* of a death trap than most other theaters in town. Most of the rest of them were ignoring the rule about doors opening outward as well, and papers had been known to run lists of all the "death trap" theaters that were ignoring much of the fire code.

But when the Iroquois Theatre opened in November 1903, playbills actually advertised it as "absolutely fireproof." In hindsight, it seems as though they were tempting fate from the start.

The gilded, marble theater itself *was* reasonably fireproof, but the things they put inside it certainly weren't. People in winter clothes, for one, are pretty flammable. Canvas scenery and oil-based paints are known to burn as well, not to mention the hemp-stuffed seats.

The first show booked to run in the theater was *Mr. Blue Beard* (often, from day one, mistakenly referred to as *"Mr. Blue Beard Jr."*), a musical comedy revue starring a famous comedian of the day named Eddie Foy and featuring such immortal songs as "Come and Buy Our Luscious Fruits," "Oriental Slaves Are We," and "A Most Unpopular Potentate." None of these had anything to do with the plot, which, to the extent that the show had one at all, was about a guy who kills his wives and hangs them up on meat hooks in his closet.

This, for the record, was a children's Christmas show.

It was, by all accounts, a really stupid show—but it was considered perfectly acceptable family entertainment, and like most big stage musicals of the day, it was a tremendous spectacle, featuring a cast of hundreds and elaborate sets and costumes, with dancers, aerialists, and Eddie Foy running around in a dress singing a song called "Hamlet Was a Melancholy Dane." It may have been dumb, but it was still a treat to watch, and pretty much standard theatrical entertainment for its time. Ticket sales were brisk.

For the matinée on December 30, about two thousand tickets were sold—even though the theater only held about 1,700. Hundreds of spectators had no seat of their own and had to resort to standing at the back of the balcony. But if anyone *did* complain, no one wrote it down. The first act went off without a hitch and most everyone, by all accounts, was having a good time. There *were* stories about people who remember walking in and thinking, "This place is a death trap," but I've never run across an anecdote of someone saying, "I was just whispering to the person next to me that the show really sucked cheese..." though this seems to have been the opinion of most critics who had reviewed it.

Midway through the second act, Eddie Foy noticed that the orchestra had stopped during what was supposed to be a double-octet dance number called "Let Us Swear It by the Pale Moonlight." By most accounts, a calcium light (which was providing the pale moonlight) had arced and sent a couple of sparks into a muslin drape on the wall, causing it to catch fire.[1]

According to some accounts, the drape had caught fire at least once before, and generally just burned itself out when the flame hit the top of the drape. But this time the flames started to catch on the scenery that was being stored

---

1. This is usually listed as the cause of the blaze, though some say it wasn't really the light, and instead blame sparks from the massive electrical circuit board beside the stage (which, in surviving photos, looks about as safe as your average powder keg).

in the rafters—as many as 280 pieces by some counts, mostly made of canvas and painted with oil-based paint. No sprinkler system had ever been installed.

Foy (who had been raised in Chicago and was a boy during the Great Fire three decades before) interrupted the show and told people to remain calm and stay in their seats—he knew that a stampede toward the doors could be deadlier than any fire. When it became clear that the fire wasn't just going to burn itself out, he begged them not to get excited, but to leave the theater slowly and in an orderly fashion while stagehands lowered down a special fireproof curtain to keep them safe.

"Remember," he may have told the audience, "this building is absolutely fireproof." He even stayed on stage—long after it was safe for him to do so—and tried singing a song to keep them calm.

But as a giant piece of scenery crashed to the stage in a fiery heap, the cast and crew all seem to have said something along the lines of "Screw this, I'm outta here." They made a beeline for the backstage door—which was locked. As some of the crew worked to open it, others worked to lower the fire curtain, the giant asbestos curtain that could be lowered between the stage and audience to keep fires from spreading. Every theater was required by law to have one of those.

There were a couple of things they didn't realize, though.

One is that they'd cut some corners with the fire curtain. Every theater was required to have an asbestos curtain, but the Iroquois was using one made from a blend of asbestos, cotton, and wood pulp. Records reported by the *Tribune* indicate that this saved them around $56—the material was not only cheaper than the pure stuff, but it also needed to be replaced less frequently. However, cost-effective though it may have been, it was pretty much useless against a fire. It burned to ashes almost instantly.

The fire curtain might have at least held the flames in check long enough for people to escape, though, if it had been lowered properly. But a stray light rig blocked its path and prevented it from forming a proper shield between the stage and the audience, and the flames soon made their way to the gas tanks, at which point all hell broke loose.

Another thing that Foy and the crew probably didn't realize is that, since it had been snowing off and on for some time, the ventilation on the roof had been nailed shut. This kept the snow from getting in, but it also turned the whole building into one big chimney. When the backstage door was opened, it created a backdraft that caught on the flames onstage, turning them into what people later described as a "balloon of fire," a "globe of fire," or a "cyclone of fire"—a massive fireball that shot out under the partially lowered curtain and flew over Eddie Foy's head and into the audience, and then into the balcony, where several hapless people were instantly burned to death.

Now, imagine that you're sitting in this theater. There's a famous man in a dress singing a song and telling you to be calm, but you just saw a *massive fireball* shoot out at you. Some people are probably already dead. Naturally, you panic and run for one of the many fire exits.

But there's a problem—you didn't realize that the owner, who was always concerned that poor people would sneak in through those exits to see the show for free, was keeping most of the fire exits locked. They could be unlocked from the inside, but not easily—it was a fancy new kind of "French" lock that people had trouble figuring out, especially in a crowded, unlit room. Exits were supposed to be lighted, but the owners had felt that exit lights were distracting when a show was in progress, so the only light was the light from the blazing fire.

So imagine: you push your way to a fire exit, and it's sealed shut. With all the pushing, no one can get enough space to figure out the locking mechanism. By the light of the fire, you can see that everyone else is having the same problem, and you figure that your only way out is to get through the front doors onto Randolph Street. You start to run, and (because this is just a story) you get into the hallway ahead of everyone else. You rush out the exit, down the hall, across the promenade, into the lobby, thinking, *If I can just get through those doors, I'm safe!*

Then you get your hand against the door, and you realize you've made a huge mistake. You expected the doors to open *out*, toward the street, as they had been required by law to do for a couple of decades in Chicago, but these ones actually opened *in*, toward the lobby (not to mention the fact that, by most accounts, they were also locked). So instead of crashing through the doors, you simply crash *into* them, and are immediately crushed against them by all the people crashing behind you.

Some people were trampled beyond recognition.

And things were no better up on the balcony.

Up there, there was only one hallway that led back down below, and the owner had blocked *that* off with a metal accordion gate to keep the people in the cheap seats from sneaking down into the better ones. Another stairway appeared to lead to an exit, but really only led to a bathroom door, against which many bodies were soon piled. A few tried to jump off the balcony to get below, and presumably all died in the process—I've never found an anecdote about anyone escaping like that successfully.

Some say that the fire escapes had not been built yet, and drawings of the alley do appear to show a couple of doorways to nowhere, but those are probably actually windows. Contemporary accounts don't seem to mention anyone falling out of these doors, but the fire escapes that *were* in place were basically useless; those that were built seem to have been designed to handle a small handful of people moving in an orderly fashion, not teeming throngs in a panic (which is what you should probably expect when there's a fire in a crowded theater), and the stairs got jammed when people burned to death halfway down. The rush onto the galleries and through the windows pushed as many as two hundred people over the rails and into the alley below, where the pile of bodies is said to have been several feet high. Some were saved only by having dead bodies break their fall.

Now, the building on the other side of the alley was a part of Northwestern University that had been built into the old Tremont House hotel at the time. When the people in the building saw all the people falling down into the alley, there were able to extend a ladder across from their window to the fire exit so that people could try to crawl their way across to the next building. It was a good idea but didn't work out so well—the window was iced over, the ladder was fairly rickety, and when you get several people crowding onto a ladder like that at once, it's impossible to hold it steady. A couple of people (perhaps as many as thirty) were saved, but many more probably fell to their deaths. There were a couple of accounts of people escaping into the alley only to be killed by the people falling from the ladder above.

The Iroquois Theatre as it appeared at the time of the fire.

It's difficult today to determine the exact body count from the fire—the newspapers all had different figures. There's a list of around six hundred victims that we know of who died on the scene or of their wounds, but many bodies were probably claimed by the families before they could ever be counted. Some estimate that over a thousand people—mostly women and children—perished.

And the first people to arrive on the scene were not all firefighters or rescue workers; many were of a particular type of criminal class known as "ghouls." The fire hadn't even stopped burning before the ghouls raced in and began yanking necklaces off necks, shimmying rings off fingers, and pulling money out of pockets. A regional paper recounted the story of a man who was caught cutting a woman's finger off to get her ring, and was pinned by a crowd who cut his hand off at the wrist and threw it into the smoldering rubble, where it was found a couple of weeks later. This sounds like hearsay, but in those desperate hours after the fire broke out, anything could have happened.

One common story is that the nearby Thompson's Restaurant was used as a morgue, and the owner was caught stealing the gold fillings out of the bodies' teeth. This story isn't true, but it seems to have *some* basis in fact; one man, Louis Witz, *was* convicted of stealing $200 and a watch from a body at Thompson's, making him just about the only man convicted of wrongdoing in connection with the fire.

Many bodies were taken to a temporary hospital set up across the corner in Marshall Field's, or to a morgue at the nearby C. H. Jordan's Saloon. Others were laid out in the cold, bloody alley, the one that the *Tribune* called "the Alley of Death and Mutilation," and which later accounts shortened to "Death Alley."

The next day, the citizens of Chicago were out for blood. Soon the mayor had been indicted, along with the theater owner, the theater manager, and the building inspector. The lawsuits dragged on for some time, but nothing came of them. Eventually, everyone got off on technicalities—courts ruled that based on the way the fire-code laws were written, they were not enforceable *laws*, but *guidelines*. Suggestions. A judge ruled that William K. Davis, the owner, was *morally* responsible for what happened, but that he couldn't be held *legally* responsible.

Only months later, the theater was briefly reopened under the name Hyde and Behmann's Music Hall. It then became the Colonial Theatre in 1905, and stayed that way until the 1920s, when it was torn down to make way for the new Oriental Theatre, which is there to this day.

All that remains of the original theater is a single sub-basement-level foundation wall, but ghost sightings began almost immediately after the fire and continue even in the new theater. Employees at the Oriental are not allowed to talk about this sort of thing (they aren't even supposed to talk about the fire unless someone asks about it), but when one spends as much time in the alley as I do, one hears stories from employees who come out for smoke breaks fairly often.

According to many, when one is in the theater after hours, standing on the stage, it's not unusual to see what are known as "soft shapes" (the ghost-hunting TV shows would call them "shadow people") moving through the auditorium—almost invariably racing from the stage area to the area where the exits would have been, as though these were the shadows of people running for their life. I've sometimes seen just that sort of thing out of the corner of my eye in the alley as well.

One day, during rehearsals for *Wicked* in 2004, all of the doors in the building suddenly flew open. An electronic command can *close* the doors, but not open them.

Other times, actors have been sure they saw people sitting in the balcony, watching rehearsals. When security arrives to shoo them out, they find that the doors are locked, and no one is there. Ana Gasteyer, who starred in *Wicked* there, went on the TV show *Celebrity Ghost Stories* and said that she encountered the ghost of a woman and her two children dressed in outfits that appeared to come from 1903 (though they were dressed more like Pilgrims in the reenactments).

Other employees say that they've occasionally heard the sound of screams piercing the air in the middle of the night, and many have reported the ghost of a little girl who manifests in an odd way—by flushing a backstage toilet, then giggling.

There have been many stories over the years about a ghostly woman in a tutu, presumed to be Nellie Reed, a trapeze artist who was one of only a couple of performers killed in the fire (most modern sources say she was suspended above the stage when the fireball shot through, but contemporary accounts say she was backstage and died of smoke inhalation). I thought I saw her silhouette in the alley a few times, but she seems to be one of those ghosts that's better known among ghost hunters than she is among people who work in the building.

Ghosts in the Alley

Since ghost tours are generally unable to bring groups into the building, they've typically focused on the alley behind it. It is often said to be one giant "cold spot"—a good ten degrees cooler than any other part of the city. Police officers have told me that they take breaks in the alley during the summer because it will be cooler than it is in other alleys. Another cop (who may have been joking) said he'd felt a rush of heat, like a fireball had flown through, while patrolling the alley. The "shadows" spoken of inside the building are sometimes seen in the alley as well, and ghostly-looking photographs in the alley are not uncommon.

If you look at ghost pictures online, you're probably familiar with the sorts of pictures people hold up as ghost photos—weird blobs of light (orbs), mists, strange shapes in bricks/wood/foliage, mysterious faces, even the occasional humanesque form. I have seen all of those sorts of pictures in the alley, from vague shadows and orbs (which serious ghost hunters tend to ignore) all the way up to full-body specters who have a head but no face.

Running a tour in the alley, 2009.

Once a person even snapped a photo that seemed to show a pants leg floating in mid-air, right near the spot where the bodies would have fallen; my standard joke there is that the scariest part of that picture is the fact that, if the ghost's leg was right in front of my chest, then their butt must have been right in my face. Phantom pants are not exactly common, but phantom clothing in the alley is not unheard of; lately there have been a few shots of what appears to be a green dress hovering in the air.

More Nearby Ghosts

The ghosts of the fire seem to stretch beyond the boundaries of the original theater—it must be remembered that many people died of their wounds at the makeshift hospitals and morgues set up in every available adjacent space. According to rumor, some employees at the Garret's Popcorn next door to the theater find their bathroom so spooky that they hike over to the nearby McDonald's when they have to go. Employees at the Borders bookstore that once stood two doors down told me that one of their own bathrooms was notably spooky as well.

In addition to this, it should be remembered that the fire victims certainly weren't the only people who ever died in the area. In fact, female employees occasionally tell me stories of the ghost of a very gruff man haunting the basement level, where they hear his voice cussing them out. This doesn't seem like a fire victim (few of whom were men), so it could go back to *before* the days of the theater; back in the days when the neighborhood was called Hairtrigger Block, the site where the theater stands was occupied by an outfit called Seneca Wright's saloon.

One night in 1866, a notable neighborhood gambler named George Trussel was in the saloon when Mollie, his on-again-off-again girlfriend/wife, came in and demanded that he take her out for a night on the town. He tried to shove her back out the door, and she responded by shooting him three times. He stumbled out back to the stables (right about where the alley would be now) and bled to death while Mollie cried for him at the police station. Every now and then I've had people shout, "Look out, George! Here comes Mollie!" while we're in the alley, just to see if anything happens. He's the best guess anyone can make for the identity of the unpleasant man in the basement.

One Ongoing Myth

It's frequently stated that John Wayne Gacy met up with many of his victims in the Trailways bus station on Dearborn and drove them away in a van he had parked in the alley. The reality is that he met one victim—just one—in the Greyhound station that stood on the other side of Dearborn from the alley, where the Goodman Theatre is now. There's nothing to link him to the alley; his main hangout downtown was at Bughouse Square (see chapter 25).

One Enduring Mystery: The Lost Time Capsule

When the Iroquois was built, a "time capsule" was buried in a cornerstone. No one seems to know whatever happened to it.

If You Go

The theater is not open to ghost hunters, but the alley is almost always available to the public. If you buy a ticket to a show or arrange to take a tour of the theater itself, you can do a little bit of stealth ghost hunting, and employees may break ranks and share stories with you—but don't expect much access. Audio recording and EMF detection in the alley are basically useless, since there's so much else going on in the environment. Cameras and the naked eye are the best tools you can use.

It's quieted down somewhat since 2007, when they cleaned the alley up. Perhaps this just made it less spooky, and therefore less likely to play tricks on the mind.

Also: watch out for Arnold Palmer. From the first time I began taking tours into the alley, some odd graffiti in the alley has read, "Arnold Palmer Sells Drugs Here."

CHAPTER 2

Gallows Ghosts

For most city hangings, the gallows were set up in a prison that stood at the current location of the fire station at Dearborn and Illinois, in between the Loop and the Magnificent Mile, though a few other hangings were held at various locations in the city. Rumor has it that suspected looters were hanged from every available lamppost during the Great Fire of 1871, but these stories may be mythical.

Riding the CTA buses can be an adventure, and for some reason, the #9 buses that run up and down Ashland Street tend to be particularly full of weirdos. I hardly ever get on the bus without someone next to me telling me a gross bathroom story, or talking me through the details about some conspiracy theory involving Hitler, or trying to sell me random objects like gold necklaces, fancy cologne, or laser-disc copies of *Mary Poppins*. This is part of the fun of living in the city.

Still, there's something particularly disturbing about the drop you feel when that bus hits a large pothole between Polk and Taylor. It was on this spot that a couple of public hangings were held in the 1840s, and it's hard not to think to yourself that you've just made the same drop that the convicts did.

Chicago was still a young city when public executions were banned in Illinois, but a few of them took place in town before the ban. The first, the hanging of John Stone for the murder of Lucretia Thompson, was held in 1840 on the dunes near where 26th Street is now, near the place that would soon be set aside for one of the city's first two official burial grounds. Nearby this site would be the current home of Mc-Cormick Place, which is not generally listed among haunted places in Chicago, though one employee tells me that the East Building is so spooky that he won't go in there.

The next couple of public hangings were held in the middle of Reuben Street (now Ashland), between Polk and Taylor Streets. This would probably have continued to be the hanging site if the state hadn't banned public executions, forcing them to be held within the confines of the jail. The first few "private" ones were held in the old prison and courthouse at Clark and Washington, including one disastrous execution in which the rope broke, sending the convict, Michael MacNamee, several feet down to the floor, where he landed on his head. He was a bit dizzy and quite likely suffered a concussion from the fall, but he was immediately taken back up to the scaffold and hanged properly.

That old jail was still standing amidst the rubble after the Great Fire in 1871, and was kept in service while a new one was planned and built. The criminal court was moved to what is now Hubbard Street, just west of Dearborn Street. A jail building was built behind it, fronting Illinois Street, and another jail was later added adjacent to that one at the corner of Illinois and Dearborn. A fire station stands on the spot today; the jail and criminal court are now on the Southwest Side.

The fire station at Illinois and Dearborn marks the site of the old jail, where around ninety men were hanged by the neck until dead.

But that "new" courthouse, rebuilt in the 1890s, is still there on Hubbard, and is sometimes said to be haunted itself. It's just offices now, but it still contains a number of old holding cells and large vault doors. When I did a late-night ghost hunt there, a couple of people working late shifts told me stories about ghostly women in white (which usually makes me think they're just telling me what they think I want to hear), or of hearing the sound of typewriters in the middle of the night.

My investigation there was not exactly a serious one (it was the kind where the guy who got us access to the building showed up with a six pack), but nothing there gave me the impression it was haunted.

The jail and gallows site behind the courthouse may be another story, though.

Ghosts of the Old Jail

Numerous books and tours have pinpointed the alley between the court building and the jail as the location where criminals were hanged, but this isn't quite accurate. The misconception probably springs from scenes in the movies *His Girl Friday* and *The Front Page* in which reporters in the court building look out the window at workmen building the gallows in the alley below. The gallows *were* sometimes set up in the alley, but only to hang sandbags in order to test the mechanisms and get the "spring" out of the rope (when you hang someone, you want them to drop and stay dropped, not bounce back up and down). For the actual executions, the scaffold would be rebuilt within the walls of the "old jail." If you go by the fire station today, look at the middle garages—that's about where the gallows would have been, as near as I can triangulate from a couple of newspaper diagrams showing where they were. Today, firefighters sit on folding chairs, chatting with passers-by, outside of the red garages. But until 1927, when the state switched to the electric chair, dozens of men met their doom there.

There were a number of notably grim executions. A couple of men had to be hanged while tied to chairs. There was also another occasion when the rope broke and the convict, George Painter, landed on his head. Unlike Michael MacNamee, who was barely shaken, Painter was bleeding so much that he was probably already dead. However, the sentence said he must be hanged by the neck until dead, so his bloody form was hauled back onto the scaffold, where they wrapped a new rope around his neck and slid him down the trap door so his limp body could dangle for a while.

The first known reports of a ghost haunting the old jail came in the 1880s—though they were probably explained right away.

In 1886 there had been a rally at Haymarket Square, a near-west neighborhood around Randolph and Desplaines Streets, in support of workers who were going on strike in an attempt to get an eight-hour workday. The second the permit for a rally expired, police started marching toward the ralliers with guns (this was an age when organized labor was regarded as a genuine threat to democracy; anti-union policies and sentiment may be on the rise today, but they're nothing compared to the situation in 1886). As the police began their march, someone hiding in a vestibule threw a homemade bomb at them. One officer was killed, and the rest began firing into the crowd. By the time the dust settled, seven more officers were dead, along with an unknown number of people who were just there for the rally. No one in the press seemed to care much about the people killed in the rally; after all, most were communists and anarchists (the two terms were often used interchangeably back then), and many of them were foreigners. No one outside of the radical papers spoke of justice for the ralliers, but cries were heard near and far to make the world "safe for democracy" by punishing the organizers. They never did figure out for sure who threw the bomb, but all of the speakers from the rally were arrested, and five men were eventually sentenced to be hanged.

But on the morning of the execution (which was a huge media event attracting reporters from all over), only four were actually facing the gallows—the fifth man, Louis Ling, had committed suicide by biting into a dynamite cap and blowing his own head off the night before. Several reporters who had assembled to witness the hanging heard a strange wailing noise that they thought might have been his ghost, but most thought they were just hearing the jailhouse cat (which always starting wailing around the time of hangings, according to a few anecdotes published by reporters of the day).

The other men, though, went to their death shouting slogans and singing songs. One loudly proclaimed that it was the happiest moment of his life. Say what you will about their politics, these guys had balls the size of grapefruits.

By 1906, the idea that the jail was haunted was taken as a matter of fact by the prisoners, as well as some of the guards. In the middle of the night—particularly on nights before a hanging—prisoners would say they could hear the sound of the scaffold being erected. This was hours *before* the construction would actually begin. During a period around 1906, the sound was said to be heard nightly, even in the days *after* the execution, when the scaffold had been taken apart and put into storage, and some prisoners reported seeing grim apparitions of executed men in their cells. "The forty-fifth man to have died upon it," the *Tribune* wrote, "has gone to join the army of those who, the superstitious believe, are back as shades to haunt the grim walls of their parting place."

Strange "manifestations" were commonly seen and heard before hangings; on the night before one man was hanged, the trap door of the scaffold fell down all on its own when no one was in the room. The rope that held it in place had been cut neatly in half by unseen forces that the jailer was never able to explain.

Though the belief in ghosts seems to have been more common among the prisoners than the staff, the guards admitted that enough strange things happened in the jail to scare anyone. "I don't believe in ghosts," one of them said, "but somehow I am getting creepy in this place. Last night I sat here and heard someone pounding. I got up and the sound stopped. I went to the place I thought the sound had come from, but there was no one. I asked some of the prisoners, and they said they had heard the pounding...I wouldn't say that [the jail is haunted]; it would make me look foolish. But I want to tell you that I wouldn't stay in this place alone."

One prisoner even managed to be transferred to the "new jail" built adjacent to the original building after spending just one night in the old one. He was haunted by visions of men being executed, including the most notorious outlaws of the day, the Car Barn Bandits: three young men who were sort of the last of the cowboy criminals in Chicago, having killed several men in a crime spree that included robbing the barns where train cars were held and at least one attempt to actually rob a passing train.

One of the bandits, Peter Niedermeier, is probably the man most commonly said to haunt the jail. According to legend, when he was brought to the scaffold, he cursed everyone involved in his execution. "You can't kill me, you scoundrels!"

he shouted. "I will come back, and when I do come, you will be sorry for what you have done!"

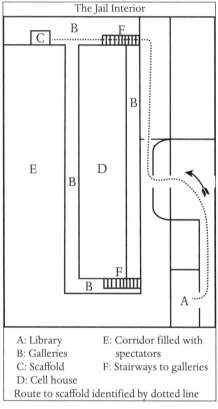

A diagram from the 1880s showing where the gallows were set up; this would be about where the middle garages are in the fire station today.

The jailer didn't believe in ghosts—he chalked the stories up to the superstitions of lonely men, perhaps mixed with the strange noises that occurred in any old building, the banging of steam pipes, and the occasional practical joker. However, he did his best to put the more easily frightened prisoners in the newer building, since they were always better able to sleep there. It was less spooky than the old building, where the hangings took place.

Remaining Haunts

Stories of the ghosts faded away a great deal after the old prisons were torn down and the newer jail facilities were opened at the current location on 26th Street and California Avenue. But they haven't gone away completely. I recently spoke to a man who worked near the building who said that, on occasion, he and his co-workers had seen men walking up toward the garage and vanishing into the morning air. It's no one they would recognize on sight, though. I've studied local hangings extensively enough that if I saw the ghosts myself I *might* recognize them, but there are no known photographs of a great many of the men who died on the spot.

But I have also spoken to people who told me that there are firefighters in town who refuse to work at that station—or at least to stay there overnight—because it gets so spooky in there. Some firefighters don't seem to be bothered there at all, but others apparently report a general aura of creepiness, and talk of hearing sounds like people singing when they get up at night to take a leak. The "singing" angle makes it a bit easier to narrow down who the ghost might be, since only a few people were noted to do much singing on the way to being hanged. But, remarkably, a few men were.

One was Nicholas "The Choir Singer" Viana, who was hanged on his nineteenth birthday after killing at least a dozen people as a boy thief for the Cardinella gang, which was not unlike the gang from *Oliver Twist*; Sam Cardinella would lure boys into his pool room, where he taught them to commit crimes. Viana sang "Il Misere" as they brought him to the "death cell" (the morbid name for the prison library), where he spent his last night and sang "Mother o' Mine" to his mother the night before his death; a prison official later said that his singing "beat any show you ever saw." Some expected him to sing on the scaffold before he was hanged, but he didn't. Perhaps he's making up for it now.

At least one of the Haymarket anarchists sang on his way to the scaffold as well. On the morning of the hanging, Adolph Fischer led the prisoners in a rousing chorus of "The Marseillaise" shortly before he was led from the "death cell." There are also stories about Albert Parsons singing "Annie Laurie," an old folk ballad that would sound particularly creepy coming out of a ghost, in his cell:

> *For bonnie Annie Laurie*
> *I'd lay me down and die*

But the gallows singer that everyone remembered best in later years was Carl Wanderer, who was hanged in 1921.

Carl Wanderer's Last Song

One pleasant summer's day in 1920, Wanderer had walked up to a drifter outside of a cigar shop on Madison Street, near Halsted, and said something along the lines of, "Hey, buddy, I'm in the doghouse with my wife. She's pregnant and she doesn't think I'm enough of a man to be a father. If you'll come pretend to rob us, so I can punch you out and look like a hero, I'll give you ten bucks!"

Wanderer's story as to exactly what they'd arranged varied whenever he told it, but this seems to have been the main substance of the agreement. The stranger agreed, and Wanderer loaned him a gun to make the holdup look real. The next day, as Wanderer and his wife walked home from a silent film version of Jack London's *The Sea Wolf*, the stranger confronted them, pulled out the gun Wanderer had loaned him, and ordered them to hand over their money.

Wanderer calmly pulled out a gun of his own and shot the "ragged stranger" to death, firing five shots into his chest.

Having done that, he turned to the side and shot his pregnant wife to death as well.

This had been Carl Wanderer's plan all along. He didn't want to be a father; he wanted, depending on who you believe, to get back into the army, to hook up with a former army buddy with whom he was having an affair, or to marry a sixteen-year-old girl he had been dating on the side. So he'd cooked up a plan to kill his wife and blame it on the "poor boob" who had been robbing them, and who would by then be too dead to defend himself.

In any case, he was briefly hailed as a hero who had bravely defended his wife from an evil robber, but within a few days the police noticed a lot of holes in his story. They were particularly suspicious that he and the "ragged stranger" owned the same expensive model of pistol.

"Oh, gee," Wanderer said. "They were both my guns, see, but I pulled *both* of them out, and the drifter took one away from me."

Though many a gun enthusiast today is proud to carry as many firearms as possible to the movies, police at the time thought it was awfully odd that Wanderer would have needed two guns to walk home from the theater. How many people did he think he was going to have to shoot?

Before long, he broke down and confessed that he'd wanted to rejoin the army, and thought that it was better that his wife be dead, partly to spare him having to leave her, and partly so that he could get her $1,500 in savings. "I want to be hanged," he told reporters when he read a confession in prison. "I hope to join her in death. I wonder if she will forgive me. Well, I loved her too much to let another man get her. But I didn't want her myself." He concluded the reading of his confession by ordering pork and beans for supper.

Wanderer was initially brought to trial just for the murder of his wife and sentenced to life in prison. One of the newspapers was so incensed that his life had been spared that they reputedly published the names and addresses of the entire jury, all but encouraging people to go harass them. Newspapers, meanwhile, described Wanderer pacing his cell, appearing to talk to his wife's ghost.

Perhaps it was out of concern for the jurors that Wanderer was rushed back into court to stand trial for the death of the "ragged stranger." The lawyers tried all sorts of tricks to get him off the hook—such as saying the way Wanderer played poker proved he was insane, or arguing that since the stranger had never been positively identified, he didn't legally exist and therefore could not have been murdered. But none worked, and Carl was sent to the gallows in 1921.

Public executions had been illegal in Illinois for a good seventy years by then, but prisoners were still expected to put on a show for the assembled reporters and officials. (Sometimes the prison officials would even sneak friends in, and sometimes the friends were so numerous that the execution was effectively a public one—attendance was over a thousand for the execution of three guys who had killed a man and mailed the body to Pittsburgh in a trunk in 1885.) Before the assembled crowds, prisoners were expected to make a little speech about how nice the warden had been, how sorry they were, and perhaps something about Jesus.

Wanderer refused to do any of this—instead, as near as I can tell, he decided to torture everyone a little. Rather than making a speech, he made them sit and listen as he sang "Old Pal, Why Don't You Answer Me," one of those horribly maudlin parlor songs about dead people that were popular at the time. Most tour passengers are ready to hang *me* by the time I finish singing two lines of it, but Wanderer sang the whole song through.

One reporter said he "should have been a song plugger," but others said that he deserved to be hanged just for his voice.

So perhaps that's the singing that people say they hear there now—Carl Wanderer, repeating his last words.

Some Other Victims Who Might Want to Come Back

George Painter: Accused of killing his wife, Painter went to the gallows protesting his innocence, and the rope broke—he was the guy who landed on his head, cracking it open so badly that he appeared to be dead already from the fall.

James Tracy: Immediately after cutting Tracy down in early 1882, scientists pumped electricity into his body to see if they could reanimate him. They were able to manipulate his facial features by moving the wires (*"Now he's happy ... now he's sad ... now he's smelled a fart ..."*) and were able to get his heart beating, but his neck was broken, so there was no bringing him "back to life."

Sam Cardinella: The early gangster who led a group of kids, including Nicholas Viana, who committed dozens of murders and hundreds of holdups, Cardinella lost a lot of weight in prison and had (or faked) a breakdown on the scaffold—he had to be tied to a chair to be hanged. But the shorter drop and lower weight were all a ploy to keep from breaking his neck, so his henchmen could try to bring him back to life. Prison officials thought it was odd that the "hearse" his friends had brought to take the body away looked more like an ambulance, and held it up in the jailyard. Inside, they found a team of doctors trying to revive the dead man.

The jail physician believed that if the "hearse" hadn't been held up in the jailyard, there was at least a slim chance they could have pulled it off—and legend had it that they'd already successfully tested it in Nicholas "The Choir Singer" Viana, who, according to whispers told among prisoners for years, was successfully reanimated and then allowed to die again as punishment for betraying the gang. His body, too, had been taken away in an ambulance, and Cardinella spent his last moments with his family the night before his hanging, whispering Viana's name.

Johann Hoch: Another serial killer—sometimes said to be an associate of the famous H. H. Holmes—who went to the gallows protesting his innocence. Some authorities believed he had married more than fifty women and poisoned about a third of them. I like to assume that he's the ghost at Dunning Memorial Park who grabs women's ankles (see chapter 19).

If You Go

The corner of Illinois and Dearborn is crowded these days, so doing any ghost hunting there would be tricky business, and the firefighters aren't likely to let people into the station to look for ghosts. The *good* news is that if you use an audio recorder outside of the garages and capture a voice singing Carl Wanderer's last song, even the most hardened skeptics won't dare to say that it was just someone blasting parlor songs on their car stereo.

CHAPTER 3

The *Eastland* Disaster and the Haunted Morgues

The Eastland *disaster site is in the Chicago River between Clark and LaSalle Streets; Wacker Drive runs alongside it. The Reid Murdoch Building, one of a few buildings used as a morgue, is still standing, though it's missing a large section that was torn out when LaSalle was expanded, leaving the clock tower slightly off-center.*

In 1915, the Western Electric Company hired excursion boats to take its employees on an annual trip to Michigan City, Indiana, for a picnic on the dunes. Several thousand tickets were sold to eager passengers, marking what may be the last time in history that a group of Chicagoans got all excited about a trip to Indiana, which some refer to as "our New Jersey."

The Eastland *in happier times, sailing the Great Lakes.*

The most famous of the ships they booked was the *SS Eastland,* which was known as "The Speed Queen of the Lakes." The other ship, the *Theodore Roosevelt,* was far less well known, and no matter what it said on people's tickets, everyone seemed to intend to get on the *Eastland.*

The official capacity of the *Eastland* as of the beginning of the summer was 2,200, but they probably should have been lowering it down from that. The boat was already known as a fussy, top-heavy ship that was given to rocking back and forth, and now they had added a massive new cement deck weighing between thirty and sixty tons, which didn't help matters.

Also, there were new laws on the books stating that every ship had to have enough lifeboats for everyone—one of the laws that had been passed after the recent sinking of the *Titanic.* It was a good law, obviously, but the *Eastland* wasn't really built to hold so many lifeboats—they had to retrofit it a little and tie extra boats to the top. This made it even *more* top-heavy and, ironically, less safe than ever. But the weight wasn't the worst of it: some geniuses who worked on the ship reasoned that if they put up enough lifeboats for 2,500 people, they could *raise* the capacity up to 2,500. And that's exactly what they did.

The summer of 1915 was mild, and a very slow year for the pleasure boat industry—the most they'd had on board the *Eastland* at once for most of that summer was only about half of the new capacity. But on the day of the Western Electric Company picnic, it was filled to the full capacity—2,500 passengers and seventy-two crew. This was a few hundred *more* people than had been on the *Titanic*, and the actual number of passengers was probably higher; many historians believe that they crammed it even *beyond* the new capacity.

And barely half of the passengers, if that, had boarded the vessel when it began to list (tilt) back and forth as it sat there in the dock between Clark and LaSalle.

But the passengers were all there for a good time; it doesn't seem to have occurred to them that anything could be wrong. According to many reports, every time it listed dangerously to one side or the other, passengers would laugh and applaud.

Meanwhile, down below, the crew was having some trouble with the ballast tanks that were used to regulate the distribution of weight. Apparently, the portside tanks were letting water in, but not letting it back out. One story goes that a large crowd ran over to the port side to watch another ship go by, further raising the amount of weight on the port side.

It may have been this mad rush to port that made the ship list enough that the furniture below deck began to slide across the floor. This meant that in addition to having the port side overcrowded, and in addition to having full ballast tanks on the port side, all of the furniture was on the port side as well.

This combination of troubles finally proved to be too much; the great ship tipped over and wound up lying on its side in the river between Clark and LaSalle. Its hull came to rest on the riverbed, and eight or nine feet peeked out over the waves, turning the starboard side into an island in the water.

A boat tipping over in a shallow river might not sound too alarming—the river was only about twenty feet deep, and those thrown overboard were just a few yards from the shore. It wasn't like the *Titanic,* where they were above the very darkest depths of the ocean, miles away from any possible help.

But there were some major problems.

One is that many of the passengers probably didn't know how to swim. Another is that they were dressed in 1915 fashions—and it had been a very mild summer. Once you got those heavy clothes wet, you might just as well have been wearing an anchor.

Worst of all, though, was that there were layers of people below the surface, frantically reaching to grab whatever they could find to pull themselves up. Most of the time, all they were able to find was people's legs. Many people were jerked down below, never to return.

And those were just the people in the water. Down below deck on the ship, many were crushed to death by the falling furniture, and others were suffocated under the weight of the people falling on top of them.

The Eastland *lying on its side. The port side of the ship
would have been lying on the river bed, but the river wasn't deep
enough for the ship to sink completely. That's the side of the ship,
not the sidewalk, that the crowd is standing on.*

Passersby did whatever they could to help. One guy started throwing lumber from a truck into the water to act as
buoys (though, according to some reports, he did more harm
than good—in addition to treading water in heavy clothes and
kicking people off their ankles, the unfortunate people now
had to deal with a guy throwing 2x4s at their heads). Another guy started throwing in doll parts, the only thing he could
find. Another threw in orange crates. A group of onlookers
put in a special effort to save a man dressed as Uncle Sam.

Firefighters with Engine Company #13, the same company called to the scene of the Iroquois fire twelve years earlier, were able to walk out onto the side of the ship to survey
the scene. They determined that the most good they could
do would be to break into the ship and try to save the people stuck below. They broke in against the objections of Captain Harry Pederson, who frantically tried to stop them from
damaging the ship (he later tried to explain that he was suffering from a headache that kept him from thinking straight).

Eventually, the captain had to be loaded into a boat and hustled across the river to the Reid Murdoch Building, where he was held in secrecy to protect him from lynch mobs. He never captained another ship.

Below the deck of the ship, the firemen found that they were largely already too late.

It's difficult to know just how many people died—every source has a different number. The *Tribune* initially said that 919 bodies had been recovered, and that the final death count could be as high as 1,200. The most commonly agreed-upon figure today is that 844 people were killed, but that number may be low; officials were saying that eight hundred–some bodies were in the morgues at a time when they still estimated a few hundred more had yet to be recovered.

Ghosts on the Ship

Ghost sightings from the tragedy began almost immediately. When the ship was righted, it was anchored near the Halsted Street bridge, where it quickly developed a reputation as a haunted ship.

The ship was in bad shape. The railings were twisted, the upper deck a wreck—it certainly *looked* haunted. By night, passersby would hear groans and creaks coming from the ship and would run like hell to get away from it.

Meanwhile, on board lived a man named Captain Edwards. He had been given the lonely job of living aboard the ship to guard it from "incendiaries" who wanted to blow it up.

Edwards told the *Chicago Daily News* that he didn't believe the ship was haunted, but admitted to getting spooked. "It's all right in the day. Just a matter of killing time," he said. "At night it's a bit different … when the noises on the bridge die down and the river begins to talk, sort of lapping against the dock and against the boat like it was full of secrets. That's all imagination, and I wouldn't mention it except I've been listening to it for ninety-seven nights ... sometimes there's a bang toward the stern and a queer creaking ... sometimes something begins straining and ends by giving out a screech. I'm not saying I'm afraid ... [but] when there's an extra loud bang I get out of bed and take a lantern and go see ... every night nearly, sometimes two or three times."

The captain noted, though, that he was more afraid of living people than dead ones. Plenty of living people wanted to blow the ship to smithereens.

In fact, he laughed when asked about ghosts. "I've never seen any," he said. "If there's a place where ghosts are likely to haunt, this is the one. But the creaking and the screeching are only pieces of timber falling. I tell you what, though. You should come past here at ten o'clock at night and watch the people cross the bridge. They don't stop to look long. They sort of scoot over, and sometimes I hear one cry out, 'Look, there's a light!' and start to run. The light's me, of course, sitting in the pilot house."

In May 1916, the ship was finally returned to the Great Lakes. Crowds on the bridges and behind the windows of the Reid Murdoch Building, which had served as a temporary hospital and morgue, gathered to boo as the ship passed. The *Tribune* quoted viewers as shouting, "Take it out to the lake and sink it!" "Blow her up!" "Put her at the bottom where she put her passengers!" The crew, the paper noted, looked like a ghost crew in the cool spring drizzle.

The ship was eventually sold to the U.S. Navy, which used it as a training vessel on Lake Michigan for years under the name *Wilmette*. After World War I, a captured German U-Boat was brought to Chicago; under the terms of the treaty that ended the war, all captured ships had to be sunk within a year. The former *Eastland* was used to sink the U-Boat in the lake; papers at the time said that it was the last official shot of World War I.

The ship remained in service for more than thirty years without any major incident—but people who were stationed on it were known to get creeped out. One sailor, Ernie Pyle, who would go on to find fame as a journalist, later wrote that the ship was "still in sinking condition ... it constantly shied to the right and once in a while felt as if it wanted to lie down." The Navy kept it in service for decades before selling it for scrap around the time of the Korean War.

Ghosts in the River

The most obvious place to look for ghosts, outside of the ship itself, would be the actual site of the disaster in the Chicago River between Clark and LaSalle. Stories have circulated about people hearing whispers in the water or seeing pale faces float up toward the surface, and then vanish.

Occasionally I'll see pictures in which the waves seem to form an image of a person's face. It's easy to brush these off as optical illusions, except that the good ones seem to come in batches—I'll go months without seeing a really good one, then suddenly we'll go through a period where a couple of people get one every tour.

Others report being overcome with an overwhelming sense of sorrow and sadness while walking across the LaSalle Street bridge. High-schoolers on school group tours always want to try this out, for some reason.

Rumor has long had it that people in old-timey costumes are sometimes seen thrashing around in the river by that same bridge, but this is one of those ghost stories for which a first-hand report is tough to pin down; the "old-timey people" are the kinds of ghosts that every ghost hunter hears about, but you never meet anyone who's actually seen them. Rumor has it that police respond to calls about ghosts in the river from time to time, particularly in periods when there's nothing in place to commemorate the disaster, such as when the plaques get stolen, but I've never seen a police report to back this up.

The closest I've come to seeing the "old-timey people" myself was a winter morning a few years ago when I was running a daytime tour. The river was covered in sheets of ice at the time—not one continuous sheet, but a sort of jig-saw puzzle of jagged chunks. As we stared down at them, something that looked like a woman's bare arm reached up and grabbed one, like someone was trying to pull herself up from the icy depths below. It lingered for a second before disappearing. There was no way anyone could have been alive down there at the time; I've always tried to convince myself that it was just a branch or a fish, but those should have slid back in, not disappeared. I'm not prepared to say it was definitely a ghost, but saying "branch" in this situation is about as convincing as saying a UFO sighting was just swamp gas.

This sighting—my only one there, other than seeing people's pictures—was right near the LaSalle Street bridge. Indeed, a majority of the ghost sightings at the disaster site seem to take place around that bridge, which didn't exist at the time of the disaster—instead, there was a streetcar tunnel that took LaSalle Street underneath the river in that place.

Given the history of that tunnel, it's possible that we're dealing with ghosts from *two* disasters here—both the *Eastland* and the Great Chicago Fire of 1871. The tunnel was originally built as a pedestrian tunnel and, at the time of the Great Fire, was the only way out of the Loop when the bridges burned. According to some reports, fires in the buildings on LaSalle were sucked into the tunnel at one point, turning it into a death trap for the people inside.

For my part, I've certainly heard strange noises down by the river—but since the Riverwalk runs right against Lower Wacker Drive, in close proximity to a number of restaurants, it's difficult to determine whether the noises and voices heard there aren't from a perfectly natural source.

Haunted Morgues

Several sites were used as morgues following the disaster. When the space on the south shore was found to be inadequate for caring for the dead and injured, many bodies were taken to the first floor and basement of the Reid Murdoch Building, a grocery warehouse across the river from the capsized vessel. Soon, every room of the place was stuffed, and bodies lay on desks, tables, and the bare patches of floor.

People who work in the Reid Murdoch Building (which is now occupied by offices and restaurants) have plenty of stories about objects flying across the room in the middle of the night. Moving chairs seem to be particularly common—people on the upper floors often tell of chairs zipping across the floor with enough force that it seems as though someone must have pushed them. This is pretty standard poltergeist stuff.

After the bodies at the Reid Murdoch had been embalmed by the team of fifty embalmers who were pressed into service, they were taken to the Second Regimental Armory building on Randolph Street. There, the bodies were laid out in neat rows of eighty-five, and by ten o'clock on the morning of the disaster, the armory was full of citizens searching for their loved ones among the dead.

Some 30,000 people filed through the building, viewing the hundreds of bodies, though many of the earliest to enter were simply curious, not relatives of the missing. Coroner Peter Hoffman announced through a megaphone that, in the name of common decency, he would arrest anyone who had no missing relatives thought to be among the dead.

All were eventually identified, though in many cases the identification may not have been correct. Newspapers told of one man who needed to show a photo of his sister to several friends to get their opinion on whether a body was hers; he was given the body even though it had been identified as that of two other girls already. There were many similar stories of people being stopped from taking the wrong body at the last second, and at least one was exhumed after burial to correct a mistaken identification. In all the hurry and hysterical confusion, it's inevitable that mistakes were made, which may be used as a reason that the building seems to be haunted today. One wouldn't normally expect a morgue, where no one actually dies, to be haunted, but while ghosts seem to be more commonly seen haunting the places where they died, there are numerous exceptions, particularly in places that lack commemoration, that have been vandalized, or where mistakes were made.

The nearby armory sure seems to be haunted—the old building is now the southwest portion of Harpo Studios, where Oprah Winfrey filmed her show until 2011. There's still a lot of editing and production work that goes on there, and a few friends of mine who've been called in for a day or so of backstage work say that certain areas of the building are absolutely terrifying to be alone in.

It's generally been said that the staff was forbidden to talk about the hauntings, but none of the Harpo workers to whom I've spoken over the years knew of any such rule. Most have been more than happy to talk to me, and almost all seem to have stories of contractors getting freaked out by stray voices of children. Some even say they have to warn contractors who come in to work on the building about the ghosts; one sheet metal worker in the place confirmed this for me, saying that employees told him that if he heard any noises, it was just the ghosts.

A couple of employees have told me that the ghost of a rather irate man haunts the second floor—they speculated that this was the ghost of Captain Pederson, the captain of the ship, but he didn't die during the tragedy, so it's an unlikely story. If there's a ghost, it's some other angry man.

Others on staff say that it's not uncommon to hear the sound of children laughing and playing at times when there are certainly no children in the building (people who work in nearby buildings have often reported the same thing in *their* buildings, some of which also may have been pressed into service during the tragedy—the "armory annex" on the other side of Aberdeen Street certainly was). Others speak of seeing shadowy figures in the hall out of the corner of their eye. Others have spoken of a little girl who appears, then disappears, near some vending machines. I sometimes wonder if there's something biological about young girls that makes them more apt to become ghosts upon death than other people; there doesn't seem to be a haunted house in town that isn't home to a ghostly little girl.

The story I hear from people the most, though, concerns one of the bathrooms. The middle stall of one of the bathrooms is normally kept closed, but many staffers have heard a woman crying from behind the door. They speculate that this is a sort of echo left behind by someone who had been to the morgue to identify one of the bodies.

Perhaps the most famous Harpo ghost is the "Gray Lady," a woman in a long gray coat seen floating down one of the halls. Some say she's shown up on security cameras. This ghost, known as the Phantom of the Oprah (g'night, folks!), seems to be one of those ghosts that is well known to ghost hunters, but relatively unknown to the people who actually work in the building. She was perhaps better known to staffers in the 1990s, when the story that Oprah's studio was haunted first circulated, but most staffers today don't even seem to have heard of her.

How Oprah Winfrey reacted to all this is a story that changes with the teller. Some say she loved the ghosts, others say she refused to speak about them, or that she refused to be in the building alone at any time (though it's hard to imagine the circumstances under which she *would* have been alone in the building at any time; there are always people there). In an October 1996 episode of her show, she referred to sightings of "extraterrestrial people" in the building and added, "That's why I'm not here after midnight—and that's true." Whether she seriously had a rule about not going there after midnight because of the ghosts or was just chatting to fill air space, as one does, is certainly up to debate.

Rosie O'Donnell, who briefly filmed a show of her own in the space after Oprah left, said in a comment to the Chicago Unbelievable blog that she loved ghosts, but she hasn't commented about the building since.

A few other sites were used as temporary morgues—including a "floating morgue" beneath the Wells Street bridge that was set up to house any bodies found when the boat was raised a few weeks later (none were)—and many undertaking establishments throughout the city were put in service as well; a recent rumor has it that one was on the site where the Trump Tower now stands. The only other major morgue that I know of—the one used when a building as large as the armory was no longer needed to house the unidentified dead—was Sheldon's Undertaking Room at 912 West Madison. That building is long gone, but for the building that occupies the space there now to be the subject of hauntings would hardly be unusual.

Other undertaking establishments at which bodies were held on the day of the disaster:

P. J. Gavin's, 642 N. Clark (3 bodies)

Western Casket Co., 90 E. Randolph (29)

Central Undertaking, 318 Federal (8)

Carroll's, 822 N. Clark (9)

Arntzen's, 810 N. Clark (9)

Bradley's, 1820 W. Harrison (1)

Maloney's, 1004 N. Wells (3)

Sbabaro's, 708 N. Wells (1)

The Armory Annex

One Enduring Mystery: The Missing Movie

In the weeks immediately after the disaster, a live film of the tragedy was shown all over the country. Filmed mainly from the fire escape of the Reid Murdoch Building, it showed the boat on its side, with firefighters climbing over it and divers out plying their trade recovering the dead. Stretchers were seen being taken away, along with scenes of nurses and firemen working in the Reid Murdoch Building itself, as well as scenes from the Second Regiment Armory. A few girls who survived posed for the camera. The Tribune company began to show it in theaters under the name *Great Eastland Disaster* at once, offering to donate all profits to the *Eastland* relief fund. It was banned in Chicago, but exhibited in nearby Forest Park.

At least forty prints of the thousand-foot film were struck, and were being exhibited around the country within seventy-two hours after the disaster. In Flint, Michigan, it was shown on a double bill with (get this) a Charlie Chaplin film. "In a thousand feet of moving pictures," the ad screamed, "*Chicago Tribune* camera men were on the scene making their record of heroism and death. Come and See it for Yourself. Just as if you were one of that crowd of thousands standing on the docks and bridges. SEE the battle for life in a river seething with death. The volunteer heroes, the life-saving crews. This picture tells the whole story. Also: Charles Chaplin in *The Knockout*. Don't miss this great show."

Like most silent films from 1915, no print seems to survive, but prints of long-lost films like this are discovered all the time, and it seems as though this one would have been kept as evidence for insurance reasons, or during the long legal proceedings that followed the wreck. Could a print still be in the vaults?

If You Go

You really can't go ghost hunting at Harpo Studios, which seems to be the most actively haunted location related to the disaster. I've been inside a couple of times for tapings of TV shows, and in those situations there are so many other people around you, everyone full of hurry and excitement, that it would have been very difficult to pick up on any lingering creepiness.

Your best bet, then, is to go right to the source of the disaster—the stretch of river between Clark and LaSalle. On cold mornings, one definitely gets a sense of foreboding if one walks along the river knowing the story of what happened there. However, for ghost hunting, all you can really do is stand around taking pictures of the water. I've seen plenty of neat pictures that were taken like this, though, and you never know when you might see something creepy in the water.

The Riverwalk makes access to the river itself between the two bridges fairly easy. As usual, most ghost-hunting equipment is fairly unreliable in such a busy location.

CHAPTER 4

The Murder Castle of H. H. Holmes

The H. H. Holmes "Murder Castle" stood near W. 63rd Street and S. Wallace Avenue, overlapping a little bit with the post office that stands on the grounds today. As the legend of Holmes has grown, the number of victims he's said to have killed in the secret passages and vaults that line the building he called "The World's Fair Hotel" has gone from dozens to hundreds.

One day, while running a tour of H. H. Holmes sites, Hector was driving the bus back downtown when a customer screamed—there was a dead body, she said, lying by the side of the road.

We turned around, and saw there was, indeed, a humanesque form beside the road. I cautiously approached it, mindful of urban myths that robbers sometimes pose as dead bodies in order to lie in wait for victims. It turned out to be a stuffed canvas dummy.

Really, how we had mistaken it for a body at all sort of baffled me, but just talking about the Murder Castle of H. H. Holmes, the site of which we'd just visited, certainly puts you in the frame of mind to see corpses everywhere.

In 1885, a man came to Chicago calling himself Dr. H. H. Holmes. Born in New Hampshire under the name Herman W. Mudgett, he had just graduated from the University of Michigan medical school. What led him to Ann Arbor from his native New Hampshire, where he left behind a wife and son, is not really known, though it's easy to imagine that he'd heard of the school's reputation as a hub for body snatchers. Nearly all medical schools in those days had a "no questions asked" policy when it came to buying human remains, and digging up bodies was a sort of a rite of passage for young surgeons. Even with that in mind, one who researches articles from the 19th century about grave-robbing finds that the University of Michigan comes up a lot. Holmes's fellow students later remembered that he took particular delight in the pleasures of the dissection room, and this recollection is one of very few bits of reliable information we have about him.[2]

In fact, there's hardly anything we can say about the man with much confidence, partly because he himself was a chronic liar. Nothing that he said about himself can be taken as gospel. Further complicating matters is that much of what was said about him, both during his life and since, was

---

2. Another bit of reliable info, from a doctor's report, tells us that his sexual organs were "unusually small." This may be the most reliable information on Holmes there is, as a matter of fact; much of the rest came from vague memories of old schoolmates, gossiping reporters and neighbors, women and employees he had conned, or Holmes's own confessions, which weren't the least bit reliable.

strictly hearsay. To dig into the history of H. H. Holmes is to wade into a hopelessly complicated riddle.

It's generally agreed that he arrived in Chicago around 1885, when he was still in his early twenties, got work in a pharmacy owned by one Dr. E. H. Holton, and eventually bought the business (some believe he killed Dr. Holton and his wife; from what we can gather, what he actually did was buy the business without actually paying them, which was his usual method of operation). Though he could have easily made a comfortable living as a practicing physician and pharmacist, he soon had buildings and businesses all over the city; over the next nine years, he can be associated with a few offices in the Loop, a candy store on Milwaukee Avenue, and a few glass-bending furnaces scattered throughout the North and South Sides. He had a wife and a house in the north suburbs and various girlfriends in the south suburbs, where the drugstore was located. Operating first and foremost as a swindler, records indicate also that he had conned furniture shops all down Wabash Street.

During the World's Fair in 1893, he owned and operated a building on 63rd Street, across from the old drugstore, that he referred to as "The World's Fair Hotel." This was the now-famous building that the rest of the world would come to know as the "Murder Castle."

The Castle

The first floor was given over to businesses, the third was hotel rooms and flats, and the second was a maze of secret passages, blind hallways, hidden rooms, and trap doors. There was even a soundproof vault where people could be locked for days at a time and no one could hear them screaming. Hard evidence of what went on in the place was slim, but when police investigated it after Holmes's eventual arrest, it was clear that it had been designed with sinister purposes in mind.

The building was situated just down the road from the site of the World's Fair, which registered some twenty-seven million paid admissions, including countless tourists who were away from home for the first time. At least one paper later noted that an awful lot of people had gone to Chicago for the fair and never returned.

But for Holmes to have used the castle for killing people during the fair would have been a very bold move, since the city already knew all about the building and many of its secrets by then. A few months before the fair opened, there was a huge article about the building and its secret rooms in the *Tribune*. At the time it was thought that Holmes was using these rooms to hide furniture that he'd never paid for.

Some months after the World's Fair ended, Holmes approached Benjamin Pitezel, a regular partner of his in crime, and suggested that they go to Philadelphia and fake Pitezel's death in order to cash in his $10,000 policy. Pitezel went to Philadelphia, but his death wasn't faked—Holmes simply killed him and proceeded to swindle his widow out of most of the money. With that done, he began traveling with three separate groups: one containing his latest wife, one containing Pitezel's widow and two of her children, and a third containing the other three Pitezel children—Alice, Nellie, and Howard. This, among other things, sets him apart from the kind of people we now think of as "serial killers." Most of them pick one type of person to kill, but Holmes is known to have killed men, women, and children.

But he had apparently blabbed about the scheme to get Pitezel's insurance money to one Marion Hedgepeth, a train robber with whom he'd briefly shared a jail cell in St. Louis some months before. Fidelity Mutual Life Insurance took Hedgepeth's testimony to confirm something they already suspected about the case being fishy and tracked Holmes to Boston. When he was arrested there, three of the Pitezel children who were supposed to be in his personal care were missing. He told everyone that his wife, Minnie Williams, had taken them to England, and this seemed, for the moment, to satisfy everyone. Holmes became a sensation, but newspapers were talking of his success in defrauding the life insurance company by faking Pitezel's death, not murdering him.

Then, in the summer of 1895, while he awaited trial, the bodies of Alice and Nellie Pitezel were unearthed in Toronto, confirming that there was certainly murder in the case, and not just the murder of Benjamin Pitezel.

Now that it was known that there was murder in the case, people remembered the building full of secret rooms on 63rd Street, and police began an intensive investigation of the place. In July and August of that year, they dug out every inch and interviewed all of the neighbors and residents.

A number of shell-shocked people who had worked for Holmes came forward and said that he had always been trying to get them to let him take out an insurance policy on their lives, presumably intending to kill them and cash in. It's commonly said now that he killed an awful lot of people for the insurance money, but I think only Ben Pitezel was dumb enough to fall for a scheme like that.

Very little evidence was actually found in the castle, outside of some bones that may or may not have been human, some clothes that appeared to be bloodstained, and a mysterious furnace hidden behind a basement wall. However, at least six people connected to Holmes during his years in Chicago had vanished and couldn't be found.

In the end, Holmes was only tried and convicted for the murder of Ben Pitezel in Philadelphia, for which he was hanged in 1896. By then a fire had ravaged the castle building, necessitating the removal and replacement of the top two floors, but the building itself remained standing until the 1930s, when it was torn down to put a post office over the grounds.

Holmes "mug shot," taken when such things were a new concept.
Most stories about him are wildly exaggerated,
but they don't really need to be.

People largely forgot the story for half a century or so, but since the publication of Erik Larson's bestselling book *The Devil in the White City*, Holmes stories seem to get wilder by the day. It's common to hear that he killed at least two hundred people, skinning some alive and trying to create a race of giants by stretching others on a medieval-style rack in the castle basement. It's also common to hear that he had an obsession with determining just how much pain a human body could endure. Most of this just comes from tabloid gossip from the 1890s and pulp rewrites of the story from the 1940s, but the fact remains that the man can be confidently said to have killed at least ten people, and those are just the ones that we know about. And ten is plenty.

Castle Ghosts

Stories of the castle being haunted started during the original 1895 investigation, when detectives found a letter from Holmes to a man currently operating a business in the castle, asking if he ever saw "the ghosts of the Williams girls," referring to Minnie Williams and her sister Anna, both of whom had vanished by then. In May 1896, a whole crowd gathered around the building on the day Holmes was executed, wondering if his ghost would immediately repair to his old stomping grounds. E. C. Davis, a jeweler who worked in the building, remarked that "some people" were always seeing ghosts there. Some superstitious neighbors spent the night with friends and relatives on the other side of town. A police officer on the beat was repeatedly asked about the ghost that night, and replied, "Devil a ghost have I seen, and devil a one do I want to see this blessed night. If I see one I'll run the spalpeen in, I will!"[3]

---

3. *Spalpeen* was an Irish term for "rascal." This quote has been translated from the thick Irish brogue in which the paper transcribed it.

In following years, stories occasionally circulated about the castle being haunted—a 1902 newspaper article spoke of residents seeing apparitions and suffering from nightmares. I once had a passenger on my tour who remembered the building from when it was standing; she told me that as a little girl, she always crossed the street to be far away from it when she was walking down 63rd Street—the building gave her the creeps, though it wasn't until years later that she learned the history behind it. Several other people who grew up in Englewood during the 1920s and 1930s and are still alive today seem to remember being superstitious about the place as well, though the story of what happened there was mostly forgotten by then. Like a few other places associated with Holmes, there was simply an aura of menace and unease about the place.

The castle building was purchased by the government in 1937 and torn down to make way for the new post office that was built on 63rd Street; the new building overlaps just slightly with the castle's original footprint, most of which stood on the grassy knoll just east of the new building. The elevated railroad tracks that run alongside it were grade-level in Holmes's day.

The post office, too, has occasionally inspired a ghost story, but nothing *too* specific. Mostly there are just stories about people in the building saying that it gets a little spooky at night, or that lights occasionally flicker on and off. One person wrote to me to say that his mother worked for the postal service in the 1960s and 1970s, leading him to spend many nights in the place; his time there was mostly occupied by playing in the mail carts, but he always had a vague sense that someone was watching him through the "dark" windows on the east side of the place, which would have been looking right into the space where the Holmes building stood.

It's long been said that some original structure from the castle remains down in the basement. As far as I know, I'm the only person who ever had a chance to do any real ghost hunting down there; I got into the site during the shoot for a new show that was being filmed for the History Channel in June 2012. I was officially only there as a historian, but I felt sort of obligated to do some ghost hunting while I was at it. At the time, I considered myself to be an advance scout for a major investigation that was scheduled to be held there in the fall of 2012, but as of this writing, that investigation has been postponed indefinitely; the post office isn't letting people in anymore, apparently by order of the postmaster general. So what evidence I picked up may be all we have to work with.

The tunnel in the basement of the post office that stands over a portion of the grounds where the Murder Castle once stood, and where the strange sound was recorded in 2012.

Fortunately, I got some of the most interesting things I've ever found on any ghost hunt, ever. Even as skeptical as I am of equipment readings, I got some interesting stuff.

A shadow in the basement: an H. H. Holmes victim,
or just a camera issue?

I got a few odd "shadow" photos—shots with a mysterious black mass covering up a portion of the frame. It was a large mass in the first shot, and I noticed it right away. I checked my camera for anything obvious that would cause such an issue, then took another shot of the same spot. The mass was still there, but smaller, then smaller still in the next shot, then gone in the fourth, as though it had been the shadow of something standing beside me that slowly slinked away.

As a ghost hunter, I wouldn't grade these any higher than about a C+. I was able to dismiss a couple of the most obvious explanations (such as saying it was the camera strap) at once, but it still seems like it's probably something to do with the camera, not a dead person, that caused the black spaces in the pictures. Maybe the aperture just didn't open all the way. There *does* seem to be something in the place that messes with cameras, though; the guys from the film crew were having some serious battery-drain issues, and my own camera was acting funny down there as well.

The Voice in the Tunnel

The most unusual feature of the basement today is the tunnel. If one climbs up a stepladder into a hole in the wall, there's a small tunnel that leads right into the footprint of the old castle basement. Postal employees told me it was an escape tunnel Holmes used, and I'm not quite sure I believe them (it seems more likely that it was for steam pipes or something), but part of it *is* lined with bricks that look about right for being from the 1890s, and the little brick wall is odd in and of itself: it serves no apparent purpose; some of the bricks show fire damage; and the top few rows seem to be "dressed" for being exterior bricks.

For lack of a better idea, as I sat alone in the tunnel I started whispering the names of the three victims I'm most confident were killed there: Emeline Cigrand (a stenographer), Julia Conner (who was having an affair with Holmes), and Pearl Conner (Julia's daughter).

I didn't hear anything odd in the tunnel in response to my whispers, but when I played the recording back, there was a voice, louder and clearer than my own, that sounded like a little girl singing. Now, I'm not usually that interested when people play me their EVP files—usually I feel like I need to use my imagination to hear much of anything. But in this case, the voice is louder than my own.[4]

The voice was clear, but what she was saying wasn't; the nearest I could transcribe, it sounded like she was saying, "Sorry Beefalow," which sounds like the world's worst Chef Boyardee product. Almost everyone *else* who hears it, though, seems to think she's saying, "Why did she go?" which could be a reference to Julia Conner, the mother of the girl thought to have been killed there.

Could that have been the voice of Pearl Conner? There was certainly no little girl anywhere near me at the time, and I didn't hear a thing down there with the naked ear. I'm usually averse to saying that equipment readings are evidence of hauntings, but this one was clear enough to require no particular imagination to make one think it's a ghost.

---

4. It can be heard on the Chicago Unbelievable blog's "Murder Castle Audio/Video" section.

If You Go

Bugging the post office is a bad idea, and many people today are scared even to go into Englewood, which has become the city's go-to place to mention when you want an example of a crime-ridden neighborhood. However, even if you can't get into the basement itself, it's worth remembering that *most* of the castle would have been located on the grassy space just to the left of the post office. No one will stop you from looking for ghosts on the grassy knoll during the day.

Also, try walking around the block and taking a look at the Disco Salad Bar.

For much more information on the castle, see my e-book short *Inside the Murder Castle* (Llewellyn Worldwide, 2012).

CHAPTER 5

H. H. Holmes and the Ghosts of Sobieski Street

"Sobieski" was the old name of a one-block section of See-ley Avenue (which is a half-block west of Damen Avenue), just below Fullerton. Here Holmes appears to have operated a "glass-bending factory" that was suspected of being used for cremations; he sure wasn't bending any glass there. I began to take people there as a historical curiosity on "serial killer" tours, but so many strange things happened there that I had to add it to the ghost tours as well.

We see a lot of odd things when we drive the tour bus down the dead-end street that was once known as Sobieski Street. One time, and only once, there were chickens crossing the road, which I thought only happened in jokes.

Another time we saw a van that was a-rockin' parked beside the vacant lot. I could just imagine the guy saying, "Come on, baby. I know the perfect little dead-end street.

No one ever goes there." Then, just at the exact wrong moment, here came the tour bus!

And sometimes things get scarier there. One winter's night, as we were turning the bus around (no easy trick on a dead-end street), there was a terrifying THUD and the bus came to a stop, as though we'd backed into something. I was afraid that the driver had backed us into a tree or a fire hydrant; there was snow falling, and the windows were too fogged up for us to see behind us very well. Then, to my great horror, a couple of customers said there had been a woman behind us, terrifying me further.

But when I ran out to see what had happened, there was nothing anywhere near the bus—we were several feet from any tree or fire hydrant or anything else that could have made such a noise or stopped us in our tracks, and certainly no woman and no footprints in the fresh snow to indicate that one had ever been there. The driver was freaked out, but I was sort of relieved; all things being equal, if we're going to hit something, I'd rather it be a ghost than a living person.

There's no telling who this could have been the ghost *of*; neighbors says that in the 1960s, '70s, and '80s, police used to find bodies in the vacant lot pretty regularly. But this site was also thought to be a "body dump" used by H. H. Holmes.

The Glassworks

As I discussed in the last chapter, there was not a lot of solid evidence found at the "Murder Castle"; and it's unlikely that even H. H. Holmes would have been brazen enough to dispose of too many bodies in such a crowded building, as it's hard to get rid of a dead body in such a place without people smelling it. In fact, though some fragments of remains that may have been human were found there, the bones may have been soup bones, and the quicklime pit seemed to be unused. Indeed, it may be that the basement of the castle was set up deliberately as a decoy that would keep the police busy in case he was ever caught. Pearl and Julia Conner disappeared early in the castle's history, but after the March 1893 *Tribune* article about the building and its secret passages, Holmes had to have known the castle could be searched one day.

And shortly after a fire at the castle halted the investigations there, newspapers announced that *another* "castle" had been found.

I'm occasionally accused of having made up the story of the Holmes "body dump," but I didn't. The story was broken in several newspapers around the country in late August 1895, after it was discovered by a man named Robert Corbitt, an amateur detective who had been working on the Holmes case. Corbitt is, to be sure, a bit of a wild card in the Holmes story; he was often known to state a belief that Holmes was innocent. I noticed an interested pattern in digging up data on Corbitt: he would say Holmes was guilty, then something bad would happen to him, then he'd say Holmes was innocent.

Whatever we think of his abilities as a detective, it must be admitted that he had access to more Holmes data and locations that modern researchers could ever dream of, being present at the castle excavations, in possession of a number of Holmes's personal documents and letters (more than the police had, it was said), and able to conduct interviews with people who knew Holmes.

In August of 1895, he told reporters that he and the police believed Holmes was doing whatever cremating he needed to do in a building that he'd called a "glass-bending factory" on

Sobieski Street, a short North Side street ten miles north of the castle (which seems like less of a distance when one considers that Holmes had a wife several miles farther north in suburban Wilmette, where he remained a reasonably familiar face to the neighbors). Corbitt's "discovery" of the factory came during one of his periods of saying Holmes was guilty; a week or two later, Corbitt was reported missing in Milwaukee, and reemerged to say Holmes was innocent again.

Holmes constantly spoke about starting a glass-bending business, and he had several costly pieces of equipment built that he said were for this purpose. He told a contractor that that's what the giant furnace in the castle basement was for, and demonstrated it to a few people who seemed rather unimpressed with his skills as a glass bender (but who don't seem to have asked why a trained physician would be so keen to get into the glass-bending business rather than practicing medicine). None of the facilities he built to bend glass, though, was quite as big as the factory Corbitt discovered.

To actually call this other building a second "castle," as the papers did, was stretching things a bit: it was just a shabby brick building with a two-story house behind it. But neighbors identified Holmes as the owner from a photograph, and Pat Quinlan, who was sort of the "Igor" of the Murder Castle, as the man who had emptied out all the garbage a short while before, while the cops had been occupied with investigating the castle. When the factory was "discovered," all that remained was some of Holmes's paperwork, some ashes, and clues indicating that it had recently housed a furnace that ran the whole 150-foot length of the place—this would have made it about ten times the size of the furnace found in the Murder Castle.

Unlike the bustling intersection of 63rd and Wallace, where the castle stood, Sobieski Street was a *great* location to get rid of bodies. It was an isolated area fronted by railroad tracks, with few neighbors who spoke English. A coal yard nearby would have been a perfect place to dump ashes, and the Luetgert Sausage Factory was near enough that it could have covered any odd odors. That factory, too, would one day be said to be haunted, after Adolph Luetgert was convicted of killing his wife and melting her body down in a curing vat there (see chapter 6).

The precise location of the glass-bending factory is hard to determine, as papers were a bit vague in their description. They said only that it was "where 65 Sobieski Street ought to be," and that it was just northwest of where the Northwest Line railroad tracks intersected with Robey Street (which is now Damen Street). This, though, is more than enough information to get an idea of the grounds—"Sobieski Street" was only about a block long. Today the street is a part of Seeley Avenue, extending about a block south of Fullerton Avenue before it dead-ends at the railroad tracks. A fire insurance map from 1911 shows an abandoned brick building with a two-story house at the rear that seem to match the descriptions of the place still standing there, right where a large garage stands today.

Strange Goings-On

That little no-thoroughfare gets a bit spooky at night today. The dead-end street goes along a vacant lot that gets so overgrown that I sometimes worry that customers might have Vietnam flashbacks, and there's usually a nasty-looking windowless van or two parked nearby, and sometimes a car that appears to be abandoned. Just from looking around, you'd never know you were in Chicago at all, let alone the fashionable Bucktown area.

*The site of the glass-bending factory,
as photographed by Jen Hathy.*

Sometimes, little things in the environment make it seem even spookier. One night we drove up to find three hawks with dead white birds in their mouths, sitting at the end of the road.

Another recent night, we found the place covered in snow. This was a bit shocking since there was no snow anywhere *else* on the tour route that night.

A couple of large trees stretch toward the sky toward the end of the road, and one of them is known to drip some sort of blood-red sap. I don't care what the scientific explanation for that might be—it's freakin' spooky.

In addition to the night when we thought we'd hit someone, "Sobieski Street" is also the only place on the tour where I ever thought I saw a full-body apparition. As we drove away from the place one night, a woman in a long dress was standing in the middle of the road. As we approached, she stepped in between a couple of cars that were parked along the curb. When we passed by the cars, the woman was gone.

Perhaps it was just a living woman who was now standing behind the cars, out of sight. But everyone on the bus saw her standing there as we approached, and no one saw her as we pulled away.

It's only been recently that anyone has gotten photographs there, but starting in 2012 we had a rash of pictures showing what appeared to be three-dimensional shadows. They looked like shadows of people, but in 3-D, and they weren't leaning against walls or the ground, but were free-standing in the parking area. One of the more recent ones shows what appears to be a man in a bowler hat leaning against one of the two trees at the end of the road.

Lexie Manke took this photo with a strange silhouette one night on the tour. It appears to be a man in a bowler hat. Holmes wore one of those, but so did nearly every other man in Chicago in the 1890s. I initially thought it was me in the photo, but other shots from that night show I was in a completely different sort of hat at the time.

The "Holmes Light"

One other factor working in favor of the idea that Holmes used the space as a body dump is the fact that it was very close to the homes of three of his known victims. It's quite possible that he was using the place not just to dispose of bodies, but to create a few new ones as well.

Minnie Williams, the only one of his wives who vanished, may have lived for a time in the two-story house that sat at the rear of the place. She and her sister Anna—who vanished long before Minnie did—lived for a short while in 1893 in an apartment on Wrightwood Avenue, just a short hike from the glass-bending factory.

Another young woman named Emily Van Tassel was an employee at Frank Wilde's Fruit and Grocery Store, a shop Holmes owned on Milwaukee Avenue, not far from the factory. Holmes's exact role in the store is tough to determine; he may have been Frank Wilde, but it also may have been his partner Ben Pitezel. What little information we have on Emily Van Tassel is a bit confusing—enough so that police weren't 100 percent confident Holmes had been involved in her disappearance, though her mother was convinced of it. If he was, it seems likely that it would have been much easier to take her to the factory than clear down to the castle. Oddly, in one version of his 1896 "confession" (which was mostly nonsense), Holmes called her "Anna Van Tassaud." In another version, he called her "Rosine Van Jassand."

In any case, she's the one I think is most likely to be haunting the place, if anyone is.

In the first couple of years that I took people there, the most popular attraction was a flickering light attached to a nearby house—it came to be known as the "Holmes Light."

Most nights it just appeared to be a bad light that flickered a lot (it's been disconnected completely now), but every now and then there would be a night when it would turn itself off and on like clockwork whenever someone said the names "H. H. Holmes," "Minnie Williams," "Anna

Williams," or (especially) "Emily Van Tassel." I tried to keep a sense of skepticism about it, but I was present on nights when the light really *did* seem to be responding to those names. Some nights the light would just flicker at random and I'd stand there looking like an idiot (one of my bigger skills), but on some nights I could stand there and test it again and again. It wouldn't change or flicker much when Hector or I said, "Ernie," "Bert," or "Oscar," but it would switch itself on or off as soon as we said, "Emily Van Tassel." Many customers accused me of having a remote control to operate it. I didn't blame them.

This brings up an interesting question: can hauntings be used as clues to solve flesh-and-blood mysteries? Police were never sure what happened to Emily Van Tassel, and listed her as a "maybe" when listing Holmes victims. It would never hold up in court, but if there's any reason to believe that Emily is haunting the area around a building once owned by H. H. Holmes, that would be the first clue we've had in over a century.

More North Side Holmes Locations

The glassworks was far from the only building outside of the famous "castle" that Holmes operated in Chicago. He had a few different offices and apartments in the Loop—three on Dearborn Street alone. A house he shared with one of his wives remained standing in suburban Wilmette until the 1990s.

In the Loop, Holmes and many of the gang from the "Murder Castle" operated the office for the ABC Copier Company in the Monon Building, at what would now be 436-444 S. Dearborn, near the Manhattan Building. It was torn down in 1947, and Congress Parkway now goes right over the location.

In Wicker Park stood Frank Wilde's Fruit and Grocery Store. The address was variously given as 1151 or 1152 Milwaukee Avenue, but 1152 was probably never an actual address (it would have been in the middle of a cross street). After the 1909 renumbering, 1151 would be 1513 N. Milwaukee, the site of a newer building, currently home to an AT&T store. Police in the 1890s became convinced that Holmes was Frank Wilde, though it seems to be one of his associates who actually ran the place.

Not far from the Sobieski Street "castle," Holmes rented an apartment for Minnie Williams at 1220 W. Wrightwood (which would be 1140 now). There's a new residential building there today.

If You Go

Like many places, "Sobieski Street" *seems* more isolated than it is. The nightmarishly muddled intersection of Damen, Fullerton, and Elston is barely a block away. Hence, most ghost-hunting gear that requires a quiet, stable environment will be particularly unreliable. Keep in mind that there are residential buildings nearby, and that if you wander off of the street itself, you may be trespassing. An ominous sign about trespassing includes the phrase "no dumping"—a fine sign to find at an old body dump.

The "Holmes Light" has now been disconnected, but strange smells, sounds, and photographs are still reported regularly. Neighbors often report a general sense of creepiness in the area.

CHAPTER 6

The Ghost of Louisa at the Luetgert Sausage Factory

1735 W. Diversey Avenue

This is a private condo building now, but it was here that "Old Man Luetgert" killed his wife, Louisa, and boiled her body down in a sausage-curing vat. Stories of the site being haunted started to circulate immediately after Louisa vanished and even figured into the subsequent trial. Located at 1735 W. Diversey, it's only a brisk walk from the H. H. Holmes "Sobieski Street" site.

It's tough for me to tell people the story of the Luetgert Sausage Factory murder. As soon as you've said "murder" and "sausage," any story that *doesn't* end with someone getting eaten is bound to be anticlimactic.

But Louisa Luetgert didn't get ground into sausage by Adolph Luetgert, her brute of a husband who fancied himself the Sausage King of Chicago. Rather, he just had her body boiled down in a "caustic soda" that he brewed up in a sausage-curing vat. Still, when stories went around in 1897 that a sausage-maker's wife was missing and was suspected to have been murdered, you can imagine what it did for sausage sales in the city.

Adolph was known as a man of a violent temper—some say that a tavern he owned at Webster and Clybourn Avenues is haunted by the woman and children he killed there. The actual building he owned is long gone, and there's no evidence that he killed his first wife or kids (records show them dying of natural causes), but he *does* seemed to have killed a guy outside of the place by shoving a giant wad of chewing tobacco down his throat. Old Man Luetgert had a temper, for sure.

His second wife, Louisa, was known to feel the wrath of his temper as well. Neighbors could hear them fighting from all over the neighborhood, and when she disappeared, they immediately suspected the worst. Eventually, the police found a ring with Louisa's initials on it and some bone fragments in the curing vats. More bits of bone and hair were found in the goopy run-off of junk from the factory that filled the nearby potholes. Only a year before, these bits wouldn't have been enough to convict Adolph; bone fragments hadn't been enough even to bring H. H. Holmes to trial in Chicago. But this was a case that would change history: Dr. George Dorsey, an anthropologist from the Field Museum, was able to establish that the bone fragments were the bones of a single human, and they were admitted as evidence.

Luetgert died in prison. Rumors that he said he was seeing Louisa's ghost in his cell are bunk (he was still insisting that she was alive), but he *may* have claimed to see her in the factory itself.

Stories that the factory was haunted began with Old Man Luetgert himself, when he was under investigation for the murder of his wife in 1897. One day he stomped into the police station and loudly accused them of "hiring" ghosts— apparently, he had seen the ghost of Louisa and believed that the police had hired someone to dress up like her to scare him into confessing. The police found this amusing, but one neighbor, Agatha Tosch, had to swear during the trial that she hadn't dressed up as a ghost to scare Mr. Luetgert.

In 1901, some years after the crime, a Des Moines newspaper reported that several neighbors had seen Louisa's ghost, including John Seifert, the factory watchman, who lived in the house adjacent to the factory; Gustaf Haus, who lived in the Luetgerts' adjacent house; and August Beck, who ran a saloon across the street. Seifert had even reported the ghost to the police, and Detectives John Quinn and William Blaul were sent to investigate.

Quinn saw a light in the window, and entered the place with a revolver at the ready (ghost hunts in those days usually did involve firearms). The light darted before Quinn, his partner, and Seifert like a bolt of lightning passing from the first floor down the stairs into the basement. Following it down, they found the light hovering on the exact spot where the infamous curing vat had stood, and now taking on the distinct form of a woman. Quinn chased it around the room a bit, and ended up crashing his face right through a window pane as it disappeared. The presence of so many full names in the article lends it some credence, but the whole thing sounds like a scene from *The Ghost and Mr. Chicken*. Detective Blaul seems to have liked to tell ghost stories; he appears later in this book as the source of an early ghost sighting in Lincoln Park.

Is Louisa Luetgert still haunting the basement
where her murdered body was boiled down?

Often said to have burned down in the early 20th century, the Luetgert Sausage Factory building is actually still there, part of a condo complex on Diversey, and ghost activity in the factory continued to be reported through the century. When a family purchased the building some time later, they felt (according to surviving descendants) that they got a good deal because no one else wanted a haunted building. In the 1940s, one of them would regularly hear footsteps going up and down the stairs to the basement where Louisa Luetgert's body was boiled down in a curing vat; he may have just been joking when he blamed the footsteps on her ghost.

If You Go

The building is private now, and the owners certainly don't want any ghost hunters lurking around, but be on the lookout for white lights floating around outside on Diversey.

CHAPTER 7

The Congress Hotel

520 S. Michigan Avenue

It's safe to estimate that more people have died at the Congress than at any other local hotel. Once known as the Auditorium Annex, and now officially known as the Congress Plaza, over the years it has hosted everyone from refugees to stars, from gangsters to presidents, and more than a couple are said to have stuck around.

One odd side effect of working in the ghostbusting industry is that no matter how hard you try to be level-headed and rational, you're still likely to get articles written about you that make you look like a nut.

In 2006, I found myself the subject of a very amusing tabloid article that described me as a "courageous ghost hunter" who had "dedicated his life to exposing the horrifying entities haunting the mean streets of Chicago." I've been called worse, I guess.

The article went on to describe a night in the Congress Hotel when I was "chased down the 12th floor hallway by a malevolent spirit."

Other people who were present that night contend that I "screamed like a little girl."

The truth is that I had gone up to the 12th floor to check on some equipment that was set up there, and when I returned to the elevator, I felt an overwhelming sensation that something was behind me. I ran to the elevator and wouldn't look back for anything. That's my story, and I'm sticking to it.

But I'm certainly not the first person ever to be scared on the 12th floor of the Congress.

There are some types of buildings that just *always* seem to be haunted. For instance, you never hear of an abandoned mental hospital that isn't supposed to be haunted by former inmates. In larger cities, there are two types of buildings that seem especially prone to haunts: theaters and hotels.

Most of the theater stories are pretty easy to explain; old theaters are full of creaks and noises and open spaces that can play tricks on your mind, and, anyway, if you ask the average theater person to tell you a ghost story, they *will* do it.

Hotels have the same creaks and noises, but if you do enough research, you'll probably find half a dozen or so deaths associated with any given older one. Usually, it'll be a handful of old people who died of natural causes, a couple of suicides, and perhaps a murder or two.

At the Congress Hotel, on South Michigan Avenue, I've found the names of dozens of people who died in their rooms, in the lobby, or in the tunnel that once connected the hotel to the Auditorium Theatre across the street.

It's only rarely, when I have a very small group, that I can take them inside of the hotel these days, but it's always a memorable stop when I can. The place was built in 1893 to accommodate visitors who came for the World's Fair, and it retains a bit of that vintage elegance. It is, in fact, one of those old buildings that seems as though it *ought* to be haunted as soon as you step inside.

There are lots of nonsense stories about the place circulating around: that Al Capone used to own it, or that serial killer H. H. Holmes used to stalk victims there, or that Stephen King based his short story "1408" on a sealed-off room. I get asked about them a lot, but the Capone and Holmes things are flatly untrue, and I don't know anything about any sealed-off rooms; the Stephen King thing seems to have grown out of an older myth that room 666 was sealed off (in reality, there were offices where room 666 would have been). There are plenty of stories I *can* verify, though, and naturally I prefer to focus on those.

A Dark and Splendid History

By the 1930s the Congress Hotel was world-famous. Presidents stayed there frequently, as did movie stars, opera singers, and gangsters. You can still download radio broadcasts of Benny Goodman playing in the ballrooms.

But while all old hotels have played host to a handful of deaths, the Congress seems to have played host to many more than its share. Most of them were old people dying of natural causes, though some of those deaths were fairly notable; for instance, G. H. Palin, the sloganeer who coined the phrase "Safety first," died there (it would have been a nice bit of irony if he died falling down the stairs or slipping in the shower, but it was a heart attack).

And then there have been a number of bloodier deaths. In 1908, there was an attempted murder-suicide, involving a love triangle, just outside of the front door. A husband and wife, shot by the wife's jealous lover, reconciled as they lay bleeding on the sidewalk. The wife's name was Ruby Pishzak—newspapers couldn't resist commenting on the "ruby-red blood of Ruby Pishzak" in headlines. She survived, and wound up divorcing her husband after all.

Also in 1908, a ballroom in the Congress was frequented by a man named Roy Gormley who spent money like a sailor on shore leave—indeed, he seemed to be trying to run himself broke. And, as it turned out, he was. One night, Roy offered the orchestra leader $500 if they would play "The Dead March" from *Saul*, a tune perhaps best known for being played when soldiers are buried at sea. The orchestra leader said they didn't know it, so Roy hummed it. They must have managed an acceptable rendition, because Roy gave them the money and bought a round of drinks for the orchestra—plus another round to be delivered the next week. Then, having finally spent his last dollar, Roy retired to his room, where he committed suicide.

In the 1920s, at least one man died there of drinking poison moonshine—ever a danger in the Prohibition era, when several gangsters lived in well-appointed suites at the hotel.

Theodore Roosevelt, who is sometimes said to haunt the place, didn't die in the building—but, from a certain point of view, his career did. It was in the Florentine Room that he announced, in 1912, that he was leaving the Republican Party to run as the candidate of the Progressive Party (better known as the Bull Moose Party). In one of the most remarkable campaigns in American history, he had managed to beat William Howard Taft, the incumbent Republican president, in the primaries; but when, in that era of less democratic political conventions, Roosevelt didn't win the party's nomination, he decided to form a new party. In the November election, however, he lost in a four-way race to Woodrow Wilson, and Roosevelt never held elective office again.

The north wing of the hotel is from 1893, and the south wing was constructed in 1902 and 1907, around the time that the name was changed to the Congress from the Auditorium Annex. Part of the new construction included the massive ballroom known as the Gold Room, which was the first ballroom in the city to be air-conditioned. That and the Florentine Room are the oldest ballrooms left today. Many others, like the Elizabethan Room and the Pompeiian Room, have vanished so thoroughly that no one at the hotel even seems to know where they *were* anymore.

Indeed, the hotel itself is sort of a ghost today—a surviving relic of an era when all the classy people went to hotels to hang out, and the performers in the ballrooms were the biggest talents in America.

But plenty of the regular kinds of ghosts get reported there as well.

Ghosts are known to appear right at the entrance: there's one that's variously known as "Twenties Man" or the "gangster guy." He sometimes appears right in the front hallway in an overcoat and a fedora, and appears to be a guy from the 1920s (he's also been seen on the second floor). He doesn't say much but seems to appear and disappear. One woman on my tour recently described walking into the hotel and noticing the man standing there as she tried to find her elevator, then turned her head and he was gone. When she mentioned this to a doorman, he asked her, "Was it that guy from the 1920s? We see him now and then."

One thing frequently seen in online reviews of the hotel is that the TVs turn themselves on and off at random. This drives the engineering staff nuts. They've tried to replace wiring and to replace the TVs, but nothing works. Some guards blame the phenomenon on the ghost of "the Judge," one of the last elderly people to move into the hotel permanently. In his declining years, he acquired a remote control that worked on the TVs in the hotel rooms and would amuse himself by sitting outside of rooms, turning guests' TVs off and on from the hallway. Some say that the TVs turning themselves on and off now is just the ghost of the judge, up to his old tricks again like a regular little rascal.

The "Shadow Guy" and the "Little Boy"

At times when I was able to get groups in regularly, I got to know the security staff pretty well, and they kept me abreast of paranormal developments. Just recently, a security guard told me that they'd received a call from a man saying that something—a ghost, he was sure—was moving around in his closet.

"Will you look inside the closet and see if there's anything there now, sir?" security asked.

"Hell no!" the man replied.

By the time security arrived (to find nothing in the closet), the man had packed up and was in the hall, ready to move to another room, if not another hotel.

Other guests have reported a shadowy figure that is said to appear mainly to people associated with the military (according to several employees, it once scared a roomful of Marines so badly that they rushed to the lobby in their underwear and refused to go back). Given the military connection, it's been speculated that this may be the ghost of the first man to die violently in the hotel: Captain Louis Ostheim, a U.S. Army officer, who was found in his room with a bullet wound in his temple in 1900.

Ostheim had recently returned from the Spanish-American War, and was suffering from night terrors—really violent nightmares from which he would wake up screaming, probably a result of post-traumatic stress disorder. His friends believed that he had awakened and shot himself in the midst of a nightmare before becoming conscious enough to realize that it was all a dream, though it could always have been cold feet as well—he was to be married the next day.

I've been in plenty of places where we saw mysterious humanesque shadows zipping by, and they aren't really all that scary. When you see one, you just think, "Hey, there goes one. How about that?" This one, however, seems to be scary enough to frighten people out of their rooms. Could it be that the terror in his brain that led Captain Ostheim to shoot himself lingers along with his shadow?

But the most tragic Congress Hotel story of all is that of the little boy whose ghost is seen on the top floor of the north wing. Some have also seen a little girl (of course), leading me to wonder if it may be the ghosts of Donald and Zudel Stoddard, a brother and sister who perished in the Iroquois Theatre fire, trying to find their mother, who was waiting for them at the Congress. But as sightings of the boy are far more common than reports of the girl, I tend to tell people that the most likely identity for the ghost is Karel Langer, who was six years old when he died, and assume that the ghostly little girl is probably an exaggeration, not a ghost that anyone actually sees.

In 1938, the Langer family fled their hometown of Prague when Hitler took over Czechoslovakia. They had to sell the factory and mansion they owned for next to nothing, and wound up living in basement in Humboldt Park on the West Side of Chicago. The mother of the family, Adele, was driven to madness, it was said, by the persecution she and her family had suffered, both in Prague and in Chicago at the hands of hostile German Chicagoans. The fear that she was going to be sent back to Czechoslovakia when their visa expired weighed heavily on her mind as well, and she seems to have suffered a nervous breakdown.

In a fit of what was determined to be temporary insanity, she checked into the Congress Hotel with her sons, Karel, who was six, and Jan, who was four, in early August 1939, and asked for a room on the top floor (the 12th). There she threw both boys out of the window before jumping out herself. All three died.

Ghost hunters don't agree on much, but one thing that many believe is that a lack of commemoration will lead to more ghost sightings. The next day, photos of Adele and Jan, the four-year-old, appeared in many newspapers, but there was no picture of Karel. Perhaps that's why he stuck around. I hadn't yet heard the story of him when I felt like I was being chased down the hallway.

In any case, every security guard I've spoken to agrees that the 12th floor is pretty creepy at night. One even told me that he once stood stock still at the end of the hall and watched the other end grow farther and farther away.

The Gold Room

The ballroom known as the Gold Room is sometimes said to be haunted by the ghost of a man with a peg leg.

I'm not making that up. *Someone* might have, but it sure wasn't me.

When I first assisted on an investigation of the place, security told us that they'd recently received several reports from customers saying that a homeless man with a peg leg was lying around in the hallway. They would go to run the guy off and find no trace of him. Some reports (which I've never been able to verify independently) state that a hobo with a peg leg was murdered in the hotel in the 1920s.

Initially the hotel workers told us this was on the seventh floor in the south wing, but one guard told me that he'd shown up in the Gold Room as well.

The Gold Room is the most impressive of the ballrooms that remain in the hotel today—a real throwback to the days when hotel ballrooms were really *something*. A few ghosts get reported there; some people have told stories of a bride and groom walking around the balcony, and some have sworn they heard an orchestra tuning up there in the middle of the night. But most of the ghostly activity on the second floor seems to take place *around* the ballroom, not in it. One guard told me that the ovens in the nearby kitchen have been known to turn themselves on, despite the fact that they aren't supposed to be connected to anything anymore. On one occasion—and only one—I saw strange colored lights dancing about on the ceiling in the lobby outside of the ballroom.

The Florentine Room

But as spooky as the Gold Room can seem in the dark, ground zero for ghostly activity in the Congress Hotel is, without question, the Florentine ballroom. Some longtime security guards have refused even to go near the place.

Step into the Florentine Room, and you'll probably immediately notice that the atmosphere there is markedly different from the atmosphere in the Gold Room. On some nights, it's absolutely terrifying just to walk into the room. Even on nights when it doesn't make the hair stand up on the back of one's neck, the old wooden floor creaks as you walk across it, and the series of Florentine-style paintings on the arched ceiling seem to be telling some sort of story that you can't *quite* comprehend.

It was here that Theodore Roosevelt made his grand announcement that he was leaving the GOP, which was no longer radical enough for him (and had been careless enough to renominate Taft instead of him), to lead the Bull Moose Party in 1912. He never held elective office again, and is sometimes said to haunt the place. A photo of a mysterious silhouette was taken here in 2008—it seems to show a stout man standing upright in a Roosevelt-like posture. I'm standing to the left of it in the shot; I like to imagine that it's a picture of me with Colonel Roosevelt.

The silhouette in a photo by John Stephenson. Colonel Roosevelt?

One night after seeing a TV show about "era cues"—the practice of playing music from a ghost's era to see if the music could persuade the ghost to show up—one tour customer asked me what sort of music they played at the Teddy Roosevelt rallies held in the ballroom. I agreed that trying an era cue might be fun, so before turning the lights on, I wandered to the piano and picked out a rough version of "Battle Hymn of the Republic," the 1912 Bull Moose campaign's theme song, using single soprano notes that echoed through the darkened hall. Nothing unusual happened, but it sounded so deliciously spooky that I decided to do it every chance I got.

And so, every time I was in the room after that, I would play a few bars of the song, usually leaving off in the middle of a line. Most of the time, nothing happened—but on two occasions, as I walked away, there was a distinct sound of another piano note in the air. One time there was a stray baritone note that rang out while I was plunking at the keys on the other end of the scale.

Stories of phantom music in the room are fairly common. Many guards say they've heard music coming from the room (one specifically mentioned calliope music, which he theorized was from the room's stint as a roller-skating rink). Others talk about hearing a guy humming in there, which makes me think of Roy Gormley, they guy who hummed "The Dead March" for the orchestra before ending his life.

The Phantom Gunshot

The most famous story of the ballroom, however, has become the story of the "Phantom Gunshot."

Now, it's no secret that the hotel was once a favorite of gangsters. Al Capone never owned the place, but he certainly spent some time there—his gang even held a guy hostage there for a while. In the days before the gangs really started fighting in the mid-1920s, members of nearly every gang in town were living there, more or less in peace. Tony Genna, of the "Terrible Genna Brothers," had a $100-per-night suite (quite a sum in 1920s money). Vinnie "The Schemer" Drucci, whose gang would soon wipe out the Genna brothers, lived there around the same time.

According to legend, there was once a mob murder in the service hallway that runs alongside the Florentine ballroom. Whether this is true or not is totally unknown—when gangsters kill each other in service hallways, they don't exactly fill out paperwork that you can dig up at the library later.

But one night, we thought we heard the ghostly sound of a gunshot coming from that hall.

Here's what I wrote on the Chicago Unbelievable blog at the time:

> *Shortly after we wandered into the darkened ballroom, I felt as spooked as I'd ever been in that room. Enough so that I quietly broke out a keychain to try Hector's "pendulum trick," at which I normally scoff.[5] Suddenly there was a huge BLAM coming from one of the service hallways off to the side—I honestly thought someone had fired a gun at us.*
>
> *There were no footsteps following it. No scream, no sound of a body hitting the ground. And when we opened the door to the hallway, no one was there.*
>
> *We spent the next several minutes scouring the area, trying to see if there was any way to explain the gunshot sound. There were some people who thought they detected some movement in the door to the hall itself, as though it had been cracked ever so slightly ajar, then shut at the time of the sound, but there wasn't nearly enough movement to cause anything like the noise we heard. Even when we*

---

5. Hector sometimes holds up a pendulum and asks it if there are ghosts in the room. It's fun. I feel kind of silly talking to rocks, but the results we get with it are no less reliable than what you'd get from any commercially available ghost-hunting gear.

SLAMMED the door, it sounded more like a door slam-
ming than a gunshot. The slight movement could have just
been impact from the force of the noise (which, again, was
REALLY loud).

When we ventured out, I went down to the office and
spoke to security, saying, "Okay, guys, nice one—how did
you do it?" They insisted that they hadn't faked us out,
and showed me logs indicating that no guard had been on
the floor at the time.

Over the next year or so, we heard the "gunshot" again a
handful of times—and caught a security guard in the act of
faking it at least once by setting off a firecracker and hiding
in a locked closet (however, the firecracker was a different
sound than the gunshot). These days, now that some time
has passed, I'd say that odds are *pretty* good that they set it
up every time, but I have to give them credit for this one—
they certainly scared the heck out of us, and I sure can't
prove it was them the first time.

Nor can I explain how they could have made *all* of the
loud noises we heard in there—some of them actually came
from the ceiling, and seemed loud enough that they would
have broken right through if they were just stomping on
the roof.

If You Go

Union members on the hotel's staff were on strike for ten
long years, so I never recommended actually staying there,
though I had no moral qualms about just popping in to look
at the hotel's stuff and use the bathroom. But the strike
ended in May 2013, so there's no reason not to book a room

on the 12th floor. If you go after 5:30 in the off-season, after management has gone home, several of the security guards are usually happy to tell ghost stories if there's nothing else going on for them to deal with. Whether they can show you the ballrooms depends on (a) whether there's a function going on in them, and (b) whether the staff likes you. So be polite.

For best results, be upfront, make it clear that you're interested in the history of the building (not just the "paranormal" stuff), and be friendly. Do *not* just go sneaking around or hiding out in the ballrooms, or you'll be asked to leave. Reputable ghost hunters don't go sneaking around in places when they could get proper permission (even though I must admit that it can take some of the fun out of things).

CHAPTER 8

Abraham Lincoln's Funeral Train

Within view of the Congress Hotel stood the depot at Michigan and 12th where Lincoln's funeral train pulled into town and where a ghost train has been reported from time to time. The funeral carriage would have passed right by the site of the Congress Hotel.

After Abraham Lincoln's assassination in 1865, his body went on tour. There were stops in most every major city between Washington, D.C., and Springfield, Illinois, and the body was laid in state at each stop so that the citizens would have a chance to pay their last respects. Many spectators had never seen the president when he was alive, and in those days when photographs weren't as ubiquitous as they are now, this would have been their first real-life view of Lincoln. It was hardly the best way to see him; the embalming process turned his face a dark purple hue over the course of the tour. Stories about this filtered down south, where a few of his louder detractors snorted that they'd always known he was secretly a black man.

For many years, people all over the country reported encounters with the ghost of the train that had carried Lincoln's casket. The way I first heard the story, people in Chicago not only saw the train but also saw the casket itself, and the ghost of Lincoln himself dancing around it with the flesh dropping off of his face.

The Lincoln funeral train, 1865. The ghost of the train was one of the more famous ghosts of the 19th century.

Lincoln Lying in State

The courthouse at the time of Lincoln's lying in state in Chicago; the blurry mass is the massive crowd filing in and out.

It's a grisly and memorable image, but it doesn't stand up to research very well.

The funeral train did come to Chicago, rolling around the perimeter of the lake en route from Michigan City, Indiana, the previous stop. It pulled into a depot that stood at 12th Street (now Roosevelt Road) and Michigan Avenue, which, incidentally, was within spitting distance of the spot where the Democratic National Convention had nominated General George B. McClellan to run against Lincoln for president only months before (an event that the *Tribune* described as a real amateur hour, and that the Lincoln-hating *Chicago Times* described as an event not unlike Caesar coming into Rome).

The casket was loaded into a hearse that drew it up Michigan Avenue to Lake Street, and then over to Clark, where it was put on display in the rotunda of the old courthouse that stood at Clark and Washington.

This courthouse, incidentally, was only blocks from the Tremont House hotel, where both Lincoln and John Wilkes Booth, his assassin, had stayed in Chicago (at separate times, obviously). Booth was the theatrical hit of 1862 in his run at the McVicker's Theatre, which was near Madison and State. Just imagine how odd it must have been for people to file past the corpse, remembering Booth, only blocks away, making speeches plotting to kill a king in his roles as Hamlet or Macbeth, both of which he played at McVicker's. Stories eventually circulated that he was either haunting that theater or hiding out in it, having faked his death (as nearly all outlaws killed in shootouts are said to have done).

In 1867, stories went around that the jail and courthouse were haunted. All through the autumn of that year, mysterious noises were heard, and strange "shapes" were seen by the jailers, as well as the specter of a man. A story about it published in the *Tribune* created a bit of a sensation, and crowds estimated to number in the hundreds came to the jail to hear the ghostly sounds for themselves. They were not disappointed; at ten o'clock at night, a sound was heard that the paper described as "a wail so pitiful and full of agony that everyone hearing it started to their feet, while the prisoners in different cells ceased their laughter and conversation and listened." The ghosts were never quite explained; most assumed that it was the ghost of one of the few people who'd been hanged there, but the fact that Lincoln's body had been laid in state there is certainly worth noting.

Sightings of the ghost of the funeral train that carried the president's remains were common around the country for years, and most ghost researchers would describe the ghostly train as a "psychic imprint" type of a ghost, a sort of "visual echo" created by the intense mental energy of the people who came out to view the train. The fact that no one has seen it in years, to my knowledge, actually works in this one's favor—one would assume that these "psychic imprints," if they can be created at all, wouldn't last forever.

Less plausible, though, is the part about Lincoln's flesh dropping off of his face as the train approached Chicago. The body had been re-embalmed several times during the trip, and by the time it reached Chicago, President Lincoln was basically a mummy.

In fact, in 1901, Lincoln's coffin was dug up to be moved to its current location in the tomb in Springfield, after a long period in which it had been moved hither and yon throughout the grounds of the elaborate tomb, occasionally even being hidden under the floor while the mourners and the curious filed past a sarcophagus that was actually empty. When the workers and officials had the coffin out in the air, it was determined that they ought to open it up and make sure Lincoln was still inside of it; there were *lots* of conspiracy theories stating that he wasn't, and there had been at least a couple of attempts (one of which was nearly successful) to steal the body and hold it for ransom. This would be the last chance to put to rest the rumors that Lincoln wasn't in the coffin.

So the coffin was opened, and the body was found not only to be present but also to be recognizably that of Abraham Lincoln. A bit of red dust covered the chest (it took them a while to realize that this was the remains of a flag that had been draped over him and had rotted away in the casket).

But while the flag had mostly disintegrated, the face was still recognizably the face of Abraham Lincoln, albeit that it was now a deep copper color (which makes me extremely tempted to make a flip remark about him looking just like he does on pennies).

If You Go

The depot is long gone, but Michigan and Roosevelt remains a busy intersection, so a ghost train pulling up to the spot would be difficult to miss! The old courthouse was replaced a short while after the Great Fire in 1871; City Hall stands on the site now. I don't know of any reports of ghosts in there, but I'd be shocked if the security guards didn't have a few.

CHAPTER 9

The St. Valentine's Day Massacre

2122 N. Clark Street

The little field where 2122 N. Clark ought to be was the site of one of the most famous mass murders in history.

The facts are these:

In 1920, the Eighteenth Amendment to the Constitution went into effect, banning the sale of alcohol in the United States. Wine makers were forced to sell "grape concentrate," which hurt sales until they started adding warning labels stating that if you weren't careful, you could *accidentally* ferment the juice and turn it into wine. Beer breweries were forced either to shut down or switch to making nonalcoholic "near beer" (alias "pee water") instead.

And yet, the appetite for booze remained strong nationwide. If anything, it got *stronger* in some areas, as a whole generation of previously upright citizens were introduced to the fun and thrills of breaking the law. By one estimate, the number of places where you could get a drink in Chicago roughly tripled, despite the fact that a drink that cost a nickel before Prohibition now cost exponentially more.

Naturally, the jump in demand, drop in supply, and subsequent rise in price for booze was the best thing that ever happened to the local gangsters.

The major gangs divided the city into territories and operated more or less in peace for a few years, with John Torrio, head of the South Side (and boss to young Al Capone), acting as the peacekeeper. But after Dean O'Banion was murdered by the Genna brothers (who worked for Torrio), a war ensued, and leaders of gangs dropped like so many flies. By 1929, the two major gangs were run by Al "Scarface" Capone and George "Bugs" Moran; there were lots of individual organizations in the city, but every gangster was either a "Capone guy" or a "Moran guy."

On February 14, 1929, five men associated with Moran's North Side gang (plus an optometrist named Reinhardt Schwimmer who liked to hang out with gangsters, and John May, a gangster-turned-mechanic who'd been trying to go straight, but needed money) congregated at the SMC Cartage Company, a garage on North Clark Street, presumably waiting for Moran himself to arrive. Instead of Moran arriving, a police car pulled up, and the garage was entered by two men dressed as police officers and a couple of men dressed in plain clothes. Neighbors heard some loud noises, and then the men dressed as cops walked out, pushing the men in plain clothes in front of them, making it look as though there had been a regular liquor raid.

Moran himself wasn't there at the time; he had seen the police car, thought it was a raid, and ducked into a nearby coffee shop (often said to be the one now known as Mello's, in the building that was used for exterior shots of the apartment building where Larry and Balki lived for a few seasons of the 1980s sitcom *Perfect Strangers*).

The frantic barking of Highball, a German shepherd[6] tied to the axle of one of the trucks in the garage, alerted the neighbors, who found that seven men had been lined up against the wall and shot. Six were already dead—the other two, including one Frank Gusenberg, died soon after.

Gusenberg was a gangster to the end—when asked what had happened, he looked up, nearly dead and bleeding from the bullet holes, and said, "Nobody shot me." One paper claims that he said, "Cops did it."

This had been, clearly, a straight-up assassination. The victims had thousands of dollars in their pockets that the killers left untouched.

Newspapers around the country printed hideous, gruesome photographs of the crime scene. Those who thought Reinhardt Schwimmer had no brains in his head to run around with gangsters just for bragging rights could see his brains for themselves, lying next to his hat and his shattered skull.

The "fun" of Prohibition was officially over the minute those papers hit the press.

Immediately, suspicion fell on the Capone gang, and it was assumed that the massacre had been an attempt on the life of Capone's chief rival, Bugs Moran. One theory goes that the men dressed as cops had lined up the men against the wall and said, "All right, which one of you mugs is Bugs

---

6. Some say he was an Alsatian shepherd—I honestly wouldn't know. I can't tell based on the surviving photos.

Moran?" When no one said they were him (since none were), they simply killed all seven of them.

Capone himself was in Florida at the time, but his gang seemed like the obvious culprit. His main hitman, "Machine Gun" Jack McGurn, was held for a time, but eventually let go due to lack of evidence. He had spent the morning in a hotel room with a blonde showgirl, whom he later married.

Indeed, though it's generally thought that the "massacre" was an attempt on the life of Bugs Moran, exactly what happened, and who was involved, is still unknown. Every few months there's a new theory—perhaps the most common today is that Capone brought in some gangsters from Detroit or Missouri to handle it.

Others, however, doubt he would have trusted such a sensitive operation to people he didn't know he could trust. The "orthodox" solution is still that the hit was arranged by Jack McGurn, Capone's hitman and confidant, who perhaps brought in some outside help that the North Siders wouldn't recognize, and was possibly aided by "the murder twins," John Scalise and Albert Anselmi, whom Capone had used as assassins before and who weren't exactly known as great thinkers. Shooting all seven people would have been just the kind of boneheaded move Scalise and Anselmi might have pulled, and some speculate that it was Capone's anger at this overreach—which brought a lot of heat onto the organization—that led to Scalise and Anselmi's own deaths. In any case, they didn't last long; a few months after the massacre, their bodies were found on a roadside, shot full of holes and beaten to a bloody pulp with blunt instruments usually said to have been baseball bats.

But this is really just one of dozens of theories that go around about the massacre. In any case, no matter who was responsible, the massacre was a turning point for both the North and South Side gangs—it was pretty much the end of the North Siders (no one wanted to work for Moran after that) and turned the public against Capone, whether he was involved or not, and finally motivated the federal government to get involved in the case. A couple of years later, Capone was finally arrested on tax-evasion charges.

He was scared enough in the aftermath of the massacre to get himself arrested (quite probably on purpose) in Philadelphia on an illegal-weapons possession charge, which allowed him to lie low in a Pennsylvania prison until things cooled down. He emerged from prison into a different world; Miami, where he'd been spending most of his time, no longer wanted him, and the Feds were building a case against him for tax evasion in Chicago. In 1931, he was given an eleven-year sentence. After his release, he lived out most of his remaining few years in his Miami estate, seldom venturing out and largely ignored by a world full of people who thought he had died in prison years before— the fate of many who have the discourtesy to outlive the eras they help define.

So Capone was gone—but the story of the SMC Cartage on Clark Street wasn't over yet.

Ghosts and Curses

The bullet holes remained in the north wall of the building, where the men had been lined up. A few decades later, when the building was torn down (after generations of curiosity seekers had snuck in), the entire north wall was sold to a man who rebuilt it, brick by brick, and set it up as a urinal wall in a Roaring Twenties–themed restaurant in Canada— guys would stand to pee just where the gangsters stood to be shot, and were supposed to aim for the bullet holes.

The restaurant didn't last long. When it closed, the bricks were sold to a collector, and many have shown up on the collector's market since—often priced as high as $1,500 per brick. You usually have to take the dealer's word for it that these are *actual* bricks from the massacre, and the fact that they might be cursed comes with the territory.

Early on, stories began to circulate about gunshots, screams, and sobs being heard inside of the building, but the most famous ghost story, by far, was that dogs would go insane when they were walked past the location—reacting, presumably, to a psychic imprint left by Highball, the lone survivor. Even if the dog wasn't killed, one could theorize that he was so freaked out that some sort of mental "imprint" could be left behind.

If such an imprint was ever there, it's faded considerably—it's to be assumed that such "residual energy" would fade over time. I've heard enough accounts of dogs going crazy at this location in the past to believe it *used* to work, but in recent years I've seen many, many dogs walk past the spot, and I never saw any of them react in any way. The story has, perhaps as a result, narrowed—it used to be said that any dog would go nuts at any time; nowadays, some say that the dog has to be a German or Alsatian shepherd and that the date *has* to be February 14.

The location is now a small empty lot next to a senior apartment complex; a tree in the middle roughly marks the spot where the north wall would have been. Some say that on nights when there's snow on the ground (again, sometimes it has to be *fresh* snow, and *on* February 14), you can see faint impressions in the ground where the bodies would have been. One tour passenger who lived nearby confirmed that he'd seen this firsthand—they don't look like outlines of bodies, but there are, he told me, often five or six roughly humanesque impressions in fresh snow. I thought I could see it once myself, too.

People who go into the senior apartment complex next door to ask about the St. Valentine's Day Massacre tend to find themselves being escorted off the premises, but every now and then one of the residents will be outside when I bring groups there, and some have stories to share.

One woman came up to me one day and told me that she'd recently gone to Target in order to buy a giant dress. She was a small woman herself but wanted a big dress to hang over her mirror, because every now and then she'd look in it and see a man in a pinstriped suit and fedora.

"These are souls that are stuck in purgatory," she explained, "which is where they're going to be until Judgment Day."

I sometimes think that I must have a sign on my back reading, "Tell Me About Judgment Day." Still, even if the story was just the woman's icebreaker for her sermon, hers isn't the only story about a man dressed as a gangster that has filtered out from the building.

Was Capone Haunted Himself?

Legend has it that Capone himself believed he was being harassed by the ghost of James T. Clark, one of the gangsters killed on the scene. Stories go that while he was living in his Miami estate, his staff would hear him shouting, "Jimmy, for the love of God, leave me alone," or even that members of the staff saw the ghost sitting at the foot of Capone's bed, smiling and smoking before fading away, leaving nothing but the cherry from the end of the cigarette hanging in the air. His valet, Hymie Cornish, is said to have witnessed this. During the buildup to his 1931 trial, Capone is even said to have hired a psychic, one Alice Britt, to confirm that Clark was haunting him and get rid of the ghost.

However, researchers have pretty much concluded that the whole story about Capone being haunted is false. Alice Britt does not seem to have existed at all, and Hymie Cornish doesn't appear to have been a real person either. Both of those names only appear in print or on record in rehashings of the Capone story, which, unfortunately, seem to have been invented outright around the 1970s; no one has found a version of the story told before then. Even if Capone *was* seeing ghosts, we would probably just chalk it up to his brain being destroyed by syphilis.

If You Go

Every Chicago ghost hunter should check this site out at one point or another, but there's not a lot left to see, and I've never been all that impressed with the ghost stories about the place. I have seen a couple of pictures from the place where the ground appeared to be blood-red in the photos, but beyond that, this is a place that I *wish* I had better stories about. People on tours always want to see the massacre site, and it's gone down in several books as a notably haunted place, but I never seem to see anything there myself.

However, if you're in the area around February 14, and it happens to be snowing, and you happen to have a dog—it's definitely worth a shot!

CHAPTER 10

Old Town Tatu

3313 W. Irving Park Road

When I first investigated this place, it was already said to be haunted by ghosts from the days when the building was a funeral home. But it seems to have gotten more haunted since.

I must admit that I rolled my eyes when first told that I'd be running an investigation of a tattoo parlor (which, it was said, was not really a bastion of sobriety). The fact that it had once been a funeral home didn't convince me—after all, we usually expect ghosts to haunt the places where they died. Who dies in a funeral parlor?

But upon stepping into what was then known as Odin Tatu, I could see right away that the place was awesome. Despite all the modern touches, the plasterwork, the woodwork, and the stained glass all still gave it a distinctly "funeral parlor" vibe—as did the gravestone in the fireplace. When the tattoo people moved in, they found the gravestone in the attic. It made them nervous knowing the thing was up there, so they moved it down to the fireplace. Even if the building wasn't haunted, it was going to be a cool place to explore.

The staff had *lots* of stories about ghostly goings-on there. They told us about a mask that often fell from the wall, no matter how well it had been fastened, about shelves dropped of their own accord, and of ashtrays flying across the room and landing upside down without disturbing an ash. Others had vague stories about feeling as though they saw someone out of the corner of their eye, and one (presumably a *Scooby-Doo* fan like me) told us stories about hearing a ghost in the basement going, "Woooooo."

A couple of employees told us stories of the ghost of a little girl that they'd heard (or at least felt) in the front lobby, though no one claimed to have seen her. The speculation here was that it was not the ghost of a girl who died here, but a "psychic imprint" implanted on the environment by a girl who had accidentally been left behind after a funeral and was scared out of her wits.

The best stories came from the owner, Richie "Tapeworm" Herrera, whose enthusiasm for the building and its history was infectious. He told us (in very colorful language) about seeing a ghostly man in a brown suit, and another in a powder-blue suit, staring at him from the kitchen (the former embalming room, he said) while he worked. This would presumably be the ghost of some poor sap who died in the 1970s, when powder-blue suits were a thing.

And that was just down on the first floor. In the upstairs apartment, where Tapeworm lived, there were rooms where no one had ever been able to get a good night's sleep, and rooms that suffered from odd electrical disturbances. Windows opened and closed of their own accord, and ashtrays flew across the room as though thrown by unseen hands. They'd land upside down, but not a single ash would be disturbed when they were put right side up.

Down in the basement (which the guy leading the investigation told us was once the original embalming area and the site of the crematory oven), I got perhaps the strongest "haunted" feeling that I've ever felt as I wandered toward a dark corner. There I felt as though a hand was on my shoulder, and I felt a deep temperature drop.

The girl next to me, who was reputed to be a psychic, felt it too and called out, "What's your name?"

Just then, through the earphones I was wearing connected to my audio recorder, I heard a distinct voice say, "Walter."

Tapeworm began to freak out when I told him this; according to him, there were three generations of the Klemundt family that had owned the funeral home—the last of whom was a guy named Walter. This recording would go on to be shown on a TV show or two.

However, there was never any owner by that name. When I first learned that, I suspected the entire thing had been a hoax, but it turned out that the Klemundt family had believed the place was haunted for years, which removes the employees from any suspicion of having invented the *whole* thing, even if some of them might have been trying to stretch things a bit.

The building (at least the above-ground portion) was built by John Aloysius Klemundt in 1923; he was a graduate of the Art Institute of Chicago and had been in the funeral business himself since 1909. It was by no means the first funeral home in the city, as is sometimes claimed, and though the story currently going around that the woodwork was salvaged from the only South Side building to survive the Great Chicago Fire isn't quite right (the fire didn't burn much of the South Side), John Klemundt *did* salvage lots of architectural details from old mansions, many of which are still in the building. For thirty years, the structure was a "chapel" building that was used for both funerals and weddings, though it fell into disuse when a newer chapel was built next door (the next building to the west is no longer a chapel either, but you can sort of tell that it used to be when you look at it). The back kitchen, where Tapeworm saw ghosts watching him, *is* said to have served as an embalming room until the 1970s, but the basement was never more than a woodworking shop, and certainly never housed a crematorium.

Tapeworm was wrong about a man named Walter having been the owner of the building—the only owners of record were John A. Klemundt and John F. Klemundt. Assuming he hadn't hidden someone behind a wall to shout out the name, exactly who the "Walter" on the recording would have been is sort of an open question. One interview I conducted with a man associated with the building told me that Tapeworm was actually thinking of *another* guy named Walter who had lived there once—one who wasn't dead yet.

In interviews with the Klemundt family, the team from the TV show *Ghost Lab* established that there w*as* a Walter in the family: Walter Loeding, a relative of an in-law of the family. The way the story was told to me, Walter didn't have a suit in which to be buried when he died in the late 1960s, so the family provided one (a brown one). According to the person who first told me the story, during Walter's funeral a man in a powder-blue suit crashed his car into the funeral home and died! Obituaries confirm that Walter Loeding was a relative whose funeral was held at the building where the tattoo parlor is now, but if the car wreck happened, it somehow didn't make the papers.

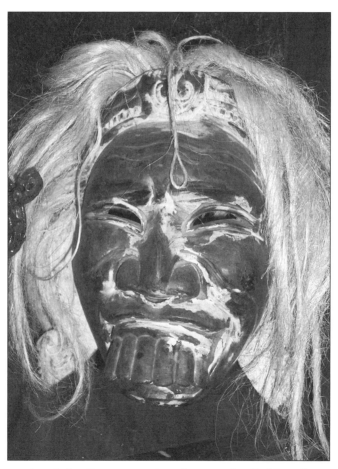

A mask that Tapeworm said was known to fly off of the wall.
Some people find the mask inexplicably terrifying.

Tapeworm

Stories of the building being haunted were already old by the time the tattoo parlor moved in—and even though the circulating stories are a mix of fact and fiction, the place only seems to be getting *more* haunted as time goes by. In fact, in recent years, the hunt for ghosts of the funeral home has been overshadowed by the hunt for the ghost of Tapeworm, who died shortly after investigations on the building began.

On that first investigation, the most memorable story Tapeworm told us was of the two occasions on which he felt as though some mysterious, invisible entity was trying to push him down the stairs to his residence.

"That freaks me out," he said, "because everyone knows that you can't fight *back* with these cats. So the first time it happened, I looked up, and I went, 'Listen, motherfucker! If I fucking die in this fucking place, it is fucking *on!*'"

Around three weeks after the investigation, Tapeworm had a heart attack in his second-floor residence and *did* die in the place. He was thirty-seven.

A few months later, a Halloween party was held at the studio, and one of the employees found a missed call on his cell phone from Tapeworm's old phone number. Employees now report that only people who were friends of Tapeworm in life can get the equipment at his tattoo station to work, and they told me many times that the ghostly activity there seemed to quiet down when they played music Tapeworm liked (metal), and that it increased when they played music he hated (techno).

Since his death, I've occasionally been known to say that if there was *ever* a ghost that I truly believed in, it was the ghost of Tapeworm. Many times when I was back in the basement, I felt as though someone was flicking my ears or pulling my hair—just the way that guys like Tapeworm would pick on a nerd like me. Once I took a picture of a back wall, and the flash illuminated a silhouette that shouldn't have been there but which sure looked like Tapeworm to me.

If You Go

Most of the staff is happy to talk about the ghosts in the building.

CHAPTER 11

Lincoln Park Ghosts

Lincoln Park, particularly the portion from North Avenue to Fullerton Avenue, has something of a grim history: it served a few decades as a cemetery, and in the early days of its era as a park, one of the ways that it distinguished itself was that it was a very popular place to go to kill yourself.

Down at the south end of Lincoln Park, on the grounds occupied by the Chicago History Museum, stands a little gray building about the size of a one-car garage. Thousands drive past it daily, and most who notice it at all assume it's a tool shed or a power station. Actually, it's a tomb.

In 1857, hotel owner Ira Couch died while spending the winter in Cuba. His body was returned to Chicago, and his brother commissioned a $7,000 tomb for him. It was constructed from fifty tons of stone from Lockport, New York, and required a team of eight horses to carry it through the city. Seven thousand dollars was a really good chunk of change at the time—a few years later, the "Wigwam" building, in which the Republican Party nominated Abraham Lincoln for president, cost about the same amount to build.

At the time, City Cemetery was the plot of land now known as Lincoln Park. The city had initially designated two plots of land as burial grounds—one around the spot where 26th Street meets the lake today and one near the Old Water Tower, on Chicago Avenue. At the time, it was thought that few, if any, Chicagoans would ever live north or south of the Chicago River, which branches out to form a border around what is now the Loop, and those two locations seemed nice and remote. However, the city grew faster than anyone imagined, and both cemeteries were soon overtaken and abandoned.

In those days, people who died in cities were often buried in little churchyards, and those places tended to get overcrowded very quickly. Stories abound of churchyards where the coffins were stacked one on top of the other, until the one on top had to be stamped on to stay below the ground, and of churchyards where every turn of the shovel drew up some human remains. Putting aside a big patch of land for burials far out into the outskirts seemed like a very progressive move in the 1840s, when Chicago set aside the huge tract that would one day be Lincoln Park.

Tens of thousands were buried there over a period of around twenty years, but no tomb was quite so large as the Couch family mausoleum. Around the end of the Civil War, people began to worry that, since the City Cemetery was no longer the outskirts of town, the dead bodies might be contaminating the drinking water, and an order was made to close down the cemetery and move the bodies elsewhere, so that the land could be repurposed into a park. Exhumations continued until well into the 1880s, though no one ever seems to have thought they came close to getting *all* of the bodies. As recently as 1998, workers digging out grounds for a new parking lot found the remains of eighty-one people.

The tombstones, at least, were all moved, but the Couch tomb remained. No one is quite sure why it's still there; some say that it was left as a reminder that the ground had once been a cemetery; some say the Couch family was threatening to sue (they *do* seem to have been a litigious bunch in those days); and others say the city just didn't want to spend the three thousand dollars it would cost to move such a large tomb. I tend to think it was a combination of all three; perhaps there was a council meeting that went something like this:

> *Councilman Sacks: "Some minister is going to suggest we leave something on the grounds as a reminder that it was a cemetery once. Think that would make people less likely to come to the park?"*
>
> *Councilman Peters: "I don't know … Say, did you hear that it's gonna cost us about three thousand dollars to move the Couch vault out of there?"*
>
> *Councilman Jeske: "I heard that. I also heard the Couch family is thinking about suing to keep it there."*
>
> *Councilman Sacks: "They are? Well, for crying out loud. I don't wanna spend thousands of bucks AND have to deal with Jim Couch making a big scene. Let's just leave it there and say it's a lasting memorial to the fact that there was a graveyard there. I mean, let's be honest—we know they're not getting all of the bodies."*

Councilman Jeske: "All right, then, all in favor? All opposed? Then it's resolved: we'll just leave the thing there to save us all a lot of trouble and cash. If anyone asks, we left it as a reminder that the grounds were a cemetery. Next order of business ..."

Today, the Couch tomb is a mystery that drives me insane. No one knows who, or what, is in there anymore. The vault was built to hold about a dozen people, and the best estimates are that it's about half full (or, if you prefer, half empty), but no one seems to know for sure anymore who was in there and whether they were ever moved.

One consideration to keep in mind when trying to solve the mystery of what it's like inside is that the thing cost as much as a convention center to build. Wouldn't that imply that there must be something pretty nifty in there? Some suggest that behind the door is a stairway leading down to a subterranean crypt; it *is* hard to picture the thing having space for a dozen coffins in the portion that can be seen above the ground, or that a simple building with notches in the wall would cost so much.

The most recent clue we have came in 1911, when a park official said that he'd been inside the tomb around 1901, and that there had been no human remains inside. At the same time, though, Ira J. Couch (the grandson of the guy for whom the tomb was built) said that Ira Couch was in there with his father, his mother, and two of his own brothers, as well as a couple of others. There are a few strange things about this statement: Ira's mother died well beyond the age when it was legal to inter bodies in Lincoln Park, and his father died well before it. Furthermore, genealogists have no other evidence that Ira J. Couch even *had* any brothers. However, he should have known whether he had any brothers better than anyone a century later would, and would presumably know where they, and his great-grandparents, had been interred … right?[7]

The Couch tomb still stands at the south end of the park, the most visible reminder of the old cemetery. But what's inside?

A handful of vintage newspaper articles state that the family found in the 1890s that they couldn't get the tomb open without dynamite. This was probably hearsay but also probably isn't far off—the huge metal door in front of the tomb is sealed against the stone walls. There is no locking mechanism, and the handle is little more than a loop of metal

---

7. Just as this book was being finished, a testimony from Ira J. Couch in his grandmother's probate file proved that he did, in fact, have two siblings who were stillborn and died without names.

welded onto the slab. It's not the kind of door that one could simply open up.

Trying to find out what's *behind* that door is one of those mysteries that has driven me crazy for ages—I used to bring tour groups out to the tomb nightly, and many was the time people would scheme up ways to see in. Most of them, though, involved blowing it up.

I began to have dreams about going inside of the tomb all the time (in dreams, it was usually bigger on the inside). In early 2013, I was giving a talk about the place when I noticed a bug crawling under a crack beneath the metal door.

In all the time I spent staring at that door, I'd never realized it was only sealed on three sides. There was, it turned out, a space at the bottom just about large enough for an iPhone to fit under, and, after checking over local laws to make sure it wouldn't be illegal, I rigged up a super high-tech device called the Tomb Snooper 500 (an iPhone taped to wire hangers) that allowed me to take some photos under the crack in the door without damaging the tomb at all.

The photos revealed... another door. The giant metal door doesn't lead to the tomb itself but to a small antechamber, at the back of which is another large door that appears to be made of stone, though it's so dusty that it's hard to tell for sure. Some days my job feels like I'm inside of one of those text adventure computer games from the 1980s.

Even if we could see behind the *second* door, it's unlikely that anything would really be left inside of the tomb. Not being exactly airtight, it's probable that any coffins or remains rotted away to dust ages ago. But you never know; the 1850s, when Ira Couch died, was the age when the Fisk metallic burial case was all the rage. These ornate metal cof-

fins—which earned the Fisk Company a letter of endorse-
ment from Jefferson freaking Davis—had viewing windows
over the face, and were considered the height of class when
it came to burials. They weren't cheap, but a family who
could afford a $7,000 crypt could probably also spring for a
heck of a nice coffin. One such casket was unearthed from
the parking lot across the street from the tomb in the 1990s,
and the guy inside was in pretty good shape.

*The antechamber and interior door behind the exterior metal door,
as revealed by high-tech investigations that involved a phone and
a lot of packing tape.*

Still, for now, the mystery of who is, or was, in the tomb
will remain unsolved, as the room behind the door offers
no clues.

Other Missing Bodies

Couch and his cryptmates are far from the only bodies that were left behind at City Cemetery—when the tombstones were moved, many (some say most) of the bodies were left in the ground. David Kennison, a man who claimed at the time of his death to be 115 years old and the last surviving participant of the Boston Tea Party, is still buried somewhere in the park, though opinions as to *where* he's buried tend to differ. A memorial boulder marks the space some people who remembered his funeral said he was buried, and the nearby historical society still has some tea leaves that he said were from Boston (even though it's now pretty well established that he was completely full of shit).

The portion of the park now occupied by the baseball fields was the potter's field—the space where unclaimed bodies were buried in unmarked graves. Thousands of Confederate prisoners of war who perished at Camp Douglas, the prison camp on the South Side, were buried there. They were supposed to be moved to Oak Woods Cemetery, where there's now a memorial in their honor, but how many of them they *actually* moved is up to debate. Newspapers from the period indicated that workers were supposed to spend a year moving them but only actually spent a month on it. Perhaps they just got lazy, and perhaps they found that there weren't many bodies left to begin with—the grave-robbers had beaten them to the punch.

Grave-Robbers

Grave-robbing was a massive problem for the city (and every other city with a medical school) in the days of City Cemetery. Schools had figured out that you can't train new doctors without giving them dead bodies to practice on, but no one donated their body to science back then, so schools had to roll up their sleeves and do what they had to do. Many had a sort of "open door" policy with grave-robbers; if you showed up with a fresh corpse, you could trade it in for cash, no questions asked. Interviews conducted with "resurrection men" at the time indicate that in some periods, schools were paying upwards of thirty bucks for a good corpse, which was a month's salary to many men. And a *good* grave-robber could get five or six in one night.

There were a couple of tricks to this. One was that you had to bribe the sexton, the cemetery manager. Martin Quinlan, the city sexton in the 1850s, was caught taking bribes at least once, and was even arrested helping people from a medical school smuggle a body out.

The other trick was that you didn't have to dig up the *whole* body—all you had to do was dig down to the head of the coffin, cut a hole in it, and drag the body out with a rope.

The potter's field area was basically a smorgasbord for grave-robbers, and the Civil War soldiers seem to have been particularly common targets; some people even believe that the grave-robbers and schools had an arrangement with some of the authorities from Camp Douglas.

With all the left-behind graves and stolen bodies, one can imagine that the park built on the grounds would be said to be haunted. But the graves were only the beginning. When the land was repurposed, one of the ways Lincoln Park distinguished itself was that it was a very popular place to kill yourself.

Suicide Bridge

One long-lost feature of the park is the "high bridge," constructed in 1894, that rose forty-two feet above the lagoon. From the bridge, one could see all the way down to Jackson Park, way down on the South Side, on a clear day.

The bridge very quickly became a hangout for weirdos and drunks—one guy used to go there every night to whistle at the moon in a strange, eerie tone that scared the heck out of the cops. But it was best known as a place to commit suicide; postcards even referred to it as "Suicide Bridge." By the time it was closed and torn down in 1919, between fifty and one hundred people had ended their lives by jumping off the bridge (and one more died hanging himself from it, and another shot himself there; it had become a popular place for suicide no matter how you planned to go).

Newspapers loved to print headlines about Suicide Bridge, including the following:

> —*Policeman Spoils a Suicide: Interferes When Fascinated Crowd in Lincoln Park is Waiting for Man to Kill Self*
>
> —*Jumps from Bridge To Lagoon: Says he Tried Suicide for Fun*
>
> —*Doom High Suicide Bridge: Lincoln Park Commissioners to Spoil Convenience for Those Contemplating Self-Destruction* (Note: This was in 1909, and nothing appears to have come of it. When the bridge was closed a decade later, it was due to its poor condition.)

There was even one story, which made the papers as far away as New York, of an ostrich escaping from the nearby zoo and jumping off the bridge in 1899 (the ostrich survived).

Suicides elsewhere in the park occasionally made the news as well. One day a doctor slit his own throat in front of dozens of witnesses.

By the time the bridge was destroyed, it was a place of superstition for many, and neighborhood kids whispered to "stay away from Suicide Bridge." Hector, my driver and podcast co-host, says that kids on the North Side in the 1970s still told stories about the bridge. But as early as 1898, when Suicide Bridge was still relatively new, and the park itself had been a graveyard within living memory, the *Tribune* wrote that "there have been violent deaths enough in Lincoln Park to furnish a ghost for every shadowed nook within its confines."

Ghosts of the Park

The earliest known ghostlore from the park revolves, appropriately enough, around the Couch tomb. Around 1882, a rumor went around that every night, at the stroke of midnight, the massive metal door to the tomb would open and a "white figure" would emerge from the old crypt. For several nights, crowds gathered hoping to view the ghost, but none was ever seen, and it's easy to imagine how such a legend grew up around the tomb, which by then was one of only a couple still standing. Even as late as 1985, a tour guide named Mike Sered was telling people that a ghost could appear there if they whispered the phrase "The graves belong to the dead, not the living" (which is sometimes said to be the reason the tomb wasn't moved). It didn't work the day the *Daily Northwestern* reviewed his tour, and it didn't work when I had people on my own tour try it either.

But in 1898, it was widely said among the police officers who patrolled the place that the park was terribly haunted, and many supposedly requested to switch from night duty to day duty simply because they were afraid of the place, particularly of the ghosts of the people who died jumping from Suicide Bridge.

One snowy winter's night in the late 1890s, one Officer McCarty was patrolling the area around the playground and found the swings moving about wildly. Amongst them were "two white-clad figures" who "tossed their arms wildly about their heads…outdoing in mad pranks the goblins of Gabriel Grub."[8] When McCarty approached them, they flew through the snow, past the statue of Benjamin Franklin, wailing all the way as they made their way to Suicide Bridge, where they vanished into the wind and snow.

Another night a few years before, Officer William Blaul was patrolling the area around a refreshment stand when he saw a man leaning against a rail fence, dressed in a "Mexican-style mantle which fell from neck to knee" and a black sombrero.

"What are you doing here at this hour of night?" Blaul called.

When the man didn't answer, Blaul approached him, repeating the question. When he came close enough to put a hand on the man's shoulder, the man pulled a gun (or some gleaming weapon) from under his mantle. Blaul pulled his own gun and fired at the figure from point-blank range, and

8. Ah, the days when newspaper reporters felt no need to explain references to obscure passages in *The Pickwick Papers*.

the man simply laughed. Blaul fired three more times, and the figure continued to laugh until, after the third shot, he "melted away into the gloom of the night."

It's tough to gauge just how seriously to take this story. Detective Blaul seems to have enjoyed telling ghost stories; he was also one of the officers who was said to have chased the ghost of Louisa Luetgert through the old sausage factory.

Certainly we can't take *all* ghost sightings of the era too seriously. In 1909, regional papers told of a "ghost party" held at a house near the park, in which people showed up in ghost costumes, then adjourned to run around the park and ring the doorbells at the homes of the neighbors, hoping to make them think they'd seen ghosts. Papers said that some of them were fooled.

The Vampire Hunt of 1888

One further story from the history of the park certainly deserves some mention here.

In September of 1888, a group of residents of Lakeview, the neighborhood just north of Lincoln Park, gathered in a little garage on Clybourn, at which Albert Thalstrom, a justice of the peace and bookseller, regaled them with stories of *real* vampirism. This was an age when consumption (tuberculosis) was sometimes blamed on the bodies of those who had died from the disease "feeding" on the life of living people by infecting them with it and sucking the life out of them from inside their graves. Now and then it would lead to bodies being dug up—it happened at least once in Chicago, though details are scarce.

Thalstrom eventually turned the floor over to a man named Samuel Patton, who said that he'd been plagued by a vampire for years, ever since his time as a Civil War soldier, and that evil spirits had killed his children. The "vampire" couldn't be seen with the naked eye, of course, but Patton had invented something called "Patton's Clairvoyic Varnish for Glass," a substance that would enable you to see the vampires and spirits if you rubbed it on your glasses. He assured the people that the vampire could be seen flying up and down Paulina Street right then (for the record, it would have likely been flying right through the site of the Liar's Club, which appears in this book in chapter 14).

Most people don't seem to have taken Patton very seriously, and little is known about him now, except that he was a Civil War vet who lived until 1912 and apparently wrote a book called *Spirit Life as It Is*, which is not known to survive. Less is known about Thalstrom, who died three years later (of consumption, as fate would have it).

But the two *do* seem to have made an impression on some of the crowd. A month after the presentation, a man named Claus Larson went missing, and his wife blamed his disappearance on a vampire.

A group of local kids formed a posse, christening themselves the Vampire Hunters, and went on a hunt through Lincoln Park, where a few tombs still stood, trying to find the vampire, which they apparently assumed was the spirit of someone buried there. Personally, I tend to imagine that Patton himself organized this group for the purpose of selling the kids' parents some snappy uniforms and accessories.

Mr. Larson, for the record, reappeared after a few days, sheepishly admitting that he'd been off on a bender.

If You Go

The park is open to the public all the time. Most gear beyond cameras would be too prone to outside influences (even in the park, you're still in the city), but people with metal detectors are known to find some cool stuff. Not many ghost sightings have been made in recent years, but if you get bored, it's an easy hike to the St. Valentine's Day Massacre site.

For more on City Cemetery, check out our podcast on the subject on the Chicago Unbelievable blog, in which we discuss whether the Couch tomb would be a good score for the grave-robbers who once frequented the grounds, or look up Pamela Bannos' exhaustive website, *Hidden Truths*. Bannos is the city's resident expert on City Cemetery.

CHAPTER 12

The Haunted Hooters

Another Den of Grave-Robbers?

The "Haunted Hooters" stands at the corner of Erie Street and Wells Street in the Lower North Side. Reports of it being haunted have circulated for years, but it's only recently that we discovered the alley behind it was once a hub for grave-robbers.

The downtown Hooters restaurant on Wells has long been rumored to be haunted. Well, really, almost every restaurant in Chicago has, but the "Haunted Hooters" has gotten a lot of media attention over the years (for obvious reasons), despite the fact that no good story has come up to explain who or what could be haunting it. I never took the stories about it seriously, but I had to give some credit to the Hooters company for admitting they were stumped, not just making up some nonsense story about Al Capone having once owned the building, or about it being built on an Indian burial ground.

A while ago I was brought to the Hooters by the crew of NPR's *Wait Wait ... Don't Tell Me!* to do an interview and chat about ghosts a little. As is generally the case, I think they expected me to come off as more of a lunatic than I did. As we walked into the alley, one guy asked me, "Who's with us right now?"

"Christ, *I* don't know," I said. "What are you asking me for?"

They brought along a little bit of ghost-hunting gear they'd thrown together, and I told them what I always do— you can bring pretty much *any* piece of equipment on a ghost hunt and call it ghost-hunting gear. You can bring your electric toothbrush along, and if it starts turning itself off and on, you can blame that on a ghost. That's really no different from saying a jump in the electromagnetic field or the ion count is coming from a ghost, if you get right down to it.

In any case, nothing showed up, though the waitress told us she'd heard about "whispering" in the back room.

This lines it up with the usual stories I hear about the place—whisperings, footsteps, and a general feeling of creepiness. You get this at several places nearby; next door stands an old mansion currently called Flair House (it houses an advertising agency), one of the surviving old houses of the neighborhood known a century ago as Smoky Hollow. A receptionist there once told me that the area behind the house, out in the alley, sometimes seemed a bit spooky.

Stories of the area being haunted may go back to decades before the Hooters was built. In the 1950s, a *Tribune* article about long-forgotten haunted houses in Chicago spoke of a house on Erie Street that was said to be haunted. Having once been used by a medical college that often purchased bodies from "resurrectionists," it was said that human remains had been found in the yard (presumably around the turn of the 20th century), and that on quiet evenings, neighbors could hear the clip-clop of hooves and the sound of body snatchers unloading bodies from their wagons. Exactly *which* house on Erie this was wasn't recorded, though, and my early attempts to find out where it was proved fruitless.

However, I did eventually run across a story about a place on Erie—right about where Hooters and Flair House are now—that was involved in the grave-robbing trade, which could well be the source of the stories of that haunted house on Erie. Could the Hooters be on the same site where that house stood?

In January of 1875, the *Tribune* announced that body snatchers, "resurrection men," and other such ghouls were out of business in Chicago. New laws gave medical schools first dibs on the bodies bound for the newly established potter's field (burial place for unclaimed bodies) in Jefferson Park, so there would be no need for Chicago institutions to buy corpses from "ghouls," as they had been doing for years.

However, the problem of robbing graves continued. No such law providing schools with bodies existed in Ann Arbor, Michigan, or Iowa City, Iowa, so Chicago ghouls would simply ship their quarry there.

Only a month after saying body snatchers were out of business, the *Tribune* was providing grim accounts of a new body-snatching case that had been uncovered on the North Side. Body snatchers, it was said, were digging into the graves, opening the caskets, and drawing the body out by the eye sockets using a hook and rope—a pretty standard method for getting the bodies. Digging up the *whole* coffin was considered a real rookie mistake; all one had to do was dig down to the head and cut a hole in it.

The bodies this new band of thieves dug up were being routed through the alley behind a barn and charnel house near Erie and Wells, where they were loaded into barrels for shipment to Ann Arbor. This alley would be right about in the area around the current site of the Hooters and Flair House.

The grave-robber in charge of this particular gang was one L. R. Williams (though he variously gave his name as George Smith or George Wallace), a medical student from Rush Medical College who had been in business for a few months. He was caught during a daring chase through the alleys at Erie and Wells, then was released on a $1,500 bond. He promptly jumped bail and disappeared; as far as I know, they never caught him. How many bodies the robbers may have routed through the barn and charnel house en route to Michigan or Iowa is unknown, but at least five barrels full of bodies were found in the barn after Williams was captured.

Given the possible connection to Hooters, it's rather odd to read the *Tribune*'s lurid account of the two female bodies in the morgue during the coroner's inquest, which, disturbingly enough, was probably intended to be titillating:

> Hard and stiff, the death rigor intensified by the bitter cold, there lay upon the next slab the naked form of A BEAUTIFUL WOMAN exposed to all the indignities ... and of unsympathetic and indifferent looks and touches. Stockings covered the feet and a portion of the shapely limbs, but the rest of her person was entirely nude. The head was turned to one side in a posture that would

have been natural to animate modesty, and which, in the poor maltreated corpse, carried with it a pitying sugges-tion of womanly purity. Although the changes of death had somewhat altered the contour of her body, the behold-er could not but be struck with the shapeliness of her limbs and the general beauty of her person; but her parted lips and staring eye-balls made a gorgon horror of the face that in life had been comely and attractive …

In the other barrels were two victims of consumption (a man with a long black beard and a young boy) and anoth-er old man dead of causes unspecified. They were given far less vivid description than the dead naked women.

One wouldn't usually expect ghosts to be haunting the places where their bodies were taken—again, we *usually* ex-pect them to haunt the places where they died. But, naturally, we can't get too cocky about applying logic to the illogical, and no better story to back up the hauntings here has yet emerged.

Of course, it's probably also worth noting that the Sbar-baro Funeral Home stood less than a block away at 708 N. Wells. Most of the big, elaborate gangster funerals of the day were held there, and the procession would have gone right by the Hooters in many cases.

If You Go

Enjoy the wings and try not to act like a douchebag. The area out back can seem remarkably quiet, as can many downtown portions of Erie Street, which is still dotted with old medical college buildings, especially as you go farther east from the Hooters.

Fado

Clark Street and Grand Avenue

One of many, many haunted taverns in the city, Fado is said to be haunted by a woman in a nightgown.

I don't believe the old maxim that you should never let facts get in the way of a good story. Even on tours, where most people probably assume that I'm not really telling the truth, I try to stick to stories I can back up. Occasionally there are some stories that are just too good not to tell, but I try to flag anything I have any reason to doubt.

When I *do* make up a ghost story, it's almost always for the sake of a joke. For instance, we used to get stuck in traffic next to an adult bookstore on Clark Street pretty regularly, and Hector and I made up a story about it just to kill time:

On your left is the haunted adult bookstore. We do lots of investigations down at the haunted adult bookstore. It's haunted by the ghost of a woman who was a fairly popular stripper at one point, but who then lost her leg in a tragic shuffleboard accident. Her leg was bought by P. T. Barnum, the circus owner, who put it on display in his sideshow in a vat of formaldehyde. Soon her leg was making more money than she ever had. So she quit stripping and bought this adult bookstore, then spent years writing letter after letter to P. T. Barnum, saying, "I want my leg back. I have money. How much do you want?"

On the day she died, she finally got a postcard saying, "Honey, if you want that thing back, it'll cost you an arm and a leg!"

After the punchline, Hector and I would allow people the chance to pelt us with any vegetables they'd brought along.

I thought it was obviously just a joke, but plenty of people went to the shop after the tour to ask about the ghost of the one-legged stripper. After telling the story for years, I was roped into running a tour for a bachelorette party that wanted to stop there; going inside of the place for the first time (honest), I told the owner that it was my fault if he'd ever had to deal with ghost hunters.

"Well, that's happened now and then," he said. "We thought it was weird, because this place actually *is* haunted."

And that's Chicago for you. There's hardly a restaurant, store, school, bar, theater, or hospital in town that isn't said to be haunted. There are perhaps a hundred bars said to be haunted by the ghost of a former owner. Bars and restaurants that can't connect a dead owner to the premises will often come up with stories about Indian burial grounds or, this being Chicago, Al Capone.

And I still hear people repeating the story of the one-legged stripper as fact, along with a couple of other jokey stories I've made up. Sooner or later I'll probably even go to a website and see someone repeating the story I tell when we get stuck near a McDonald's, which is all about an employee who stole a hamburger and found himself haunted by the Hamburglar.

Fado, the Irish-style pub at Clark and Grand, is a good example of a place that started out as a made-up haunting, but ended up proving the point that you can never expect an older building in Chicago *not* to be haunted.

At the end of one tour, a rather drunken crowd offered a tour guide a hundred dollars to add one more pub stop. The resourceful guide (not me, for once) quickly improvised a generic ghost story about Fado, which was only a block away.

When I get in this situation, the story I make up is usually that the original owner, a retired circus clown, died before he could ever see the building completed, and now his clown-shoe footsteps are heard around the premises. The made-up story the other guide came up with was probably something similar.

Naturally, it turned out that the place actually *was* thought to be haunted.

A few years ago, a manager at Fado brought me in to do some research and see if I could determine the identity of their *actual* resident ghost—a woman in a nightgown—who had been seen on the second or third floor by several employees. When the restaurant was first opened, there were numerous instances of the alarm system going off on the second floor in the middle of the night. Why the second-floor alarm was going off, but not the first, was never explained.

Researching the place was a little bit tricky—Clark and Grand was not always a great neighborhood. When the building was constructed, it was an area full of saloons and single-room apartments. As late as the 1950s, the place was a strip club, and papers still talked of it as a bad area in the 1970s. Crime stories from the old days there didn't always make the news.

It was only in a longer article from the 1890s about how bad Clark Street had gotten that I found a tiny mention of a woman who lived above a low-down tavern at Clark and Grand. She was murdered in the middle of the night by a "railroad brakeman" who'd had too much to drink and was "maddened by jealousy." A bit of triangulating between the story and a few other articles indicated that the building she lived in was probably the same building that now houses Fado. The article was mainly concerned with the fact that most neighbors never even heard of the story; such a thing wasn't enough to make the news on Clark Street back then.

This is a fairly good story to back up the tale of the woman in a nightgown on the second or third floor, as she was thought to have been killed in the middle of the night— but how many others could have died in the area without anyone knowing?

If You Go

Head for the bar on the second floor (when it's open) and chat with the bartender a bit. It would be a difficult place to run an actual investigation, but most people who work there have at least heard secondhand stories. Things may have quieted down some; while nearly every server there knew of the ghosts a few years ago, the story seems less known to employees as of 2012.

CHAPTER 14

Haunted Nightclubs and Bars

The Excalibur Club
632 N. Dearborn Street

The Excalibur Club (its longtime name, although the space has recently been renamed "Castle"), the gothic-looking mansion-cum-nightclub at Ontario and Dearborn, certainly *looks* haunted. It's been *advertised* as a haunted club for years, and many of the employees truly do believe it to be the home to a number of spirits. The restaurant area is said to be haunted by (again, perhaps inevitably) a ghostly little girl who chases a ball and causes waitresses to lose their balance, and some tell of a man who hanged himself years ago from the ceiling of the "dome room." Others hear footsteps, or report being unable to open unlocked doors that seem to be held shut by an unseen force. It's famous enough as a haunted spot that I feel obligated to include it here.

However, the club has generally fallen out of favor with ghost hunters due to the fact that none of the stories hold up to historical research. Stories go around of a child dying years ago in the elevator shaft of what is now Excalibur, but those are unconfirmed (and perhaps mixed up with stories about the Metro, a club where that actually *did* happen years ago), as is the story of a man hanging himself from the ceiling of the dome room. No contemporary reference to that happening has ever been found.

Besides the erroneous stories of hangings and accidents, there are two particularly common stories about the source of the ghosts in the Excalibur. The first, and perhaps most famous, is the story that bodies from the *Eastland* disaster were taken to the building, back in the days when it housed the Chicago Historical Society. No bodies were actually taken there, though.

A more interesting story is that there actually *was* one single body in the building once—that of Jean LaLime, one of the city's first non-native settlers. His body *may* have been in the building once upon a time.

Jean LaLime was a business rival of another early settler, John Kinzie. One day, Kinzie killed LaLime (in what was ruled to be self-defense, but may have been a plain old murder or the result of a drunken brawl). According to the story, LaLime was buried on his property (which Kinzie then moved into), and was accidentally dug up years later during construction near Illinois and LaSalle. The skeleton was given as a gift to the historical society (which I'm sure was just *thrilled*), but, according to Excalibur legend, was burned in the Great Chicago Fire.

The story doesn't completely check out. The bones of someone thought to be Jean LaLime *were* dug up during a construction project at Illinois and Wabash, and a few old-timers in the city remembered LaLime's grave as being about where the bones were found; one old-timer remembered that in the 1830s that spot was said to be the place where "Old Man Kinzie" had killed a man. Experts who examined the bones at the time agreed that they were those of a white man who stood 5'4" in height, and that they may have been old enough to be those of LaLime.

The bones *were* donated to the historical society, just as the legend goes. However, all of this happened in 1891, a good twenty years *after* the Great Chicago Fire. The bones were never burned; in fact, they may have been displayed in the current Excalibur building and are still in the collection of the Chicago Historical Society. Employees there sometimes get a bit sheepish when the subject comes up; they can't *prove* the bones are that of LaLime, or even that they're the bones of a white man, so they may be subject to reburial under the Native American Graves Protection and Repatriation Act. They're currently stored in an undisclosed off-site location.

So, there was at least *one* dead body in the building that now houses Excalibur. While I'm not completely convinced that the whole thing didn't start out as a marketing gimmick, there's at least *some* backstory here.

The Metal Shaker
3394 N. Milwaukee Avenue

Employees at the Metal Shaker, a recently closed dive bar, wrote to me some time ago and told me that several people had seen and photographed the ghost of an unidentified man. Research showed that in 1962, when the building was called the Peacock Lounge, owner Andrew Zeleg was attacked while closing up by gunmen who shot him three times in the chest and three times in the head. The murderers were never caught, and the last time the case was mentioned in the *Tribune* was a short item stating that the coroner had determined that the six shots to the chest and head indicated a homicide, making me think, "Gee, Mr. Coroner, did you figure that out all by yourself?"

It will be interesting to find out if the employees of whichever business moves into this space next will see the ghosts as well!

Bucktown Pub
1658 W. Cortland Street

This place is said to be haunted by the ghost of Wally, a former owner who was known as a real jerk and has been known to knock objects off walls and onto people's heads. This story seems to be better known among ghost fans than it is among the staff.

Webster's Wine Bar
1480 W. Webster Avenue

A former employee spoke of seeing the ghost of a man dressed as a pioneer on the second floor. What makes this interesting is a plaque in front of the building noting that this was the "site of Fort Dearborn." However, it was nowhere close to Fort Dearborn, and no one I've spoken to is sure what the plaque is doing there.

Liar's Club
1665 W. Fullerton Avenue

You never know what you're going to get when you walk into the Liar's Club at 1665 W. Fullerton—some nights it's quiet; some nights it's full of bikers; and sometimes it's like the cantina from *Star Wars* in there. TVs are said to turn themselves off and on, and it was there that I once saw the closest thing I've ever seen to a person getting possessed. There was an ax murder on the third floor in the 1980s, and an event in which two men, one old and one young, got into an argument over an article of clothing in 1962. The young man beat the old one over the head with a bottle, then shoved him out of a second-floor window. He died in the hospital.

There are also said to have been other ax murders there— the exact number seems to go up every Halloween. I've only ever been able to confirm the one.

Still, the whole general region around the Liar's Club seems like a hotspot for gruesome stories. Only a few blocks down Fullerton is the H. H. Holmes "body dump." The Luetgert Sausage Factory is a few blocks northwest, and just across Fullerton was the area that Samuel Patton claimed was haunted by a vampire in 1888, inspiring the vampire hunt in Lincoln Park (see chapter 11). Just a bit south on Clybourn, a party was held in 1902 to celebrate William McFetridge's surprise acquittal in his trial for shooting his brother to death (which he admitted to having done in his home a few doors down). During the party, one man was beaten to death for refusing to cheer.

Emmit's Irish Pub
495 N. Milwaukee Avenue

In this building, the former Italian American Bank, employees report strange feelings in the vault, which is still below the building. Some say that this just comes from the Blue Line subway trains that run right beneath it.

Cobra Lounge
235 N. Ashland Avenue (near Lake Street)

Though not typically said to be *haunted* per se, there's some evidence that this was once a "panel house," a place where men would pay for a room (and likely some late-night company) and be robbed while they slept by someone who had been hiding behind a panel in the wall.

Red Lion Pub
2446 N. Lincoln Avenue (now closed)

This wonderful old-timey English pub was said to be haunted by ghostly footsteps and lilac perfume. No particularly compelling or credible story was every presented to explain the stories, but it was a fixture on Chicago ghost tours for years. A "memorial window" to a former owner's father was on the staircase; some assumed that he was the ghost. The Red Lion (which stood conveniently near the Biograph Theater and the alley where John Dillinger was shot) became a famous enough haunted spot that I'm still asked about it regularly, but it's gone now.

A new, presumably less haunted incarnation of the Red Lion is now open at 4749 N. Rockwell Street.

The Hangge-Uppe
14 W. Elm Street

Employees have said they've seen a female ghost—either from the 1960s or the 1920s, depending on who's telling the story—on the second floor, but only before and after the bar is open. Apparently this ghost doesn't care to join in with the obnoxious bachelorette parties for which the place is known.

The Green Mill

4802 N. Broadway

A wonderful 1920s-themed bar to attend, though stories about Capone being a regular there are greatly exaggerated (he kept a fairly low profile, really, and this was way on the other end of town from his main strongholds). Ghost stories abound given the place's old gangland connection, but the owner is said to hate ghost hunters. Not an easy place to investigate.

If You Go

With any haunted bar, go in and have a drink, then chat with the bartender. I usually recommend the following tips:

1. Ask about the history first. If you have some information they don't, it's a good conversation starter. Do some research ahead of time if possible. Historians aren't really *that* much less likely to be insane than ghost hunters, honestly, but acting like you've done your homework and want to learn more, not just be scared, can open a lot of doors.

2. Pick a time when they won't be busy.

3. Don't seem like a "frothing at the mouth" type who believes everything on the ghost-hunting TV shows, but don't use the word *debunk* either. Lots of ghost hunters like to show that they're "serious" by "debunking" a story right away, but even if you can think of an obvious explanation for a ghost story that an employee or patron tells you, the best thing to do is express good-natured skepticism but show that you're keeping an open mind (this is really the sort of attitude you should have to begin with). Saying, "I can debunk that" to someone's ghost story is just rude. This won't make you seem serious so much as it will make you seem like an asshole.

CHAPTER 15

The Hancock Building

875 N. Michigan Avenue

Is this, one of Chicago's most distinctive skyscrapers, haunted, cursed, or just a big black trapezoid?

During the "Satanic panic" of the 1980s, it was confidently asserted by perfectly respectable people that heavy-metal singers in mascara were convincing kids to switch religions, that every other daycare center was a front for devil worshipers, and that every time you bought a bottle of Procter & Gamble shampoo, you were giving the devil a quarter. It seems strange even to mention this now, but Procter & Gamble was hit especially hard by Satanic panic; some claimed that the number 666 was hidden in the company's logo, and many people confidently claimed that the owner had gone on a major daytime talk show and admitted to worshiping the Prince of Darkness. The rumors have died down now, and modern skeptics have speculated that the rumors were invented by Amway distributors in order to slander P&G.

When I ran a private tour for a group from P&G in 2006, I avoided making the jokes until we came to the Hancock Building.

"All right," I said, "does the name Anton LaVey ring a bell with anyone?"

No one raised their hand, so I explained. "Anton LaVey was the founder of the Church of Satan," I said. "I figured Procter & Gamble would know that!"

The urban legend, it turns out, is not something that the good people at Procter & Gamble are laughing about yet.

I have learned to ask if there are any Satanists present before I make any jokes about Anton LaVey—LaVey had a sense of humor about himself, but some of his followers sure don't. LaVey's brand of Satanism wasn't actually about worshiping the devil or any supernatural force; it had rituals and things like that, but the idea was to get a psychological transformation from them, not a spiritual one. The Satanism he advocated in *The Satanic Bible* was basically Ayn Rand's philosophy of moral objectivism with a flair for the dramatic attached.

At one point, LaVey spoke about the power of trapezoid-shaped buildings. His "law of the trapezoid" states, "All obtuse angles are magically harmful to those unaware of this property. The same angles are beneficial, stimulating, and energizing to those who are magically sensitive to them." In other words, if you lived in a big trapezoid—and the Hancock Building is probably the largest in the world—and didn't know it was magical, it was likely to screw you up somehow or another.

LaVey, for his part, occasionally claimed to have been *born* on the spot where the Hancock Building now stands.

Like most of his stories about himself, his story that he was actually born on the site of the Hancock is rather unlikely. There was never a hospital on the site, and LaVey, born in 1930, lived in an era when most well-to-do babies were born in hospitals. There also were not a lot of residential spaces on the spot at the time; most of it was a parking lot. There was one townhouse that overlaps a little bit with the footprint, but LaVey's parents didn't live there.

According to a census form taken only days before young Anton (real name Howard Stanton Levey) was born, his parents lived in Casa Bonita, a courtyard building—a very fancy one—at 7430 North Ridge Boulevard, far away from the Hancock. There's still a bit of mystery here; his father was listed as a salesman for a soap company, and it seems unlikely that a soap salesman would have made enough money to afford an apartment that went for about $100 a month (in 1930 dollars). Perhaps he was dealing in bootleg liquor on the side.

So, despite his claims, LaVey wasn't born on that spot any more than he was ever a church organist or a lion tamer (two of his other stories). He cheerfully admitted that he was an insufferable liar. "I'd be full of shit," he reportedly said, "if I didn't keep my mouth shut and my bowels open."

Some also have claimed that the Hancock was built on the site of an "Indian burial ground," the classic go-to for ghost-tour guides who are not very creative. As a matter of fact, though, one of the city's first two graveyards was on Chicago Avenue near Clark Street, not far from the Hancock, but the site of the building itself was even closer to the lakeshore back then than it currently is (the shoreline has been pushed farther out by landfills). It would have been a fairly bad place to bury anybody, and fairly few bodies were ever buried in this cemetery before the city began to grow north of the Chicago River, necessitating a move of the graves, though it's not unlikely that a few bodies are still beneath the ground nearby.

So, while most of the stories about the Hancock aren't quite accurate, this is not to say that there are no strange stories about the Hancock—go to the Signature Room or the observation deck at the right time of the year, and you'll see countless spiders outside of the windows. They aren't poisonous brown recluse spiders, as is sometimes claimed, but a species known as "bridge spiders" (or *Larinioides sclopetaria* if you want to get all fancy), a sort of orb-weaving "flying spider" that normally lives on rocks or bridges above water. However, they're hardly unique to the Hancock—spiders are a common sight outside of windows in city high-rises. Window washers have to get over any fear of spiders very quickly, as the creatures have to be removed from the windows several times per year. Security guards at the Hancock have spoken of having to brush them out of their hair.

They may be harmless, but they look pretty terrifying, and sometimes the fact that something simply adds to the atmosphere of a haunted place is enough for me.

The Curse?

Some have connected the spiders, Anton LaVey, and the occasional strange death there to the "Curse of Captain Streeter" that is said to linger in the area.

"Cap" Streeter was one of the most colorful characters in Chicago history—though finding out which stories about him are true and which are just lies that he told is a difficult task. What we do know is that Lake Michigan once extended all the way to Michigan Avenue. Then, in the 1880s, Captain George Wellington Streeter crashed his houseboat into the shore and started charging people money to dump their garbage around it. Eventually, he created (or at least claimed to create) a 186-acre landfill that is now known as Streeterville—right in the heart of the "Magnificent Mile."

Being a bit of an eccentric, to say the least, Streeter decided that the new land he'd created was not only independent of the city of Chicago but also of the United States of America. He called his new "country" the District of Lake Michigan and started allowing bums to emigrate to his new land, backing up his claim with forged deeds and a lot of cockamamie stories. Soon, the "deestrict," as he called it, was full of the cheapest, ugliest gambling halls and brothels in town. In 2006, Yahoo Maps was still marking the Gold Coast area as "Shantytown."[9]

Locals were not happy. Rich people whose Michigan Avenue mansions had previously given them a commanding view of the lake now had a commanding view of shanties full of drunks, bums, and prostitutes. There was no sanitation in the "deestrict," so the Michigan Avenue set suddenly stopped having lake views from their mansions, and instead had unobstructed views of rowdy hobos pooping in the sand (bodily functions play heavily into stories of Streeterville; police once came after Cap Streeter while he was using a chamber pot, and his wife was known to hurl the contents of such pots at would-be invaders).

---

9. They've fixed it now, but as late as 2007, Yahoo Maps was still listing "Towertown," "Swedetown," "Little Hell," "Conley's Patch," and other long-defunct neighborhoods.

But it took the city thirty years to kick Streeter off the land—and it wasn't just legal battles either. There were actual gunfights. At one point, the police broke into his houseboat and confiscated his weapons, and he held the police station hostage until they were returned.

How much of these stories is true is an open question—many of them originally came from Streeter himself, and Streeter was every bit as big a liar as Anton LaVey. I may not have much experience in the field of hostage negotiation, but I would imagine that Rule #1 is that you should never give a hostage-taker a box of guns.

According to another, more recent, legend, Streeter cursed the neighborhood on his deathbed, saying that if *he* did not own the land, then nothing good would ever be built there.

However, the "curse" story doesn't really hold up—all we know of what Streeter said of the district on his deathbed is that he willed control of it to Jack Jones, a local poet who owned the Dil Pickle Club, an "open forum" near the district that functioned as the indoor version of Bughouse Square, the nearby park where people made speeches for the benefit of hecklers up until about 1960. Jones's attempts to run people off the land were *very* short-lived.

Furthermore, if Streeter cursed the neighborhood to say that nothing good would be built there, one need only walk around the area to get the impression that he must have really sucked at cursing things. Streeterville is gorgeous today.

Though there *have* been plenty of spiders and a handful of strange deaths at the Hancock, there really haven't been many more than there are in any other residential high-rise, many of which get the same spiders.

However, some say that the fact that Jerry Springer lived there for many years justifies the curse stories all by itself.

If You Go

Some of the building is open to the public, some isn't. Though it's a regular feature of "Haunted Chicago" articles and books, I know of few actual ghost sightings there, so I can't really recommend it for investigations, though you never know what sort of story you might hear from the bartenders. The main ones I hear are from construction workers who work in the basement, where they have stories about ghosts of people who fell down the elevator shaft, though they tend to decline to elaborate (one guy told me it was a union "code of silence" thing).

But one simple tip is to save your money—instead of paying to go to the observation deck, go to the Signature Room. The view is just as good, and you can linger and stare at the city (and spiders) all evening for the price of a couple of drinks!

CHAPTER 16

Resurrection Mary

Resurrection Cemetery itself is at 7201 S. Archer Road in the suburb of Justice. It's home to the most famous of the handful of "vanishing hitchhikers" said to haunt Chicago.

In 1939, a man named Jerry Palus went out dancing at the Liberty Grove dance hall and spent the evening dancing with a lovely girl who said her name was Mary. She was nice, but seemed distant, and was even cold to the touch. When Jerry offered her a ride home, she agreed. She didn't say much, other than to point him down Archer Road, muttering, "The snows came early this year." Then, when they came to Resurrection Cemetery, she shouted, "Pull over! You have to pull over now!"

Jerry said, "I can't pull over here! This is the cemetery!" But Mary screamed, "No! Pull over!"

So Jerry pulled over and said, "Okay, but you have to let me walk you the rest of the way home." She turned and said, "Where I'm going, you can't follow."

And she got out of the car, walked up to the cemetery gates, and vanished.

Resurrection Mary

Chicago's own Resurrection Mary isn't even the only vanishing hitcher said to haunt Chicago. There's a ghostly flapper said to hitch rides to Waldheim Cemetery in suburban Forest Park.[10] A little girl is said to vanish from CTA buses in suburban Evergreen Park around 95th Street.

But Resurrection Mary is by far the most famous—not just of the Chicago hitchers but of all of them (if we do say so ourselves), and the Jerry Palus sighting is far from the only one. In fact, it's really a pretty atypical Mary sighting. Some have described giving Mary a ride home, only to have her jump from the car and run up to the gates of the cemetery and vanish, like Palus did, but more often, she's said to vanish out of the car altogether, leading the confused driver to run into the nearby tavern, Chet's Melody Lounge, to tell his story.

To find out who Mary might be the ghost of, ghost hunters have combed census records, prowled cemeteries, and chased blind leads, all on the presumption that she's not just an urban legend in the first place. There *are* several published firsthand accounts of her, which stand in stark contrast to

---

10. The flapper is usually said to look for rides at the old Melody Mill club, where stories of a vanishing hitchhiker can be traced back to the 1930s, but my own investigation indicates that the Waldheim flapper and the Melody Mill hitchhiker probably weren't the same ghost; surviving accounts of the Melody Mill story say their hitcher went to Wood Lawn Cemetery, not Waldheim.

most other vanishing hitchhikers, which usually only appear to friends of friends of friends of people you meet in line for Space Mountain.

But vanishing hitchhikers are common in folklore; in 1942 there was even a scholarly article on them published in the *California Folklore Quarterly* by Richard Beardsley and Rosalie Hankey. The researchers at the time identified a few particular variations on the story:

Variation 1 involved giving a ride to a hitchhiker who turned out to be some sort of deity in disguise. This is not known to have happened in Chicago, but it would be pretty cool if it did.

Variation 2 involved picking people up for rides and having them vanish from the car after making some sort of prophetic remark. Most of these stories were collected in Chicago, and all of the ghosts sort of failed as prophets. Many in the early 1930s spoke of the site of the upcoming 1933 Century of Progress fairgrounds sinking into Lake Michigan (which didn't happen). A similar story from the early 1940s told of a nun hitching a ride, hearing reports of the beginning of World War II on the radio, and saying, "It won't last six months" before disappearing. Even in 1942, a comment attached to the scholarly article that mentioned the story stated that "the only thing wrong with it" was that it had been more than six months, and the war was still going on.

Variation 3 is the most relevant to the stories of Resurrection Mary—in it, a woman is picked up, normally at some place of entertainment like a dance hall, and offered a ride home. She disappears out of the car at one point, and the driver goes to her address, where her mother says, "That can't have been my daughter; she died in a horrible wreck a year ago tonight," or something to that effect, at which point the driver generally recognizes a picture of his passenger on the wall. In many versions, the driver goes to her grave and finds some outerwear he'd loaned her lying on the ground.

One notable thing about Resurrection Mary sightings is that, outside of the Jerry Palus story, she actually *doesn't* fit into these categories very well. Most people who retell the legend of Mary include bits about her dying on prom night or being picked up in a dance hall, but when people tell these stories, they're really just telling the archetypal legend of the vanishing hitchhiker, not the story of Mary that emerges if you look at the actual sightings. The two stories have largely merged in Chicago folklore over the years.

Indeed, most of the Resurrection Mary encounters that have been published over the years are notable for *lacking* the details about the dance hall, or of going to her house. In none of them, in fact, is the girl ever actually identified. And finding out who the girl was the ghost *of* is a standard part of most vanishing hitchhiker legends.

In 2012 I put out an e-book short with Llewellyn Worldwide called *The Resurrection Mary Files*. In it I gathered all known published sightings of the ghost. Though the stories vary wildly, they fall into a few categories:

Type A: Someone picks up a passenger or hitchhiker who disappears—usually right out of the car.

Type B: A witness sees a strange woman who then disappears—sometimes after appearing to be hit by a car—but isn't picked up or offered a ride.[11]

Type C: A witness simply sees a strange woman on the Southwest Side of Chicago.

The following is the database of all sightings I was able to find in press archives, plus a few others that I've collected:

1932 or Earlier, Summit Encounter
Type A: Vanishing Hitchhiker

The 1942 *California Folklore Quarterly* article on vanishing hitchhikers included one account that may well be an early Mary sighting. Though "Resurrection Mary" was not called by name, one example Beardsley and Hankey gave of a vanishing hitchhiker that was said to be going around Chicago "before 1933" could easily have been a Mary sighting.

The witness said she had heard the story of a woman near the graveyard in Summit, Illinois (which had no active graveyard at the time, though Resurrection is right nearby). The mysterious woman had stopped a car to ask for a ride, given the driver a Chicago address, and then disappeared out of the car as they drove along. The people in the car went to the address they'd been given and found out that the woman had died sometime before. This is probably the earliest recorded encounter with the ghost (and puts it before the death of at least one of the most notable candidates for the "true" Mary).

---

11. This reminds me of the night we thought we hit something with the bus at the "body dump" (see chapter 5).

May 26, 1935, William Tankeczicia
Type A: Vanishing Hitchhiker
Type B: Disappearing Strange Woman (a mix of the two)

According to a story published in the *Salt Lake Tribune*, twenty-four-year-old William Tankeczicia was driving his father's car through suburban Willow Springs (which would put him near the old Oh Henry Ballroom, long said to be a Mary haunt), when he saw a ghost standing by the side of the road, trying to hitchhike. She "leered from sightless eyes and jerked a bony thumb," according to the paper.

William told his story to Peter Brown, a suburban highway patrolman, when asked why he had swerved the car sharply as he passed a cemetery, struck a post, and overturned the vehicle.

The ghostly woman who scared him into rolling the car could not be found, and no details were given as to her appearance or exactly which cemetery she was near. It could very well have been any of the many graveyards that dot the area, but I'm listing it among Mary sightings due to its location and the way it lines up with the other sightings. The fact that she was trying to hitch a ride separates it somewhat from the other "Type B" encounters when she simply appears and disappears.

1939, Jerry Palus
Type A: Vanishing Hitchhiker

Still considered the gold-standard Mary encounter, Jerry Palus claimed that he met a blonde woman in a fancy white dress at the Liberty Grove Ballroom, where he danced with her the whole night. According to most accounts of

Palus's story, she said her name was Mary and that she lived somewhere on the South Side. In the dramatization of the encounter on *Unsolved Mysteries*, aired shortly after Palus's death in 1992, the ghost specifically says she lives on South Damen Avenue, and the "Jerry" character remarks that she has cold hands, which means she has a warm heart (real smooth, Jerry).

Unsolved Mysteries showed a few clips of Palus talking: "As we walked along to the street, she says, 'Well, you might as well take me down to Archer Road ... I want to go out to Archer Road.'"

As ghost hunter Richard Crowe, who interviewed Palus, told the story, when they reached the cemetery, she said, "I must leave, and you can't follow me," or words to that effect. She then exited the car, walked up to the gates, and vanished.

Apparently, Jerry went to South Damen the next day, asked about her at the address she'd given him, and was told by an older woman at the door that her daughter, Mary, had died years ago. He recognized her picture on a piano inside the house.

A lot of this story has been subject to questioning recently; without accusing Jerry of lying, is this really the way he told the story in the first place, or just the way they presented it on TV?

Jerry's brother said it was actually a friend, not Jerry, who was driving that night. Whether Jerry actually claimed to have gone to her home at all is actually something of a question mark—some of the details (including her name) may have simply been added by the TV crew to make his encounter line up with the story of Mary Bregovy, who died in a car wreck in 1934, and whom the show was pushing as the "real" identity of the ghost.

In any case, by most accounts, by the time Jerry started telling the story, he had forgotten where she lived and what her last name was. It may be that she never told him her name was Mary at all; the reenactment of the scene on *Unsolved Mysteries* simply has her nodding when he says, "It's Mary, right?"

So the real particulars of this sighting are hard to pin down. Though Palus was obviously interviewed at length for the TV show, they showed only seconds of his actual talk. Palus died in 1992, and no complete transcript of his own version of the story seems to have survived.

The fact that he doesn't seem to have told the story at all until forty years after it happened makes the specifics a bit unreliable, but the idea that he forgot where she lived and what her name was, as most versions of the story hold, seems unlikely to me. How is a guy going to give a dead girl a ride home and then forget what her address was? I'd never be able to forget that as long as I lived, no matter how hard I tried. I suspect that Jerry's own original story was more in line with other firsthand sightings: he gave a girl a ride home, and she vanished as he drove along. In my own opinion, the part about going to her address and meeting her mother was likely an embellishment, made either by Palus or TV producers, even if the rest of the account was factual. In examining Mary encounters, one finds that this one sticks out like a broken bulb in a string of Christmas lights when compared to others, in that it lines up so much more neatly than others with the usual urban-legend motifs.

1948 (or so), Cemetery Caretaker
Type C: Strange Woman Seen

In 1983, John Satala of the Satala Funeral Home told the *Southtown Economist* that around thirty-five years before, he had taken a phone call from a caretaker at Resurrection who had seen the ghost of a "beautiful" girl roaming the cemetery grounds. Satala said the caretaker was certain that it was Mary Bregovy, one of the leading "Mary candidates" (she was the focus of the interview). Most retellings of the Mary story that mention this sighting have assumed that the sighting took place only a short time after Bregovy's death, but Satala's own dating of the affair would put it in the late 1940s, some fifteen years later.

Date Unknown (possibly post-1959)
Type A: Vanishing Hitchhiker

Satala also told the *Southtown Economist* that a neighbor had once told him that her son had picked up a girl at the Willowbrook Ballroom and offered her a ride home: "The boy said, 'How far?' and she said to keep going down Archer. As they approached the gate, she screamed and disappeared from the car."

No date was given here, nor were any names used. It's probably worth noting that going "down" Archer from the Willowbrook would be going *away* from Resurrection. That he called it the Willowbrook may place it after 1959, when the ballroom's name was changed from the Oh Henry.

Early 1970s, Unknown Man

Type A: *Vanishing Hitchhiker*

Though I'm mostly sticking to published accounts here, I'll include the story related to me by a tour passenger, who says that a friend picked up a sad-looking young woman beside the road in the early 1970s. He picked her up after mistaking her for a girl he knew from school, and couldn't exactly drive away after realizing it wasn't who he thought it was. She said little, if anything, and disappeared out of the car after a few blocks, as he drove by the graveyard.

1973, Bob Main

Type C: *Strange Woman Seen*

In 1992, a man named Bob Main told the *Chicago Tribune* that he had seen Mary on two occasions in 1973 at Harlow's, a now-defunct nightclub at 8058 South Cicero Avenue (a short drive down 79th would put you right at Resurrection from there). "This was the glitter rock era," said Main, "and we saw a lot of strange people, but one Friday night, then [again] two weeks later on a Saturday night, this woman came in. She was about twenty-four to thirty years old, 5'8" or 5'9", slender, with yellow blonde hair to her shoulders that she wore in these big spooly curls coming down from a high forehead. She was really pale, like she had powdered her whole face and her body. She had on this old dress that was yellow, like a wedding dress left in the sun. She sat right next to the dance floor and she wouldn't talk to anyone. She danced all by herself, with a pirouette-type dance. People were saying, 'Who is this most bizarre chick?'"

Main noted that she "seemed to look right through you" and had a teardrop on her cheek that looked like nail polish. No one had seen her come in, and no one saw her leave.

1973, Unnamed Cab Driver
Type A: *Vanishing Hitchhiker*

According to Chet Prusinski, then owner of Chet's Melody Lounge, which sits adjacent to Resurrection Cemetery, a cab driver came in demanding to know where the blonde in the white dress was. She had disappeared out of his cab without paying. No one was in the tavern except for Chet at the time. The story was repeated in several papers over the years, both by Chet himself and his son Rich, who eventually took over the business.

Chet left a Bloody Mary on the bar for Mary nightly and said that it sometimes disappeared, though he often said with a chuckle that some living person probably thought it was a free drink and took it.

December 21, 1974
Type C: *Strange Woman Seen*

A Halloween issue of the *Tribune* in 1975 recounted a story of two boys the previous Christmas season seeing a young blonde woman in an old-fashioned ball dress "dancing down the street, acting weird." Another paper pinpointed the date as the Saturday before Christmas.

This was reported to ghost hunter Richard Crowe, who commented to reporters at the time that "Mary's on the verge of a breakdown. She's reportedly jumped in young men's cars when they were stopped for a light on Archer, and she's been incoherent."

August 10, 1976, Pat Homa
Type B: Disappearing Strange Woman

According to reports repeated in several books, patrolman Pat Homa of the Justice, Illinois, police got a call directing him to proceed to the gates of Resurrection Cemetery. A blonde in a white dress had been seen in the graveyard—presumably a woman who had been locked inside. Homa arrived to find nobody there but noticed that the bars of the fence had been bent apart, as though someone with supernatural strength had tried to pry them open to escape. There were black scorch marks where the hands would have been.

The fact that there's an exact date and name given lend a certain credibility to the story (Homa is said to have lost his job for talking about the encounter on the TV show *That's Incredible!* though Justice police have denied this), but those who have tried to independently verify it have found nothing to back it up.

The bars *were* bent out of shape around this time, and remained visibly marked and damaged for years. Suggesting that it wasn't a ghost who bent them, but a construction worker, can generate some pretty frightening emails (trust me). However, the cemetery officials always insisted in newspapers—both to the *Southtown Economist* in 1983 and the *Tribune* in 1992—that a grounds worker had backed a truck into the bars. Other workers had tried to heat up the metal bars with a blowtorch in order to bend them back together, accounting for the scorch marks and handprints. Contractors who viewed the bars, or who now view pictures of them, seem to believe the cemetery's side of the story. I once spoke to a woman who introduced herself to me as the daughter of the man who backed a truck into the bars—according to her, the cemetery grounds workers always thought it was hilarious that people thought it was a ghost.

In any case, grounds workers have noted that with a cemetery as big as Resurrection, for them not to realize that there was still someone on the grounds when they locked the gates was not unheard of.

August 12, 1976
Type B: Disappearing Strange Woman

Police (according to a story I couldn't trace) apparently responded to a hit-and-run report and found a panic-stricken girl who had seen the body of a woman in white beside the road. The body had vanished by the time police arrived.

This was at 76th Street and Roberts Road, on the back side of the cemetery. I only found one death recorded at that intersection: that of a male cyclist in 1949.

May 1978, Shawn and Gerry Gape
Type B: Disappearing Strange Woman

According to an August 13, 1980, issue of a suburban paper, Shawn and Gerry Gape related a story of seeing a young woman lying in the highway wearing a long white gown. They swerved off the road to avoid hitting her as she ran into the road, but were unsuccessful. They braced for impact, but the woman vanished. The couple were later interviewed for *That's Incredible!*

January 11, 1979, "Ralph" the Cab Driver
Type A: Vanishing Hitchhiker

A cab driver told Bill Geist, a columnist for a suburban pull-out edition of the *Chicago Tribune*, that he had seen the ghost two weeks before. Speaking on condition of anonymity, but going by "Ralph," he told of driving down Archer Avenue a little lost, around midnight, and seeing a woman with no coat ("and it was one of those real cold nights, too") standing beside the road near the Old Willow shopping center, about two blocks north of the Willowbrook Ballroom.

"She didn't put her thumb out or nothing like that," said the driver. "She just looked at my cab…she was a looker. A blonde. I didn't have any ideas or like that; she was young enough to be my daughter. Twenty-one tops."

Ralph asked the woman where she was going, and she said she had to get home. She didn't answer and seemed tired, drunk, or simply "fuzzy" when he asked what was wrong.

She didn't say much, except to nod when the driver asked if he was just supposed to keep going up Archer. He remembered that the only really coherent thing she said was something like "The snows came early this year."

After a couple of miles, she jumped up with a start ("Like a horse, you know," said Ralph) and shouted, "Here! Here!"

The driver looked around, seeing no house. "Where?" he asked.

She stuck her arm out the window and said, "There!"

Ralph turned to see a "little shack," then looked back to his passenger to find that she was gone—vanished without a trace.

"And that car door never opened," he said. "May the good Lord strike me dead, it never opened."

Two days after this came the Chicago Blizzard of 1979, which would close the ballroom for the next two weeks. That night, the last the ballroom was open before the storm, was a "singles' night" at which the band played waltz and foxtrot music that had been popular forty years before.

1979 (or so), Joyce Laskowski
Type B: Disappearing Strange Woman

In a 1991 article, Joyce Laskowski of Elmhurst told the *Tribune* that she had seen the ghost "about twelve years ago" on Route 83, near 55th Street. It was a rainy April night, and Ms. Laskowski and her roommate were driving on Route 83 when they saw a tall young blonde woman in a white ball gown, waving desperately for help. They turned to pick her up, but she had vanished. "I'm sure it was her," she told the *Tribune*, "even though it's out of her area." Route 83 and 55th is, indeed, quite a bit out of Mary's normal range; Archer Avenue is a ways away.

1980 (or so), Cab Driver Nick Muros
Type C: Strange Woman Seen

Early one Sunday morning, cab driver Nick Muros was driving home down Archer Avenue after working at a picnic for Holy Cross Hellenic Church. Muros told *The Times*, a suburban weekly, that he had heard the *name* Resurrection Mary but didn't know any of the particulars of the story at the time.

As he approached the main gates of the cemetery, he saw a "black object" just up the road, out of the view of his headlights. (Why it was dark after a picnic is not known— had it been an overnight affair?)

Between the gates of the cemetery and the mausoleum was a girl in a flowing white dress with short blonde hair, walking slowly toward the gates. During the ten seconds or so that she was in his sight, Muros watched as she stepped onto the median strip that separates the two lanes beyond the gates. She was wearing no shoes, as far as he could see, and was standing with her palms turned up (like the raven-black-haired woman who appeared farther down Archer at St. James in 1897—see chapter 17). It was a warm night, with a full moon. Nick didn't see her disappear or offer her a ride, but told reporters that the encounter was "creepy."

August 1980
Various Sightings

The last weekend of August 1980 was a real boom time for Mary sightings; a sighting by the deacon of the Greek church on Archer was reported by the *Valley Times*. Apparently, several other people saw the same thing over the course of the weekend, but details on what they were actually seeing are sort of scarce. Most seem to have been of the "saw a strange woman" variety (type C).

September 5, 1980, Tony
Type A: Vanishing Hitchhiker

A man named Tony was driving up Archer and saw a girl in a white dress by the side of the road. He offered her a ride, and she said, "Sure." When asked where to go, she said, "Just take me up Archer." As they drove, she declined to say anything but "Just take me up Archer," even when Tony remarked that "you look like Resurrection Mary." She vanished out of the car; when he turned to look at her, she was simply gone.

This story has been reprinted in many books, but I was unable to find the original source.

September 7, 1980, Clare Rudnicki
Type B: Disappearing Strange Woman

Only two days after Tony's encounter, Clare Rudnicki, who later appeared on *Unsolved Mysteries*, was driving past the cemetery with a few other people when they saw a glowing woman walking along very slowly. One of them suggested that it was the famous Resurrection Mary. As they came closer, they were horrified to see that she had no face. She was gone when they turned around for a better look.

1981, Unnamed Employees at Willowbrook Ballroom
Type C: Strange Woman Seen

According to Nancy Buck, whose encounter from 1983 is recounted below, a couple of Willowbrook Ballroom employees saw a "strange-looking" woman in white walking slowly along Archer Avenue two years before her own sighting.

October 1983, Nancy Buck
Type C: Strange Woman Seen

Nancy Buck of Justice, Illinois, told the *Southtown Economist* that one Saturday morning in early October, shortly after

1:30 a.m. (which is sometimes given as a common time for Mary to appear), she and two co-workers from the Willowbrook Ballroom spotted a young woman in her early twenties. She had long, "dark blonde" hair and was dressed strangely.

"I mean," Nancy explained, "she was dressed kind of outdated, like something out of the '50s or earlier, and it was not a punk style." She was wearing a red velour or velvet dress that went below her knees, a long red veil, and a pair of black-and-white saddle shoes. She stared down at the ground as she walked north along Archer, heading in a direction that would have taken her to the cemetery. It seemed particularly odd that, though it was a cold autumn night, she was not wearing a coat.

October 1989, Pam Turlow
Type B: Disappearing Strange Woman

Pam and her friend Janet Kalal told *Unsolved Mysteries* that they had encountered Mary in 1989. She was dressed in white, with her hair flowing backward away from her, walking through Resurrection Cemetery as they drove by.

To their shock, the woman ran right into the road, directly into the path of their car. Janet slammed on the brakes, but it was too late. The two braced for impact, but there was none to come. The woman was gone. "There was no impact, no sound, nothing," Janet told the TV crew.

Pam said she had heard about the story of Mary from her father, who had read about it in the paper in 1939. The 1939 article has never been found, though plenty of anecdotal evidence indicates that the story *was* certainly going around by then, and that the ghost was already called "Resurrection Mary." Author Dale Kaczmarek says his parents used to go looking for Mary on dates in the late 1930s, and author Ray Johnson told me he's heard accounts of an article from around then talking about a whole network of vanishing hitchers operating on Archer.

1990s (approx.), Ed Bartunek
Type C: Strange Woman Seen

Few details were given, but in a 2004 interview with the *Chicago Sun-Times* about his experiences as a cyclist, Ed Bartunek said that he had seen the ghost during the daytime, a departure from most other sightings. "I have seen Resurrection Mary at 3 p.m.," he said, without giving a date range for the sighting. "I checked to make sure it wasn't a deer. It looked like a bride from far away. I thought it was [someone] playing a trick on me."

A few notable patterns emerge in these sightings. Some of the hallmarks of "vanishing hitchhiker" stories—such as giving her a ride home from a dance hall or prom, visiting the girl's house, or loaning her some outerwear and finding it on her grave the next day—are almost always absent from Mary sightings. It's also probably worth noting that her hair is invariably said to be blonde, and she's usually said to be in her twenties.

The Name of the Ghost: The Most Popular Candidates

So, assuming this ghost is real, who is she? Researchers have scoured the newspaper archives and records looking for the "real" Mary. Academics who study vanishing-hitchhiker lore tend to reject outright any notion that the ghost might be real, and eschew attempts to find an identity or historical basis for the stories; that's probably the most responsible way to approach these stories, but it isn't fun.

The "classical" answer to Resurrection Mary's identity is Mary Bregovy, a young woman who was killed at the age of twenty-three in a car accident at Wacker and Lake in 1934. She was buried at Resurrection Cemetery (though the Mary Bregovy whose grave is visible is a whole different person; her own grave is currently unmarked). Undertaker Joseph Satala, who prepared Mary's body, believed she was the ghost, and even told a newspaper so in the 1980s. Most importantly, she does seem to have died after a night of ballroom-hopping, which puts her in line with the way the story of the ghost is usually told.

However, there are a couple of problems with the theory. The scholarly article from 1942 indicates that the story of the vanishing hitcher on Archer had already been going around for a couple of years by the time Bregovy died. And, of course, there's the matter of the photographs—every single firsthand account of Mary I could find notes that the vanishing girl is a blonde. Mary Bregovy was a brunette.

Bregovy remains a popular candidate, though, largely due to the general belief that Mary is connected to dancing in some way. Also, we have some firsthand accounts of what Mary was like in life. By the time her story was told in connection to the ghost in the 1980s, her surviving relatives didn't remember much about her, but friends described her as "personality plus," a vivacious girl with something of a flair for danger; one friend had declined to go out dancing with her because the boys she'd met seemed "wild." This stands in contrast to most other candidates, about whom we have little reliable information.

One other candidate brought up occasionally is Anna Marija Norkus, a girl killed in a car wreck about six weeks prior to her thirteenth birthday (she's sometimes said to have died on the eve of her birthday, but the death certificate and funeral records contradict this). Some say the car she was in would have been going right past Resurrection, but this isn't quite accurate (the streets were a bit different then), and no witness of Mary has ever described her as looking twelve years old. Some connect Anna with stories of a ghostly girl who runs in front of passing cars near Resurrection (the type B encounter), but few believe that she's the vanishing hitchhiker.

This doesn't mean her ghost couldn't be seen and referred to as Resurrection Mary, though; indeed, it's commonly surmised that Mary may not be one single ghost, but a whole group of them that are simply given a collective name. After all, why should the disappearing hitchhiker and the ghost who disappears after being hit by cars be the same spirit? Since the girl who gets hit doesn't ask for rides home, there's no reason that Anna's actually being at nearby St. Casimir would stand in the way of her being the ghost people are seeing either.

For a couple of years, the most popular candidate for the "true" Mary was Mary Miskowski, a girl who lived on the 4900 block of South Damen Avenue, only blocks away from Mary Bregovy. According to legend, Mary Miskowski died on or around Halloween 1930, at the age of eighteen or nineteen, having been hit by a car while going to a Halloween party, for which she was dressed as a bride in her mother's old wedding dress. A blonde herself, she would have matched the traditional description of Mary—a blonde teen-ager in a white dress—far better than most other candidates.

Much of this information allegedly came from people Miskowski used to babysit, but it didn't really stand up to research. Census records proved that a Mary Miskowski *did* live on the 4900 block of South Damen in 1930, and that she was nineteen but still living at home at the time, just as the stories said. Stories of her death, however, could not be verified—no Mary Miskowski is listed as dying in Illinois be-tween 1916 and 1950 in the Illinois death index, and no such car accident was mentioned in the papers around Hallow-een in 1930.

I've recently found out conclusively what happened: Mary Miskowski actually died in 1956, at which point she would have been in her mid-forties. She wasn't going by Miskowski anymore, but by her married name (which I've withheld from publication to keep her surviving children from being harassed). Where the story that she died in 1930 came from is anyone's guess.

Another recently uncovered story is that of Mary Bojacz, who died in a terrible train wreck while en route to a funeral at Resurrection. Two cars had set out to attend the burial of a young girl. The front car made it all the way to the cemetery without anything going awry, but partway through the jour-ney, the second car, which contained about a dozen people, was hit head-on by a train, instantly killing all but one of the passengers—including Mary Bojacz. We're not yet sure how old she was (though we do know that she was old enough to be married, and that she was a brunette).

It should also not be overlooked that at least five girls named Mary—all roughly the right age—were buried at Resurrection after perishing in the *Eastland* disaster. Indeed, those five are only a few of the sixty or seventy girls named Mary who died at about the right age and who were buried at Resurrection in the right time period.

The name of one other Mary comes up in books and articles now and then—Mary Duranski, who was said to have died in a car wreck in the 1930s on the way home from a dance, but no data can be found establishing that she was a real person at all. There's a Mary Durancsik who was buried at Resurrection in 1918, but she was well into her forties when she died. There's also a Mary Dorencz, who was thirty when she died in 1938.

And so it goes. The list of Marys at Resurrection goes on and on, and more are being found all the time.

It should be noted, though, that most of the common candidates for the ghost are based on a fairly broad assumption that it's actually the ghost of a girl named Mary in the first place. Only one published sighting (again, that of Jerry Palus) seems to indicate that her name was Mary, and even then we're not sure if he actually heard her name at all (her name being Mary had been part of the story for years by the time he went public with his account). It could be that we just call her Resurrection Mary because it has a better ring to it than, say, Resurrection Ethel.

Another Chilling Story of Resurrection

Mary doesn't seem to be the only ghost at Resurrection— some people have spoken of strange sounds coming from the mausoleum.

One tour passenger told me a particularly frightening story: her father was a gravedigger at Resurrection, and one day, while preparing to bury a young woman, he heard a scream coming from inside the coffin. The coffin was opened and the girl was dead, inside of it, but apparently hadn't been the entire time—there were scratch marks on the inner lining.

If You Go

Going looking for Mary after a night of dancing is a popular pastime in Chicago, but few ever seem to find anything. The cemetery is closed after dark (for obvious reasons), and is not known to cooperate with ghost hunters. While the cemetery itself is said to know the current location of Mary Bregovy's body (it was moved from a temporary-term grave ages ago), the information is not given to the public.

Mary is, truly, a ghost for whom you can't really hunt. The most you can do is go to a South Side ballroom and hope for the best.

There have been scattered accounts recently of a girl dressing up as Mary and walking down the street just to mess with people. Just something to keep in mind.

CHAPTER 17

St. James at Sag Bridge Churchyard and Other Haunted Cemeteries of Archer Avenue

When ghost hunters in Chicago get together, we tend to marvel about just how many ghost stories are related to South Archer Avenue—Resurrection Mary is just the tip of the iceberg. Every cemetery in the area has a ghost of its own. Archer Woods Cemetery is said to be home to a woman in white who wanders around weeping. That's a pretty stereotypical ghost, really, but the same can't be said of the ghost in Bethania Cemetery, just adjacent to Resurrection; there a ghostly old woman curses people out as they walk past the gates in the middle of the night. This is the kind of ghost I plan to be myself one day.

The portion of South Archer around the area known as "the Sag," particularly the churchyard on the hill leading up to St. James at Sag Bridge Church ("St. James of the Sag"), has been said to be haunted for well over a century.

The Sag

In the 1880s, newspapers ran breathless accounts of a fiendish murder. One James McMahon had been asleep in bed with his wife when two burglars broke into the house; Mrs. McMahon testified that she had heard them warn her husband not to make a sound, and he replied by saying, "Aye, aye," or "All right." A second later, two shots rang out and James McMahon was dead, shot through the heart. A few witnesses thought they saw a man in dark clothes fleeing the scene, but the case was never solved.

However, in 1897 a *Tribune* story dryly noted that Mary McMahon had since married two other men, and both of *them* were murdered as well.

This was only mentioned in passing, though, in a story about McMahon's burial place at the churchyard beside St. James of the Sag Church in Lemont, twenty miles south of downtown Chicago and close to most of the other haunted spots that line the southern portion of Archer Avenue.

I don't run too many tours of the Archer Avenue area; it's just too far from downtown, and we're not even allowed to park the bus outside of most of the haunted places after dark, let alone let anyone out to look around. But even a brief nighttime glimpse of the church and graveyard at St. James of the Sag never fails to impress, especially on a foggy night when the bells are ringing.

St. James of the Sag, perhaps the oldest church in the whole Chicagoland area, sits atop a lonely hill in the Sag Valley near Lemont, Illinois, south of the Chicago metro area and just down Archer Avenue from the Willowbrook Ballroom. The old church, sometimes referred to as the "Monk's Castle" by the locals, towers above the hill on which the cemetery sits, and the headstones almost appear to be struggling to climb up the hill, leaning to the side as though they're about to tumble down into one another.

The graveyard on the hill holds a certain renown as the earliest still-existing burial ground in the area (the oldest headstones are much older than what you'll find in downtown Chicago cemeteries), and has a strange history of its own. In the 19th century, the place was commonly understood to be a "free" burial ground, where anyone who wanted to could bury a body at no charge. This may not have *actually* been the policy of the cemetery at all, but people in town certainly seemed to *think* that it was. According to an 1897 article in the *Chicago Tribune*, the land had been donated to the church in 1858 by James and Bridget Murphy, and Mrs. Murphy had insisted that a clause be inserted into the deed saying that "any poor man might bury his dead in it without any cost." By 1897, the cemetery was said to be full of "free graves" that had been dug for persons unknown.

The 1897 article described at length the brambles and tangles of roses, geraniums, and weeds that covered the graveyard in those days, and said that "beneath the floral tangle is a similar riot of bodies … in one corner suicides and murdered men rest from violence … and here and there are the graves of the unknown." Many people buried there had died in accidents in the digging of the Illinois and Michigan Canal, one of the construction projects that first attracted large numbers of pioneers to Chicago, and some were never identified (despite, in one case, having been exhumed twice for the benefit of people thought to be relatives). One spot was occupied by John McMahon, whose grisly murder was nearly forgotten by 1897.

The "free" section was a particular mess—some of the "buryings" were carried out by drunken revelers who often only dug the graves a couple of feet deep. Sometimes new bodies were buried in old plots. On at least one occasion, the priest came home to his house on the grounds to find it full of drunken partiers who, having half-buried a dead friend, were now eating all of his food. Sometimes they stole his dogs as well.

Despite all this, the priest kept up the custom of allowing free burials, asking simply that only baptized people be buried in the main part of the grounds, though suicides and the unbaptized could be buried in a special section in the northwest corner.

Many are the gruesome stories about the area. For instance, on a foggy night in 1873 there was a terrible accident when Engine 122, a freight train carrying nearly thirty cars full of coal, collided with a passenger train near the Sag. Twenty people were killed and at least as many more were badly injured; the bodies were piled on the ground within shouting distance of the cemetery, and some were probably buried there. A history of the disaster described it in haunting terms: "The cries of the suffering pierced the night air, and the crash of the collision and the roar and hissing of steam were heard at Lemont . . . their condition was indescribably horrid. Six were found already dead."

The coroner quickly ruled that the accident was the result of criminal carelessness on the part of the conductors, but by that time Edward Beane, the conductor of the freight train, was missing in action; he had jumped off the car in time to survive, but had fled the scene at once, pounding through the nearby forests on foot, only to be captured by an old friend who had turned amateur detective a few weeks later. Papers for a few days referred to the case as a "railroad murder." However, after receiving a change of venue to Will County, where there was less prejudice against him, Beane appears eventually to have been released. By the time his trial came up, papers had lost interest.

Throughout the 1880s and 1890s, stories of chilling goings-on in the area continued to be reported. Murdered men were sometimes found beside the road, and in 1886, the bodies of two women were found in a quarry pool. In 1897, the *New York Times* reported that diggers near Sag Bridge had discovered the bodies of nine "Indians," which scientists had proclaimed to be several hundred years old. One of the bodies was said to be that of a man who had stood seven feet tall.

The *Times* article even stated that nine years before, skeletons had been dug up on the same ground, and had been reburied after the people of the neighborhood reported that the spirits of the Indians had been riding through the village on horseback, demanding that their bodies be reburied. Only a few of the bodies were reburied in 1897; others were reportedly taken to the Field Museum.

This incident seems to have made little news at the time, if it truly happened at all, but certainly by 1897 the stories that the place was haunted were well known. Only days after the *Tribune* published its long story on the odd history of the "free" cemetery, it reported a chilling ghost sighting from the graveyard.

A church fair had been held in a large dance hall at the bottom of the hill. Two Chicago musicians—Professor William Looney and John Kelly—were brought in to play violin and harp. Since it was a long journey home to Chicago, they decided to stay the night after the dance, and rigged up cots on the upper floor of the dance hall.

Around one o'clock in the morning, they heard the sound of horses and a carriage rumbling swiftly by outside. In the bright moonlight out the window, the church spire stretched up above the glistening gravestones, but there were no horses to be seen. But the sound of hooves came closer and closer, then seemed to pass right by the dance hall.

The sound approached again, and when they looked out the window a second time, they saw a woman in white standing in the middle of the road. Raven-black hair hung down to her shoulders, and she glided around the cemetery as though she was on roller skates. The *Tribune*, possibly stretching things a bit, said that "deep melancholy was reflected from sepulchral eyes which rolled about with that hollow intensity indicative of some soul-eating despair."

Eventually there came a team of snow-white horses, each with a "light of electric brilliancy" shining from their foreheads, pulling behind them a mysterious dark vehicle on which no driver could be seen. It swept by the woman, who raised her arms, holding out her palms (a particular detail that would be echoed in a later encounter with Resurrection Mary[12]). By this time the woman was only twenty feet or so from the window, and a shadow began to form around her. She sank into the earth, and the horses disappeared.

---

12. Indeed, some have even suggested that the modern Resurrection Mary stories are just the way that retellings of this well-reported incident evolved over the years.

"I am willing to make affidavit to the truth of this story," said the unfortunately named Mr. Looney, "and I will go further and say I am willing to tell the priest it is the truth."

Marshal Ed Coen of the police said, "Both Kelly and Looney are fine young men, and I have no reason to disbelieve any statements which they have made ... I do not believe there was anything of a practical joke in the affair; that would be too dangerous in this locality. Everybody out here carries weapons ... any person so foolish would be likely to receive a bullet."

So, while it may be tempting to say that any stories of the hauntings of St. James of the Sag cemetery just come from the fact that the place looks so spooky, there's *plenty* of history behind it. Even now, records of who is actually buried in the graveyard are hopelessly jumbled, and in 1986 the newspapers reported on plans to have many of the sunken gravestones sodded over when the cemetery was renovated.

Much of the history of the place is now quite literally buried or faded from memory. Though the cemetery officially began in the 1850s, a 1984 report indicated that one faded gravestone, that of one Michael Dillon, read either "1846" or "1816" as the date of death. Anecdotal evidence indicates that there had previously been other burial grounds nearby, and that some of the bodies in them had been dug up and moved to St. James after its founding, so some of them could be even older than that.

By 1984, historians had lost track of the ownership of nearly seven hundred out of the one thousand known graves. The records made at the time did list a gravestone for John McMahon, the man murdered while in bed with his wife—an epitaph for the unfortunate man read "my beloved husband,"

and it's awfully tempting to wonder if the woman's two *other* murdered husbands had similar epitaphs.

The 1890s ghost sighting was certainly not the last one there, and may not have been the first. Stories circulate in ghost-hunting communities about "phantom monks" being reported in the area as early as 1847, though few details on these early sightings seem to have emerged.

A better-known "phantom monk" encounter came 130 years later, in 1977, when police officer Herb Roberts chased a group of robed figures up the cemetery hill early in the hours of Thanksgiving morning. They seemed, it's said, to glide up the hill, not even bothering to dodge the gravestones, which they seemed to float right through. I've spoken with several people who claim to have seen the police report of this incident, though I've never seen it myself.

Other sightings there in recent years have more logical explanations. For years people who broke into the graveyard at night spoke of a ghostly monk with a booming voice, though this has generally been explained as being little more than the drunken memories of people who'd been scared off the grounds by a priest who kept a megaphone handy for chasing trespassers away.

Many people who have gone to the graveyard have told of a strange phenomenon there: the ground is sometimes observed to rise and fall, as it if it were "breathing." I've spoken to people who've seen this for themselves. Even ghost hunters generally seem to think that this is a scientific phenomenon, not a paranormal one (I honestly think that the true explanation may involve swamp gas here), but this is one of those things like the tree dripping blood-red gunk at the H. H. Holmes body dump: no amount of scientific explanation makes it seem any less spooky.

If You Go

You should be able to wander the grounds during the day—like any old cemetery, it's a fascinating (if a bit depressing) place to wander around. By night, though, it's closed to the public, and ghost hunting is certainly not allowed. Officially, the Catholic church does not sanction ghosts. However, they seem to break ranks on that one an awful lot.

CHAPTER 18

Maple Lake

In the woods near St. James of the Sag is a manmade lake that claimed a number of victims. The hauntings there may even predate the lake itself.

I remember reading a slim book of ghost stories in grade school that contained the story of Joe Baldwin's "ghost light." According to the legend, Joe Baldwin was a railroad signalman who lost his head in a train wreck, and now the light of his lantern was often seen in the woods, swinging back and forth, as old Joe looked for his head, which had never been recovered. I always loved a good headless ghost story.

I noticed that the same basic story showed up a lot. Mickey Mantle talked about going to look for an "Indian light" in his autobiography, and in my hometown of Des Moines we had a "glowing grave" of some repute. These types of stories came up on *Unsolved Mysteries* now and then and gave skeptics a fine chance to blame things on swamp gas.

Recent investigations indicate that there was never any such person as Joe Baldwin. There was a *Charles* Baldwin who was killed in a railroad accident in the same location about ten years before Joe's supposed death, though. Charles Baldwin didn't lose his head but, hey, who among us hasn't spent hours looking for keys that turned out to be in our pockets? Maybe the ghost of poor Charles is out there looking for a head that's still attached. Others concluded that the light was actually the ghost still out trying to signal trains, which probably makes more sense (why would a ghost need a lantern to see, anyway?). Whatever it was, the "Baldwin light" seems to have stopped appearing when the train tracks were torn up in 1977.

We have our own ghost light here in Chicago—a reddish-yellow light that appears over Maple Lake, which sits tucked away in the woods off Archer Avenue just south of the Willowbrook Ballroom, not far away from the infamous St. James of the Sag graveyard. The lake is a manmade affair, only about twenty feet deep at its deepest point, and roughly a mile in diameter. It's said to have been created for swimming purposes, and is now a popular place for fishing by daylight hours.

I once had occasion to flip through the records of a funeral home—the one that had overseen the funeral of Anna Norkus, one of the Resurrection Mary candidates. Reading through such books of records is always a sort of depressing affair, but it was striking how many of the pages recorded the funerals of teenagers who had drowned in accidents at Maple Lake. In the 1920s, when the lake was still brand-new, it seems that Maple Lake was a popular place to do some late-night swimming, possibly while not entirely sober. Swimming at the lake was no longer allowed after the 1930s, but accidents and suicides continued to claim lives there.

Oddly, the stories of people dying in the lake don't seem to figure into many of the explanations for the legendary ghost light; most of the ones that you hear date back to the days *before* there was a lake there. Some of them just seem to be the kind of stories that develop naturally whenever a ghost light is seen, like the stories that it's a dead person looking for his head. This seems like it would be one to file in the "that's just the sort of thing some people *would* say" folder, except that one must remember that Maple Lake and the Palos Woods sits right near the Sag Bridge area. It's difficult not to cross-reference it with the 19th century stories about workers digging up skeletons, or the stories about residents being badly disturbed by spirits demanding that their bones be re-interred, that figure into the history of St. James of the Sag (see previous section).

Other stories go around about a farmer who used to plow the land being beheaded on the site. A somewhat better documented story, in that it actually has dates attached to it, states that in 1858 a farmer had built a well on the land. According to a 1923 issue of *Palos in Autumn* (perhaps the most obscure source I'll ever cite), one day he had a few friends around to inspect it, and three of them fell down to the bottom, where they died due to gasses that lurked in the bottom of the dark pit. The fact that there's actually a date attached to this gives it a bit more credence than some stories, but even that isn't quite enough to make the story automatically reliable.

The story does seem to be *about* right, from what I can find from contemporary sources; three workmen did die on October 4, 1858, while excavating a well at Palos, according to a "year in review" published in the *Chicago Tribune* at the end of that year (as near as I can tell, this was the only mention of the event in that paper). That they were excavating it, not inspecting it after a few drinks, doesn't line up perfectly with the story as it was retold in 1923, but it's close enough. However, it would be just as easy to blame the ghost light on the skeletons reportedly unearthed in the area around nearby Sag Bridge in 1897, or on the murders that took place nearby from time to time in the days when it was the domain of "rough characters."

Even if we take the bold leap of assuming that the Maple Lake spook light is truly of paranormal origin, it's impossible to tell whether we should blame it on the well incident, the murders, the drowning incidents, or even something completely different. As we ghost hunters sometimes say when we get together with stories of Archer Avenue, it just seems like there's something in the water down there.

But is there really even a light? If you ask around, it's not difficult to find people who claim to have had paranormal encounters around the woods near the lake at night—often in the form of thinking they saw a shadowy figure darting around. However, the spook light is one of those ghosts that everyone seems to know about, but that no one actually sees anymore.

If You Go

This is a difficult place to investigate now, since the light is only going to turn up visibly at night, and the lake is officially closed at sunset. In older times, when most of the sightings were recorded, the curfew wasn't enforced much, but it is now; police officers will run you off, or give you a ticket, if they catch you parking a car by the lake at night. I've taken tour groups there after dark once or twice on "Archer Avenue tours," but we can never stay long enough to see much.

CHAPTER 19

Dunning Cemetery

6443 W. Belle Plaine Avenue

The Read-Dunning Memorial Park is on Belle Plaine Avenue, which runs a block north of Irving Park Road. This marks a portion of the site that was once the city's "potter's field," in which unclaimed bodies were buried, and is still home to countless bodies. It is probably the most depressing park on the planet.

Have you ever heard of an abandoned insane asylum graveyard that *wasn't* supposed to be haunted? I sure haven't.

And yet, the site of the long-abandoned Dunning Cemetery, where the Dunning Insane Asylum buried its dead, and where the city buried unclaimed bodies for years, has only occasionally been spoken of as a haunted spot. You hear a lot of secondhand stories about ghosts hanging around in the area, and of people getting weird equipment readings, but nothing all that concrete. Ursula Bielski has been told by locals that they stay away from the area, though, and one woman even said that she wouldn't shop at the nearby Jewel-Osco grocery store because there were ghosts in it.

Wendy, my tour bus driver, swears that the one time when she went out there, she felt a hand grabbing at her ankle. She refuses to go back. And Wendy is a tough person—hailing from the South Side ("the baddest part of town"), she's the president of her chapter of the steelworkers' union, and able to pull off perfect U-turns in a school bus with no power steering.

I like to imagine that the hand grabbing her ankle was the ghost of Johann Hoch, a serial killer from the early 20th century who, when he was first caught, was rumored to have been an apprentice of H. H. Holmes. Marrying for money was Hoch's stock in trade; when police caught up with him in 1905, he had already proposed to what police guessed would have been wife #55. His usual workflow was to meet a woman, propose to her, marry her, take her money, and run, all in the space of about a week, killing the women in the process about a third of the time.

You'd think that a guy who could convince so many women he'd only just met to marry him would be a dashing fellow, but Hoch was anything but—he was a stout, wheezy little booger who looked like the guy on the Pringles can and talked like a German character on *The Simpsons*.

His last murder victim in Chicago was one Marie Walcker, a widow who owned a candy store near Lincoln Park. He met her through a personal ad and spoke with her for half an hour or so at the shop.

"I like you, and you like me," he said. "So, we can get married, yah?"

He had presented himself as a rich man who would support her, and Marie doesn't seem to have been in a position to be picky. None of his many wives seem to have been— photographs of a few of the surviving ones posed together show a crew of frumpy old spinsters who resemble the old women of River City, Iowa, who antagonize the librarian in *The Music Man*. In the days before Social Security, landing a husband, even one they didn't like so well, before they got too old or sick to keep working seemed like more of an obligation than it probably would to women today.

Three of Johann Hoch's alleged wives, looking as though they may break out into a chorus of "Pick a Little, Talk a Little" any second.

And so the two were wed, and on the night of the wedding, Hoch slipped some arsenic into her food. At the time, arsenic poisoning was a perfect crime; there was arsenic in embalming fluid, so there was no way to get a conviction once the undertaker had stepped into the room.

However, it's not a poison that kills quickly. Marie languished for many days in her bed as nephritis slowly ravaged her kidneys. From medical descriptions of her condition that came out in the trial, she was very painfully peeing herself to death. Hoch, meanwhile, sat around making a big public display of feeling sorry for himself. "I thought I had a healthy woman this time," he lamented.

The body hadn't even been removed from the bed when Johann, standing right in front of Marie's corpse, proposed to her sister, Amelia. Amelia, incredibly, said yes. A couple of days later, Marie's body was buried, and a couple of days after that, Johann married Amelia at the courthouse.

He didn't kill Amelia, though. He simply took her money and headed for New York, where police caught up with him days later. He was living in a rooming house and had already proposed to the proprietress. He was carrying a fountain pen with arsenic hidden in the barrel, which he tried to explain was headache powder.

"It's arsenic," an irate officer insisted. "A man doesn't go around with headache powder hidden in the barrel of a pen."

On the long train ride back, Hoch proved himself to be the goofiest damned serial killer ever captured.

"How come you married so many women?" asked a reporter.

"All the women for Johann go crazy," he said, in his thick accent.

"How come so many died?"

"Kidney failure, I suppose!"

This sort of exchange cracked him up. When asked the names of his most recent wives, he said that each of them had the same name: "Mrs. Johann Hoch." He then collapsed in fits of laughter.

His trial dragged on for some time, but he had made a fatal mistake by not following the advances in the embalming arts and sciences. When a mortician testified that the fluid he had used on Marie did not contain arsenic, Hoch turned pale. Several of his ex-wives had been exhumed by then, and their remains were all found to contain poison. That it was found in at least one wife who *hadn't* been embalmed with arsenic-laced embalming fluid sealed Hoch's doom.

How many of the women he *really* married, and how many of them he killed, are totally unknown today—a dozen kills seems like a fair, possibly conservative, estimate. In any case, he was (like Holmes) convicted of only one, but that was sufficient—he was hanged at the old prison on Illinois and Dearborn. Amelia Fischer-Hoch had, remarkably, forgiven him and was on hand to claim the body, but she'd poured what money she had into Hoch's legal defense fund, so the body was buried in the potter's field at Dunning.

Hence, I like to imagine that when Wendy was walking around there and felt a hand grabbing her ankle, that was old Johann saying, "Ooh! This can be wife number fifty-six!"

But Hoch's is only one of a *lot* of bodies that are probably still rotting away at or around the Read-Dunning Memorial Park on the Northwest Side.

With the closing of the old City Cemetery in Lincoln Park in 1866, Chicago needed a new place to bury the unclaimed dead bodies (at least in times when they weren't automatically giving them over to the medical schools). They set up a new burial ground near the County Farm, where they put inmates from the poorhouse to work in order to earn their keep. Dunning, a "lunatic asylum," was nearby, and soon a tuberculosis hospital would join in the mix. A persistent rumor has it that the term "crazy train" comes from the local nickname for the train that led to the asylum. All those facilities buried their dead in the potter's field.

About twenty acres were devoted to the new cemetery; the current park probably only represents a small part of the burial grounds. By Dunning Cemetery's first mention in print, in the Cook County board minutes from September 1869, there was already talk that it needed to be expanded.

Bodies kept coming in, sometimes in large numbers. More than one hundred unclaimed bodies were interred at Dunning after the Great Chicago Fire in 1871, and the next year the county board arranged to move remains from the old potter's field in Lincoln Park to the new one at Dunning (though, of course, how many of them actually got moved is sort of an open question). Records even show how much the city paid for the coffins—one M. W. Bonfield was paid $3.40 for coffins for known people, and $1.40 for coffins for persons whose names could not be determined.

The grounds kept expanding and expanding, and now there are few places around Irving Park Road and Narragansett Avenue where one could confidently say that no bodies are buried. Records were never perfect, and unmarked graves, which practically all of them were, are easy to lose track of. By the more conservative estimates, some 38,000 bodies were buried in the vicinity over the years, including several that were probably buried well after 1912, when the place ceased to be the main potter's field. As early as 1939, though, aerial photos showed no easily visible graves.

For several decades, people just sort of forgot that the cemetery was there. Then, in 1989, developers bought the land and began to put up a new neighborhood of luxury housing on the site. Naturally, they found a lot of unpleasant surprises. One worker told the *Norridge News* that they had hit one spot where there were "solid bones for two feet." But it wasn't all mere bones—on March 9, 1989, they dug up at least the top half of a man who was so well-preserved that they could still see his handlebar mustache. All through the summer of 1989, bones that were dug up in the area just lay bleaching in the sun in the spaces where the new housing developments were going up. Many were reportedly snatched up by morbid souvenir hunters.

In an effort to quiet down the many people who were fairly horrified at this treatment of the forgotten dead, a space within the land was turned into the Read-Dunning Memorial Park, a desolate-looking stretch of land with small memorial plaques commemorating the unknown persons buried there. Bodies that were found during construction were reportedly reburied in the park grounds.

Before going into ghost-hunting stuff related to the burial ground, it's probably worth mentioning that the unmarked dead may not be the only ghosts in the area. After all, ghost hunters usually expect people to haunt the place where they died, not where they were buried, and there were a number of gruesome deaths in the area. One hears a lot of horror stories about what went on at the Dunning Asylum (which is now long gone, replaced by a newer hospital nearby). One always hears horror stories about 19th-century mental hospitals, and in most cases the stories are probably nothing compared to what *actually* went on there.

Dunning's rise as both a cemetery and asylum coincided neatly with the era when medical schools were providing fine employment for body snatchers, and Dunning was by no means immune. Though rumors were constantly denied that the asylum operated a sort of "meat market"—in which doctors could select a live patient that they'd like to dissect and have that patient's corpse on the slab a day later—the very fact that the rumors kept going around should tell a bit about how people thought of the asylum (and medical schools) at the time. Plenty of inmates were *known* to have been killed by the staff, and many more were *thought* to have been.

Henry Ulrich, a night watchman at the morgue, seems to have been on the take as well. According to one alleged buyer, Ulrich offered to procure the body of a real live freak—some unfortunate "man or woman—blamed if I know" who had been exhibited as a "bear man" in city museums, with six fingers on each hand, and who was now in the asylum. Ulrich offered a sale price of fifty dollars.

"Why, he's still living," said Smith, the buyer, who later went public with the story. "I only want the dead ones."

"That's all right, doc, just say you'll give me the fifty and you can take him in one of those trunks. He's in the 'killer ward' and they'd just think he'd wandered off."

Smith stuck with bodies that were already in the morgue, but when his accusations against various Cook County officials went public, the board was, not for the first time, forced to deny to the press that there was a "killer ward." Smith did later admit that his story wasn't *exactly* the truth, the whole truth, and nothing but the truth. Ulrich, for his part, was eventually sent to jail for stealing sheets.

Grave-robbers hardly needed to rely on living bodies — they had plenty of bodies to steal among the paupers' graves, and there's plenty of evidence that they did an awful lot of work there. As of the time of the Great Chicago Fire in 1871, paupers' bodies were still initially being stored in the "dead house" at the old City Cemetery in Lincoln Park, but when there were half a dozen of them, a "full load," they would be brought out to Dunning to be buried. Sometimes they'd get behind on transporting bodies, and a dozen or more would be buried at once. Body snatchers were said to be able to get them only minutes after they were buried, despite a certain amount of police protection; there was a small firefight between guards and "resurrectionists" around 1870.

Today, Dunning Hospital has moved a short distance to the west, and the original buildings are long gone. The Read-Dunning Memorial Park, which stands on the grounds where the bodies were later uncovered (and generally left lying) is now among the better places to go ghost hunting, for my money. It's the creepiest outdoor space I know of.

There are little stone markers to "orphaned and abandoned children," the unidentified Chicago fire victims, the insane asylum inmates, and others. Not all 38,000+ of the dead are buried under the park itself—plenty more are probably still under the houses and the nearby shopping centers and fast-food joints—but a number of them surely are.

My crew went out there to record a podcast in early 2012, and I was impressed by how genuinely creepy the place seemed. It felt markedly colder inside the park than it did out of it. Though there were no pine trees visible nearby, I detected a very strong scent of pine (pine box coffins?) at one point.

*This is just a snowflake passing by my camera lens on a
chilly Dunning night, but it's pretty cool, huh?*

Other Possible Haunts

Besides Johann Hoch, several interesting people whose
ghosts you may not want to meet are pushing up the weeds
at Dunning:

Marion Hedgepeth

Known as "the handsome bandit," Hedgepeth was a train
robber and killer who is known today almost entirely because
he once shared a cell with H. H. Holmes—and helped get him
hanged. Holmes allegedly spilled the beans about his plot to
kill Ben Pitezel for the insurance money to Hedgepeth, and
Hedgepeth told the police, presumably to gain favor with
them. I've always suspected his story was nonsense, and the

fact that Holmes really *was* planning to kill ol' Ben was just a coincidence (Jeptha Howe, Holmes's lawyer, was acquitted of involvement even though Hedgepeth said he was in on it, on the grounds that a train robber's word was hardly reliable evidence). He should probably be included among the couple of dozen people associated with the Holmes trial who came to a bad end, feeding rumors that Holmes had cursed people with the "evil eye."

Hedgepeth was among the later victims of the "curse," meeting death more than a decade after Holmes was hanged. On New Year's Eve 1909, Hedgepeth was in Chicago, out of prison but not out of his life of crime. On that night, he and another man tried to hold up a saloon in the south Loop area. "Just get in line, boys!" he shouted. "This is no New Year's greeting, for I'm sure of my man when I pull the trigger." When police broke in during the robbery, Hedgepeth hustled out a back door and started to run. He was shot in the head as he ran.

At first, the authorities didn't know what they had on their hands; as far as anyone knew, the dead man was a guy named "Edward Haywood," and the body lay in the cooler at the morgue until February 1910 before they figured out that the dead man was "the Handsome Bandit" and planted his body at Dunning.

Edward Ohrnstiel

In 1898, there was a manhunt going on around the world for thirty-eight-year-old Edward Ohrnstiel, the son of a leading banker in Budapest who had just inherited about half a million dollars (in 1898 money) from his father. But he had left the country for America to nurse his broken heart when his wife left him to become an actress (she later married a French army officer). He bounced around from one financial firm to the next for a while, and wound up living in a small Clark Street apartment, where he found work as an errand-runner for a local Hungarian band to support a "mania" for collecting pictures of women, on which he'd write his wife's name. When he tired of that, he got into the habit of getting into fights in bars, and wound up on the wrong side of the law.

When his father died and his lawyers were searching for him, Edward was locked in a padded cell at Dunning Asylum. By the time they located him, he was in a coffin below a numbered wooden slab that would one day rot away to nothing, but which at least lasted long enough for authorities to find him. They might have exhumed him and moved him, but I couldn't find a record of it.

Genare Caraeilo

In 1895, Genare Caraeilo was working as a model for art courses at the art institute, where he was very well liked, and admired for his ability to sit for a full hour without moving (most models were given a break after twenty-five minutes). But in 1895, work had slowed down, and he was living on around $2.50 per week, out of which he had to feed an entire family. This poverty forced him to reconsider his career path, and he took a job doing manual labor working on a sewer on 63rd Street. On his way home after his first day on the job, he tripped on a railroad track and was crushed by an oncoming train. The *Tribune*, in one of the many times when they just couldn't resist being smart-alecky about a dead person, wrote that "Genare Caraeilo has taken his last pose. It is in a pine box which has been, or soon will be, deposited in the potter's field at Dunning." Classy.

Aspiring models should remember what happened to Genare next time they think of giving up their dreams and getting a "real job."

Morris Stack

If you ever hear the sound of drums at Dunning, perhaps it's to do with the ghost of Morris Stack, a "colorful figure" in the poorhouse who died in 1900. He was reported at the time to be 103 years old, and it was said that he'd served as a drummer boy in the War of 1812.

If You Go

Even the area around the park seemed relatively desolate the first time I investigated there; the single-family luxury neighborhood (a rarity in Chicago) that was built over the graves seemed oddly quiet, and a number of houses looked to be deserted. Perhaps it was just a symptom of the anemic housing market of the day, but it certainly called to mind a claim that the Society for Psychic Research made more than a century ago: that around 150 houses in the Chicago area could not be sold because they were haunted.

The claim always struck me as amusing; I have my doubts that a house being supposedly haunted makes it any harder to sell at all (it seems to me like a good realtor would see a unique opportunity there), but still. Could it be that it's hard to sell houses—and keep the occupants there—when you build over an abandoned insane asylum graveyard that contains the rotting remains of at least one serial killer, as well as any number of more minor criminals? The park is, at best, a grim reminder of a period in our history when the poor, the mentally ill, and orphans were treated particularly badly.

Dunning is high on my list of "suggested scores" for ghost hunters. The park is outdoors and open to the public, so you can poke around all you want without being likely to bother anyone (not a lot of people want to have a picnic in a place with a marker commemorating the orphans who were buried there). Keep in mind that as isolated as the area seems, it's very close to many houses and shopping centers, so be respectful and keep in mind that equipment readings may not be much more reliable here than they are anywhere else in the city.

CHAPTER 20

Bachelor's Grove Cemetery

*In the Rubio Woods Forest Preserve,
off 143rd Street, west of Cicero Avenue, in Midlothian*

Nestled in the heart of a south-suburban forest, Bachelor's Grove is sometimes said to be the most haunted cemetery there is, and has inspired some fascinating historical research, some tantalizing mysteries, and some Grade-A crapola.

I used to open my story about Bachelor's Grove on tours in the following way:

"There are three reasons that we don't go to Bachelor's Grove on tours. Number one is that it takes way too long to get there from downtown. Number two is that it's illegal to be there after dark without a permit. And number three is that neither Hector or myself would be caught dead in that place after dark."

"Damn right," Hector, the driver, would say. "The minute you walk in, you just feel like there's a voice in your head saying, 'Get out ... get out ...'"

I was exaggerating a bit here. I've never felt frightened in the cemetery at all (and I'm kind of a wuss, really). But Hector *does* claim that he's heard the voice, and so have many other people—some believe that there's a "guardian" spirit outside of the cemetery gates.

However, if there *is* a guardian spirit, it must be a really, really crappy guardian. It's difficult to imagine a more vandalized cemetery than Bachelor's Grove, the abandoned graveyard in the Rubio Woods Forest Preserve in Midlothian, down in the south suburbs.

A view of Bachelor's Grove Cemetery.

As with funeral homes, ghost hunters don't necessarily expect cemeteries to be haunted, since practically no one dies in them. But it stands to reason, therefore, that the ghosts one hears about in haunted cemeteries tend to be unusual ghosts. Nowhere is this more true than in Bachelor's Grove, which some have called the most haunted place in the world. Though it's been cleaned up a lot recently by diligent volunteers, and is actually probably one of the most visited cemeteries in town today in terms of the ratio of burials to visitors, Bachelor's Grove still has the appearance of a run-down and forgotten graveyard. No signs direct you to it—you have to find out how to get there on your own (though directions are easy enough to find online). Most gravestones have been missing for years, and those few that remain are mostly broken, vandalized, or both.

Stories about the little graveyard—not much bigger than a suburban backyard—are almost invariably strange. There are stories of a ghostly man being dragged into the nearby pond— supposedly the residual phantom of a farmer who drowned after getting tangled up in the reins of his horse. There's a glowing yellow figure that gets reported, a two-headed man that people see now and then, and a woman known as "Mrs. Rogers" who is seen (and has been photographed) occasionally. Stories (perhaps inevitably) circulate that Al Capone used to dump bodies into the nearby pond, but Capone and his men weren't really into dumping bodies into ponds. They were generally left in plain sight by the side of the road. The practice of destroying or hiding bodies came later.

Many of these stories can probably be traced to one simple thing: in the 1960s and '70s, Bachelor's Grove Cemetery was a popular place for local teenagers to sneak in to drink and take drugs.

And they didn't just come to the graveyard to get trashed; they came to cause trouble. In the 1960s, the police discovered the remains of a bonfire that included remnants of a couple of coffins—apparently, some locals were digging up the coffins to set fire to them. In 1973, a group of seven teenagers was apprehended attempting to dig up one of the graves. One was quoted as saying that they were doing it as a "lark." A *good* grave-robber could dig up a grave in less than an hour, but this group of seven clods seem to have spent several nights there without quite getting to the coffin. None of the seven teenagers has ever spoken publicly about what they were doing there, and those who are still alive are said to get upset if anyone brings up the incident at all, though I've heard secondhand reports from relatives saying that they weren't there for a "lark"; they were hoping to dig up valuable jewelry. One "veteran" of the area tells me that there was always a rumor that one particular coffin contained a whole lot of cash (the amount varied in stories between $50,000 and a million), and that a few of the coffins were dug up and reburied annually. He described them as looking like the oblong boxes you see in western movies.

Though it's been estimated that there were once a couple hundred monuments, there are only around twenty today, and many of them are in terrible shape. Clarence Fulton, the last independent trustee of the cemetery, once noted that some of the original gravestones had been found at other graveyards, or even in nearby police stations, but that replacing them would be a waste of time, since they'd just be stolen again.

Actual reports of ghosts inside the graveyard have been fairly slow recently—what I've heard, over and over, is that the cemetery doesn't seem haunted at all anymore, but the woods around it does. This has generally been the feeling I've gotten myself. The cemetery itself feels very pleasant to me today—I could just about take a nap there. I wouldn't want to go swimming in the fetid pond (some days you can practically *see* about twelve different diseases floating around in it), but it seems like a nice place for a picnic. I never really get that "haunted" feeling there (though I have felt a cold spot once or twice). Almost any time you go, there are likely to be a few other people wandering around, and regulars get to know each other pretty well.

The woods, though, can be another matter. It's spookier in there than it is in the graveyard, and I always, always seem to get lost out there. The woods don't seem big enough that you ought to be *able* to get lost, but I always end up wandering around in circles in there, trying to find my way back to the graveyard. I'm not the only one either. It seems that every Bachelor's Grove story I hear these days ends with "And then we got totally lost in the woods."

The woods, of course, are said to be haunted as well. In fact, the woods are the home of what may be the most famous ghost of Bachelor's Grove—the phantom house.

The Disappearing House

Many people claim to have seen a white Victorian farmhouse somewhere in the woods near the cemetery. No two people seem to see it in the same location, but nearly all of them describe the same thing: a white Victorian house, usually with a soft light glowing from downstairs. Some say that it gets smaller (or farther away) as you approach it. Rumors go around that it was the home of a caretaker who heard voices in the cemetery telling him to kill his family, and who hanged himself from the porch after following the voices' instructions, after which the community tore down the house and removed all records of it ever having been there.

In the woods, researchers have found the foundations for several small houses and at least two old wells (once my audio recorder picked up a noise like a creaking door at one of them while I was recording a podcast), but no such house was still standing in the area by the 1960s. However, many people have vivid memories of the house having been there during the 1960s or '70s—I've had people on my tours who swear that they used to have picnics outside of it when they were kids. Wendy, my driver, used to sneak into the cemetery as a teenager, and says they'd see the house on one side of the path when they went in, and another when they went out (she smiles a bit when I ask if this is because it was on the right side as they headed south and the left as they headed north, about which there'd be nothing unusual, except for the fact that the house was gone by then).

There were a number of houses in the woods at one point in time. Oddly, the relics of them never seem to disappear. I would guess that every day (especially in autumn), another ghost hunter takes home a bit of piping found in the vicinity of the foundations, but there always seems to be more where that came from.

It should be noted, though, that the story of the house has evolved a bit over time. In the early 1970s, Richard Crowe collected accounts from people who said they'd seen a white one-story farmhouse. Most more recent descriptions, and *every* description published since the 1990s, say that it was *two* stories. On the surface, this alone would seem to discredit the story, but if the house can already appear, disappear, and show up at random locations in the woods, it's not completely unreasonable to think it can sprout an addition.

In any case, the story is often told that no records indicate there was ever any such house nearby, but this isn't quite correct. There certainly wasn't any such house by the 1970s, but in addition to a number of smaller places, there *was* a two-story homestead built around the 1890s by the Schmidt family a short distance west of the cemetery (the foundation with the old stone well is probably the remains of this house). It was a sort of an L-shaped house that could have appeared as either a one- or two-story affair, depending on the angle from which you saw it, which may explain the discrepancies about stories as to whether it was one or two stories high. Exactly when it disappeared is not known; it was still standing as of the 1930s, and is sometimes said to have burned down the following decade.

More Ghostlore

Some other ghosts associated with the cemetery:

—Much folklore surrounds the "infant daughter" grave. Some stories say that the behavior of a coin dropped on it can reveal whether the woman who drops the coin is pregnant, or whether a man is single. I've never seen it work as advertised, though. The grave is a part of the Fulton family plot; some longtime residents of Midlothian still remember a "Granny Fulton" living in the area as recently as the mid-20th century.

The "infant daughter" portion of the Fulton plot.
Some say that whether coins tossed on it will land on it
depends on whether the tosser is pregnant.

—Legend has it that a couple of lost children were found in the cemetery in 1963 saying, "Blue light, blue light" over and over. A group of teenagers (one of whom went on to become an English teacher who retold the story to students frequently) went out to the woods, expecting to find some sort of pervert who took kids to a room with a blue light, or who carried a blue lantern, and whom they could become heroes by capturing, but found only a floating blue light that followed them back to their car. The blue light is still reported frequently, and police mentioned that it was a popular thing to hunt for in 1989, when they were investigating the death of a murder suspect who was found murdered himself in the forest preserve near the cemetery. A detailed firsthand account of the 1963 "blue light" story was taped by Gary Wright, a former student of the witness, but many details of it could not be independently verified.

—There are stories of a ghostly woman who carries a baby around, who may or may not be associated with the woman in the gravestone picture, and who may or may not be connected to the "infant daughter" grave.

—Ghosts in monk robes were once commonly reported, and reports of those still come in, though many people are probably just conflating Bachelor's Grove stories with the ones from St. James of the Sag. This was especially common during the "Satanic panic" of the 1980s, when a handful of ministers became convinced that every other preschool was a front for a massive organization of Satanists. It seems inevitable that rumors would go around that Satanic rituals were being held in the cemetery around then. Certainly it's a popular place for occult practitioners to mess around.

The Woman in White on the Grave

If you try hard enough, it's easy to convince yourself you've seen or heard just about anything at Bachelor's Grove, and plenty of people do. I often tell people that you don't *need* to see ghosts there; the people you meet there are strange enough all by themselves. I've met people who were using odd rituals to determine which people buried there were "evil" (roughly half, they told me). Stoned teenagers are a common sight. Some people show me pictures of leaves and say that if you look hard enough, you can see the shape of an old farmer in the foliage. And it's true, but if you look *really* hard, you can probably also convince yourself that you see the shape of Spiro T. Agnew playing a clarinet with his butt.

Any authentic stories have long gotten lost in the shuffle with all of the utter nonsense that circulates about the place. As such, I'd be inclined to brush off all the Bachelor's Grove stories as the result of imagination (or, in many cases, drugs), except for one photograph that has become one of the most famous ghost photographs of all time—the "woman in white" sitting on a broken tombstone near the cemetery gates. This one requires no imagination at all, and has continued to defy explanation.

*The famous image of the "Madonna" of Bachelor's Grove,
taken by Judy A. Huff-Felz in 1991.*

*The popular image is actually a detail of a much larger picture;
this is a scan of the original print. Courtesy of Judy A. Huff-Felz.*

The famous photograph was taken by Judy A. Huff-Felz,
a member of the Ghost Research Society, on a warm summer day in 1991, when the society, led by Dale Kaczmarek,
went on an excursion to the Grove. Judy, her mother, and her
sister were the only women present that day, and she is sure
that the woman on the grave is none of the three of them.
She was using an Olympus 35/70mm automatic camera with
infrared film.

Judy describes herself as clairvoyant and clairaudient
(meaning she sees and hears spirits). Such abilities run in her
family; though none of them use the word *psychic*, which
Judy describes as "too hokey," her sister, mother, and grandmother are also clairvoyant, and her great-grandmother was
a "spiritual healer" in Germany. Judy believes that almost every house is haunted, but that one has to be in tune with the
spirits to notice the ghosts.

The idea that every place in the world is haunted, but whether someone will be able to tell depends on how their brain is wired and how they process the "energy" in the environment, is not a new one. In 1907, the *Tribune* published a lengthy article when the theory was "proven" by a French scientist named Dr. Baraduc who claimed that humans could not typically see ghosts, but cameras could, and that the ghosts were not necessarily just the spirits of the dead, but the result of the psychic energy of every person released into the "thought atmosphere." In theaters, it was said, the ghosts of both the actors and the audiences who had been there before hovered in the atmosphere, and the actors drew inspiration from them whether they realized it or not. This is still pseudoscience, but many of the modern theories that seek to explain hauntings as scientific phenomena revolve around similar ideas.

On that day in 1991, the members of the Ghost Research Society entered the cemetery one at a time to take pictures. Judy didn't *see* the woman on the gravestone but sensed that something was there at the time. She says she's encountered a number of ghosts in the cemetery at other times, including a woman in a pale blue dress with shoulder-length hair, once accompanied by a dog, whom she describes as a "playful spirit," and who may or may not be the woman she photographed. She's never taken another photograph like the famous one she took that day, but that may simply be due to the fact that she's never used the same camera/film setup. Infrared film was hard to find, expensive to buy, and difficult to use at the time; it had to be loaded and unloaded from the camera by hand in a dark room, and most commercial photo labs wouldn't touch it when she tried to have it developed.

One thing that has frequently been noted is that the figure on the grave seems as though it must be rather small. Though it's apparently the apparition of a full-grown woman, the broken gravestone on which she's sitting seems much larger in the photograph than it does in person, implying that the figure is really fairly small. Looking at the photograph, one would imagine that stone to be about the height and depth of a steamer trunk. It's really not quite much larger than a milk crate.

Me on the famous gravestone in 2012. Photo by Jen Hathy.

If You Go

All Chicago-area ghost hunters should really go to see the cemetery for themselves. However, this has become one of those "ghost-hunting theme parks" that is so over-investigated that I seldom take sightings, recordings, or photographs seriously anymore, even when they come from people I generally trust.

Still, everyone should probably see it for themselves; as I often say, you barely need to see a ghost there, because the people you meet will probably be interesting enough on their own.

Cops patrol the area—especially around Halloween—and will give you a citation if they catch you there after dark, but it's open to the public during the day. If you want to go at night, you'll need to get a filming permit from the city of Midlothian. This isn't because the city has some sort of vendetta against ghost hunters; the cemetery is simply still prone to vandalism and drug use.

To get there, go down 143rd Street until you're just west of Ridgeland Avenue (near Cicero Avenue). You'll see a little parking lot for the Rubio Woods Forest Preserve. Park there and cross 143rd Street—you'll see a little path leading into the woods. Walk roughly half a mile down the path, and the cemetery is on your right.

But even inside of it, you aren't too far from civilization—on the end of the graveyard is the pond, and on the other side of the pond is 143rd Street. Like so many other haunted spots in town, it *feels* a lot more isolated than it is. This can mess with audio recordings—as can the fact that it's fairly unusual for anyone to be alone in the cemetery (especially in autumn).

CHAPTER 21

Hull House: Myth and Mystery

800 S. Halsted Street

Jane Addams, who ran the settlement house at Hull House, won a Nobel Peace Prize, and the house is still famous as the birthplace of American social work. Many of the ghost stories that circulate about the place have no basis in fact, but the house has been rumored to be a haunted one for well over a century.

Stories of Hull House being haunted can be traced back to at least the 1880s. It has served as a museum for nearly fifty years now but has developed a reputation for being among the most haunted places in Chicagoland. Like Bachelor's Grove, lots of truly nonsensical stories are floating around about it by now, but the real history is fascinating.

Beginning as a country mansion (though only blocks from a tough neighborhood that was called "Kansas" for some reason), the old Hull mansion in the late 19th century became a settlement house that stood out like a beacon of hope in the congested neighborhood full of impoverished first-generation immigrants, many of whom had been cast aside and neglected by their prosperous children, who saw their "old country" parents as an embarrassment to be hidden away.

This was an era when old-world superstitions still held a lot of sway with people. According to a *Chicago Tribune* article from 1888, murderers were still known to hold a firm belief in the "corpse candle," a candle made from the body of a murder victim which, according to legend, would shed a light visible only to the one who held the candle. Others put great belief in the magical powers of the severed hands of murdered men (which, it was also said, could be used to hold a candle that would only shed light for the bearer). Sometimes this was also called the Hand of Glory.

This gives you some idea what Jane Addams was up against in starting a settlement house in the area. Even twenty-five years after moving in and creating one of the most venerable social work institutions in history, she couldn't persuade people that the rumors that she was sheltering some sort of "devil baby" that was born able to swear in Italian and Latin weren't true.

And by the time she moved in, the old building she chose to call home was already thought to be haunted.

It's hard to imagine it *wouldn't* have been. By then the old Hull House was a dilapidated mansion in the midst of a slum, looking ancient even though it was barely thirty years old.

And in those thirty-odd years, it had seen its fair of tragedy and death.

Hull House as it appears following a 1960s restoration.
Some original touches remain, but most of the original bricks
are behind the currently visible ones. The "haunted room"
was probably the second-floor room on the right-hand side.

The Mansion on Halsted

You've surely seen a movie in which a family gathers around for the "reading of the will" after the patriarch of a wealthy family dies. Any lawyer will tell you that this never happens in real life. But perhaps it *did* happen now and then in the Victorian era; it certainly happened after the death of Charles J. Hull.

In 1889, Hull died in Texas. On a chilly February morning a few days later, while his remains were en route to Chicago to be interred at Rosehill Cemetery (where a statue of him now sits on his grave), his family and friends gathered in his Chicago residence on Ashland Boulevard to hear the reading of his will. He was in possession of between one and two million dollars worth of personal property and real estate at the time of his death.

But the Ashland residence was no mansion—just a modest brick row house, decorated with a few photographs and a "heroic looking bust" of Mr. Hull that presided over the proceedings.

His four nephews, one niece, and one cousin (Helen Culver, who was also his housekeeper), gathered around for the reading of the will. Most believed that the estate would be shared equally among them. But when the lawyer opened the sealed envelope and read aloud from the foolscap sheet inside, it said, "I, Charles J. Hull, being of sound mind and body … do give Helen Culver, my trusted friend and advisor for all these years, the whole of my estate."

The nephews turned pale and the niece wept. Their "great expectations" were over.

"There must be some mistake!" cried one of the nephews.

"No mistake," said the lawyer. "It's a good will. A good will. Miss Culver, let me congratulate you."

Helen Culver, who had lived with Mr. Hull as his housekeeper for many years, smiled softly. That Charles would continue to cling to Helen had been the dying wish of his grown-up daughter, Fredrika, fifteen years before.

The story of Charles Jerold Hull's life was described by Thomas Wakefield Goodspeed as "a strange story of an unusual sort of man." Born near Hartford, Connecticut, in 1820, he started bartending at a tavern in Castille, New York, when he was only twelve. He was so successful slinging whiskey that he took over ownership and renamed it the Hull Tavern when he was only fourteen. For three years, he managed both the tavern and his grandparents' farm.

The tavern was patronized mainly by "horse traders, horse racers, drunkards, and gamblers on a small scale," he later wrote. One day an angry customer, who felt he had gotten the bad end of a horse trade at the tavern, had Charles arrested for selling liquor without a license. Young Hull paid all the damages and fees, then never drank so much as a drop of alcohol, tea, or coffee again. He tore down the sign reading "Hull Tavern" and began to apply himself to education. In 1846, he married Millicent "Millie" A. C. Loomis and moved with her to Chicago, where he worked a variety of jobs on the way to becoming a pillar of the community.

He eventually became one of the city's most visionary philanthropists; he established homes and lodgings for newsboys, gave motivational speeches at prisons (and often let newly freed prisoners sleep in his own house until they could get on their feet), and even worked to help freed slaves after the Civil War, buying up West Side land and selling tracts to the freed slaves at a fair price (at a time when others were charging them five times the usual price for shacks and shanties), as well as working to help educate their children.

This, though, all took place long after he'd left his old mansion behind—the one he'd built for his family at Polk and Halsted over the course of 1855 and 1856.

Millicent, his wife, passed away in 1860; stories that she died in the house have not been verified, but there's no real reason to doubt them, since dying at home was the usual custom for Victorian women, and she certainly doesn't seem to have died due to an accident or anything. It was probably a death in her own bed due to illness.

Louis, Hull's son, appears to have died at the house as well, around the time of his mother's death. Another son, Robert, died of cholera (probably also at the house; Charles described the sight of his clothes still lying around the house after his death) in 1866. His last surviving daughter, Fredrika, lived until 1874, when she died in Baltimore after a long illness.

After his family died, the house on Halsted no longer felt like a home to Charles Hull, so he moved to other residences and converted the building to an office for a warehouse.

The Little Sisters of the Poor, a Catholic charity, eventually began to rent the entire house for $74 per month for use as a home for the aged. Six nuns housed, clothed, and fed around forty elderly inmates aged sixty or over in the house at a time, making it a rule to feed them all before eating anything themselves (some nights there was little or nothing left after forty people had been fed). "So tenderly are these helpless creatures cared for," wrote the *Tribune* in 1879, "that they never care to leave of their own accord, and there they remain until removed by the hand of death … they are nursed through sickness, and at last when the final struggle is over, their becrippled and weather-beaten bodies are laid comfortably away under the sod, where they sleep their long sleep with as much tranquility as the wealthiest millionaire in the land."

By 1880 the nuns had moved out to a larger facility, and by 1883, the "t'ole Hull House," as neighbors called it, was a secondhand store, though Charles Hull still held the deed. In 1887, the *Tribune* described Hull as "a unique character. His neighbors say he is eccentric; certainly he is original. He gets up every morning at 5 o'clock, does all the chores around the house, polishes everybody's shoes, builds the fire, and then arouses the household. Then he spends an hour or so swinging a pair of fifty-pound dumbbells."

Though he was still described as a boisterous man with a resplendent beard in the late 1880s, his health began to fail. He ignored doctors' warnings that he should get some rest and died in Texas in February 1889. Upon inheriting everything, Helen Culver, the former housekeeper, encouraged Jane Addams to move into the place and turn it into a "settlement house." Hull himself would have loved the idea.

But by then the area around the house was a bad one, indeed. In New York City, the worst neighborhood of the day was the Five Points, which no less an authority than Charles Dickens counted among the worst slums he'd ever seen. But Dickens never came to Chicago, and many said the West Side circa 1888 was worse than the Five Points had ever been. Starting a settlement house there may have seemed like a foolhardy crusade.

But if anyone on the planet could have made it work, it was Jane Addams.

Jane Addams

Jane Addams was born to a well-to-do family in Cedarville, a small town in the western part of Illinois. Her father was a friend of Abraham Lincoln, who addressed him in letters as "Mr. Double-D Addams." Hoping to become a doctor to help the poor, Jane began to study medicine in college, but health problems (including a nervous breakdown) kept her from completing her degree. She became hopelessly depressed and began to seek a purpose for her life. During this period in the 1880s, she read about Toynbee Hall, a settlement house in London that sought to improve conditions of the poor in Whitechapel, a notorious London slum, and suggested to her friend Ellen Starr Gates (who may also have been her lover at the time) that they start one of their own.

Upon traveling to London to see Toynbee Hall herself, Jane found it was everything she hoped. There, in a London that was still rigidly class-conscious, people of all classes were mixing together and helping each other out.

Eventually, she got the idea that she could do the same thing in Chicago.

Granted a lifelong, rent-free lease, Addams worked tirelessly at Hull House, which became a place where people could come to learn job skills, join after-school clubs, get medical care, and learn English. It soon included a kindergarten, a gym, a bath house, a coffee house (their most successful effort to provide an alternative to saloons) and a theater, among other facilities. The property eventually covered the entire block.

When she seconded the Bull Moose Party's nomination of Theodore Roosevelt for president in 1912, Addams became the first woman to speak at a major national political convention, and her later work for peace during World War I was cited when, in 1931, she became the first American woman to be awarded the Nobel Peace Prize. When she died in 1935, around 20,000 people per hour passed through Hull House to view her body as it lay in state. She remains one of the most admired and respected women in Chicago history.

The main operations of Hull House moved to other locations in the mid-20th century, and in the 1960s the house was restored as closely as possible to its original state. The original bricks are now behind the current ones, which form a sort of shell over what remains of the original house.

Today the house and the dining hall (moved from its original location to its current spot across the garden from the house) are all that remain, and the house is owned and operated as a museum by the University of Illinois at Chicago. Jane Addams's bedroom has been restored to a facsimile of the way it would have looked at the time she lived there, and her death mask is usually on display on the second floor.

Myth and Mystery

Every ghost tour has its own stories about Hull House today —some real, some not. If you've taken a ghost tour or seen a segment about the place on TV or in a book, you probably heard the following:

—When Jane Addams moved in, she found that the previous tenants had set up a bucket of water on top of the stairs to keep ghosts away, due to a superstition that ghosts can't cross water.

—Though she didn't believe in ghosts, Addams was so disturbed by ghostly sounds and footsteps in her bedroom— in which Mrs. Hull had died years before—that she had to move out and into another, quieter room.

—After moving out of her original room, she began referring to the old bedroom as the "haunted room," and someone—usually said to be social reformer Helen Campbell—awoke there one night to see a woman in white staring down at her.

—In 1913, a "devil baby" was brought to (or born in) the house. Some tours say it was buried out in the adjacent garden; I've even heard people say that Addams herself buried the baby alive.

—Many stories circulate about the adjacent garden and courtyard—the most common is that it was an Indian burial ground. Some even say that the Pottawatomie did a "ghost dance" on the grounds to curse the white man after the Battle of Fort Dearborn in 1812.

Some of these stores are pure bullshit: the "Indian burial ground" stories appear to be of very recent vintage, and the "ghost dance" movement wasn't started until decades after the battle of Fort Dearborn. Given the wondrous work Addams did there, any curse on the grounds would have been a pretty ineffective one.

But other stories turned out to have more truth behind them than I would have guessed. There *was* a room that the staff said was haunted, and Jane Addams herself saw a ghost in there once. The devil baby story probably came out of nowhere (and certainly Addams would never, ever have buried a deformed baby alive), but it *was* a real rumor that spread like wildfire through the area in 1913.

And, of course, the place (now a museum) probably wouldn't have held onto its reputation as the most haunted house in town if people didn't see spooky stuff there at night.

For my part, I've had enough weird nights there that I'm willing to give the place the benefit of the doubt. While I've explained away about 99 percent of the pictures I've seen and the stories I've heard, there's still that remaining 1 percent that keeps me wondering.

Addams, for her part, would probably think the ghost stories were fantastic. She might be a bit exasperated to hear that people still believe there was really a devil baby, but she spoke frequently of her own "hunger for folklore," and used to send anecdotes about Irish-American women still believing in "the little people" to William Butler Yeats. She may or may not have believed the house was haunted herself, but I imagine she'd love hearing that others still do.

And some of the stories really do seem to hold up.

The Staircase and the Haunted Room

Addams did, in fact, get the impression that people thought the place was haunted when she first moved in—she wrote about the practice of putting out buckets of water in her first memoir, *Twenty Years at Hull-House*. "The house," she wrote, "had passed through many changes since it had been built in 1856 … and although battered by its vicissitudes, was essentially sound … It had a half-skeptical reputation for a haunted attic, so far respected by the tenants living on the second floor that they always kept a large pitcher full of water on the attic stairs. Their explanation of this custom was so incoherent that I was sure it was a survival of the belief that a ghost could not cross running water, but perhaps my interpretation was only my eagerness for finding folklore."

Though Addams seemed unconvinced by her own explanation that the pitcher of water was to stop ghosts, it's certainly far from impossible. That ghosts cannot cross water is a very old belief, likely springing from similar superstitions about fairies; one sees variations on the superstition all over the world throughout history. It's why Ichabod Crane has to get across the bridge to get away from the headless horseman.

This seems to be the only mention of the attic being haunted ever recorded (except for more modern myths about it being haunted by the devil baby), and it was all Addams ever wrote about the ghosts of Hull House herself.

However, she seems to have spoken in private a bit about a room on the second floor being haunted. That the second floor featured a haunted room has been a standard part of the Hull House legend for more than a century now.

The most common version of the story today is that Mrs. Hull was widely rumored to haunt her old bedroom, which Addams had initially moved into herself. Though she didn't claim to believe in ghosts, the unearthly noises and footsteps she heard in the room eventually forced her out. Helen Campbell, another social reformer, is said to have woken up in the middle of the night to see a figure of a woman in white standing over her as she slept in the room. The woman disappeared as soon as Campbell turned on the gas jet. Other witnesses, it is said, included social reformers Louise de Koven Bowen and Mary Smith, not to mention Canon Barnett of Toynbee Hall, who visited during the World's Fair in 1893.

These stories aren't too far off from the truth, but they get a few of the facts wrong. Addams's bedroom was not the same room that was said to be haunted by a ghostly woman in white, and I've never found a source for her having to move out of her original bedroom. I've never found a good source for the story about Helen Campbell spending a night in the room and being awakened by the ghost either.

In fact, that encounter actually happened to Jane Addams herself.

Louise de Koven Bowen, a fellow social reformer and Hull House resident, included a section on the haunted room in her book of Hull House memories, *Open Windows*, in 1946. Beyond Addams's mention of a haunted attic, and the many retellings of the devil babies story published between 1913 and 1917, this is the earliest source I have found for any Hull House ghost stories, but it's a pretty solid source.

Bowen wrote that one day, Addams told her that they were having a great deal of trouble with one of the large front rooms on the second floor that overlooked Halsted Street.[13] Though it was a guest room, guests always seemed unhappy and tired after sleeping there. Rumors began to circulate that it was haunted.

Canon Barnett of Toynbee Hall was one guest who spent an unpleasant night there when he visited Chicago with his wife, Henrietta, in 1891 for an art exhibit. After a night in the second-floor guest room, the couple came to breakfast looking rather unwell—Addams said they looked "rather strange," and asked them if they'd had a good night. They replied that they had not—in fact, they'd had a dreadful experience that they refused outright to discuss. Addams never did find out what had bothered them. Henrietta Barnett's own memoirs mentioned their time at Hull House, but described nothing more supernatural than Addams going to answer the doorbell and finding no one there, which everyone assumed was the result of local boys going doorbell ditching. No boys were caught, though, so this instance can stay in the realm of possible ghost sightings.

Addams and Mary Rozet Smith,[14] her lifelong companion, decided to do some investigating of their own by spending a night in the room. "Neither one was a nervous person,"

---

13. The best I can triangulate is that it was the room that faces Halsted Street on the north side—if you're standing facing the house, it would have been the second-floor room on the right-hand side.

14. The exact nature of this relationship is another question mark; they seem to have had what is known as a "romantic friendship" for years and their letters speak of deep longings and attachment, but historians have found no hint of anything overtly sexual. Their arrangement seems to have been what was then called a "Boston marriage."

Bowen wrote. "I don't think Miss Addams was afraid of anyone or anything. Even if there had been something supernatural, she would have had a great curiosity about it. She
would have done her best to find out where it came from
and what brought it about."

Addams and Smith bedded down for the night, locked the
door, and darkened the room by turning down the gas (they
were unable to darken it completely due to faint lights coming through the window from Halsted Street). At some point
in the night, they were both awakened at the same instant by
the feeling that someone was in room. Startled, they opened
their eyes and looked up to see the figure of a woman in a rustling white dress standing at the foot of the bed!

At first, Addams thought that it was the maid and called
out, "Is that you?"

No one answered, and the figure floated out of the room,
passing right through the locked door.

Neither of the two slept in the room again. The mystery,
Bowen said, was never solved, though Addams suspected that
it had all been a dream, or an optical illusion brought on by
lights in the street and the rustling sounds coming from the
fireplace.

Bowen, to my knowledge, never actually claimed to have
seen the ghost herself, but stated in *Open Windows* that many
of her friends did. One of her friends who had a ghostly experience was Claire Paul Paige, a "strong and fearless" woman who scoffed at the stories and announced that she would
spend a night in the room herself. Just as she was about to fall
asleep, Paige felt the sheets twitching above her. She reached
out and felt nothing. Over and over she tried to lie down, and
over and over some invisible force would tug at the sheets.

Eventually the "twitching" stopped, and she ended up spending several months in the room with no further incidents.

Enough guests complained about the room, though, that the staff eventually stopped using it as a guest room altogether. It was converted to a storeroom and a dressing room for the Hull House theatrical productions, as it was adjacent to the theater and coffee house building that was eventually built next door, attached to the north side of the building. Once, when a group of young girls was dressing in the room, they reported that there was a woman in a white dress sitting on a box and looking at them. They had entered the empty room alone, and the door was locked so they could change in private. The lady vanished before their eyes, and the terrified girls declared that they would never enter the room again.

At the time she wrote *Open Windows,* some years after the dressing room incident, Bowen claimed that nothing else supernatural had happened in the room since, but said, "I know of three times when fires started in that room, for I put them out myself."

So, who could the woman in white be?

If anyone thought it was Millicent Hull in Jane Addams's day, no one seems to have written it down. However, "Millie" *does* seem to have died in the house, so she's a logical choice. In his book, *Reflections from a Busy Life*, Charles Hull included an excerpt from his diary on the day of her death in 1860: "Our Millie has gone home. She went cheerfully and gladly, seeing that her work here was done, and believing that in heaven friends and happiness awaited her arrival … she is now, I believe, with Louis [her son], with the angels, and with God."

One troublesome thing here is that one usually expects ghosts to be of people who died sudden and traumatic deaths—not of people who die "cheerfully and gladly." While this isn't the case with every ghost reported to walk the earth, it's something to consider. One *could* point out Charles Hull's interest in spiritualism and speculate that she never left after being called back during a séance. We don't know for sure that Hull ever held séances in the house, but given his interest in spiritualism and the fact that so many of his family members died in the house, it seems likely that he did. He wrote that he didn't believe that souls went to a far-off heaven—"the distance is too great"—but that they stayed among the living.

Of course, Mrs. Hull wasn't the only woman to have died in the house. Many others probably did so when it was used as a home for the aged by the Little Sisters of the Poor. However, of the two sightings of the ghost that have been recorded, neither described the ghost as an *old* woman. Mrs. Hull would have been in her late thirties at the time of her death. The nuns who ran the home for the elderly also seem to have worn white, though, and could have been any age.

Today, sightings of feminine ghosts in the windows by ghost tour passengers are in no short supply, and pictures of them are not uncommon. In 2006, when I was first bringing ghost tours to the house regularly, several children claimed to see a woman in some kind of white bonnet behind one of the first-floor windows. It happened again in the summer of 2012, though it was in a different window that year. In both periods, I was very careful not to mention anything about a white bonnet ahead of time. Was this Millie Hull? Or could it have been one of the ghosts of the Little Sisters of the Poor, who wore white head coverings themselves?

When I began researching the story, I assumed, snot-nosed skeptic that I was, that Mrs. Hull would turn out to have died in Florida or something, and that stories of her haunting the place were strictly guesses that were repeated as fact. And while they may, in fact, have been guesses, it seems as though they may have been very good ones. If there is a ghostly woman in white, "Millie" is probably the most likely candidate for her identity.

The Devil Baby

In 1913, Hull House was, in fact, plagued with rumors that a "devil baby" or "demon child" had been born somewhere in the neighborhood. According to the stories, the child was born with horns, a tail, red skin, and cloven feet (like hooves), thirty-two teeth, and a full head of hair. In some versions, it was already able to speak in three languages at birth, and was profane in each. For six weeks, workers at Hull House dealt with almost nothing besides the constant stream of people demanding to see it.

There were many variations in the story of how the baby came to exist. One, most common among Italian women, was that a Catholic woman had married an atheist who ripped a picture of the Virgin Mary off of the wall, stating that he'd rather have the devil in the house than such a picture. And, according to the story, he got his wish: his wife's first child was a devil, who emerged speaking three languages that he used to curse at priests who came to attempt to baptize him. Some versions even had him dancing and smoking cigars, or shaking a finger and warning the mother that "if you kill me, six others will come."

People usually laugh at most parts of this story today, but belief in the devil baby is still going strong. Lisa Junkin, the current education coordinator, laughed and told me they get emails about it "all the time."

Many more rationally minded people still insist that the story was based on an actual deformed baby that had been brought to the house—some speak of a baby with a condition known as harlequin ichthyosis as a cause for the deformity, though there's really no evidence that there was such a baby; stories usually state that a baby with that condition was taken to one of Hull House's "satellite" buildings during the furor, but no such buildings existed, and one would assume that if such a baby had been brought to Hull House at all, the baby would have been taken to a hospital.

Others, however, reject even these more rational explanations that the legend grew from a misunderstanding of the nature of disease, and still insist that it really was a paranormal baby with eerie powers whose presence was proof that God will punish Catholic women who marry Protestants. Many claim that the baby's ghost still haunts the attic to this day; some people claim to have taken pictures of it peering out the window. I suppose it's worth noting that people who send me these pictures generally are taking pictures of the room Addams called the "haunted room."

Though there's no evidence that the baby was real, or even that the rumor was inspired by a real baby, the tale *was* the sensation of the West Side in 1913, and Addams wrote about it extensively.

"The knowledge of (the baby's) existence burst upon the residents of Hull House one day," she wrote, "when three Italian women, with an excited rush through the door, demanded that he be shown to them. No amount of denial convinced them that he was not there, for they knew exactly what he was like with his cloven hoofs, his pointed ears, and diminutive tail; the devil baby had, moreover, been able to speak as soon as it was born and was most shockingly profane."

And so it began.

Addams noted that there were hundreds of variations on the story of the baby's origin. The Jewish version was that a woman had given birth to six daughters, and when she became pregnant again, the father raged that he would rather have the next be a devil than another girl. This is the exact same story that is sometimes told to explain the origin of the Jersey Devil that is said to lurk in New Jersey's Pine Barrens, and variations of it have gone around for centuries. "Save for a red automobile which occasionally figured in the story," Addams wrote, "and a stray cigar which, in some versions, the new-born child had snatched from his father's lips, the tale might have been fashioned a thousand years ago."

For a full six weeks, as Jane Addams walked through the house, past the Hull House telephone operators, she would hear one variation after another of "No, there is no such baby"; "No, we never had it here"; "No, he couldn't have seen it for fifty cents"; "We didn't send it anywhere, because we never had it"; "I don't mean to say your sister-in-law lied, but there must be some mistake"; "There is no use getting up an excursion from Milwaukee, for there isn't any 'devil baby' at Hull House"; and "We can't give reduced rates, because we are not exhibiting anything."

People who came to the door were often furious to be turned away. "Why do you let so many people believe it if it isn't here?" "We have taken three lines of [street]cars to come and we have as much right to see it as anybody else." "What are you saying that for—are you going to raise the price of admission?" And, of course, Addams heard the same argument that is still heard today by people who believe the baby was real: "This is a pretty big place; of course you could hide it easy enough."

Addams was initially furious, and a bit puzzled. "I suppose a deformed baby was born somewhere on the West Side," she told the *Chicago Examiner*. "But to see the way otherwise intelligent people let themselves be carried away by the ridiculous story is simply astonishing. If I gave you the names of some professional people—including clergymen—who have asked about it, you simply would not believe me."

However, as the ordeal dragged on, Addams began to see another side to the phenomenon: it revealed a lot about the tormented psyches of the women of the West Side.

A great deal about the attitude of women regarding their place in the world can be seen in a fundamental feature of nearly all of the stories they told of the baby's origin: in all of them, God was more interested in punishing the father's sinfulness than in protecting the abused mother. To many of these women, this was actually cheerful news. They seemed to have given up the idea that God would protect *them*, but something like the devil baby was proof that He might punish their husbands for their cruelty, which was some consolation.

Many of these women were recent immigrants, speaking little English and barely able to understand much of what their own children were talking about. Many had grown up with no idea that the stories and superstitions that they had been raised with were not universal, and this was one of the many difficult adjustments that they found themselves having to make. The story of the devil baby gave them a way to cling to something from the "old country," to show their unruly, disrespectful families that they were right, and that mistreating them could bring punishment.

A group of men came from a nearby factory, offering as much as two dollars to see the baby, and saying that it must be at Hull House because "the women had seen it."

"Do you really think," Addams asked, "that we would exhibit a poor little deformed baby for money if one had been born in the neighborhood?"

"Sure, why not?" one said.

"It teaches a good lesson, too," said another.

Addams was left to reflect on how strange the moral standards of Hull House must have seemed to these men, and the extent of the story's value as something for women to hold over their husbands' heads and keep them in line—the sort of commodity of which many were in dire need.

However, the devil baby did not really exist. A deformed baby on the West Side may have given rise to the rumors (fetal alcohol syndrome probably ran rampant), but there's no real reason to believe it. Certainly no such baby was ever brought to Hull House, so there's no reason to believe that it would be haunting the attic today. It's seldom noted in the retellings of the Hull House story, but the exact same story had gone around Cleveland in 1888, and in several other cities as well. The story even resurfaced in Virginia in the 1980s.[15]

Though the story could be said to illuminate the backwards superstitions of the old world, I think that one can see a glimmer of hope here. In previous times, not long before 1913 at all, when stories like this went around, people would gather at the door of the place where the baby was suspected

---

15. For far more information, see my e-book short *Devil Babies*, published by Llewellyn Worldwide in 2012.

to be and demand to be allowed to kill it. Sometimes bodies were dug up and mutilated to stop supposed "curses" and demons. In this case, people just wanted to *see* the thing. That might seem like a small step forward, but it's progress.

The Garden

No place on the Hull House grounds has inspired more bizarre myths than the so-called "Garden of Evil," the little garden in between Hull House and the dining hall. Stories of the place get particularly ludicrous. Some people are told that if they don't cross themselves before entering, a ghost may follow them home. It's a great story, but I've never once crossed myself before entering the garden and I've always made it home without any ill effects or unwanted followers.

Stories of the evil history of the ground are numerous —and frequently ridiculous. But the garden does get a bit spooky at night.

One story that doesn't usually figure in the modern garden mythos is the *actual* history of the grounds, which is spooky enough on its own. At the time Addams moved into Hull House, it was flanked by an Irish saloon on one side and an undertaking establishment on the other. A local humorist joked that the three buildings were "Knight, Death, and the Devil," a reference to a classic Albrecht Dürer engraving. The undertaking establishment was also a livery stable, and was run by "the biggest little Irishman on the West Side," according to one account by Winifred E. Wise. Though the structures on the grounds have been moved a bit, E. J. McGeeney's funeral home *was* probably right about where the garden is now.

Following that, though, the garden's only use was a brief spell as the Hull House courtyard. It's certainly not known to have been a graveyard at any time.

Other Baby Stories

The ghosts seen and photographed by tour passengers here seem almost to be in rotation. One summer we got several photographs that appeared to show a girl about eight years old. Another year we kept getting shots that appeared to show the woman in the rustling white dress. "Monks" have been photographed there off and on for decades now.

Recently, we've had a number of photographs, some of them rather clear, that seem to show a baby. One night, we even heard the distinct sound of a baby crying coming from the garden, which happens every now and then. Here, at least, we have a couple of possible stories that we could connect to the ghost.

In the early days of Hull House, a baby was abandoned at the house, eventually dying in the nursery, which likely stood around the spot where the garden is now. Addams wrote of this experience; in a case of badly misjudging the culture of the area, she had determined to have the baby buried by the county, and many women in the neighborhood were horrified that she wasn't planning a private funeral. Addams can be excused for being a bit annoyed that the women were concerned that having no private funeral would bring more shame to the mother than leaving the baby to die had, but such was the culture, and she believed her miscalculation was one of her biggest early mistakes.

Another time, a new mother rejected her baby when it was born with a cleft palate. Addams arranged for (and probably paid for) an operation, but the baby had to live at Hull House until the mother could be persuaded to take it home. To Addams's understandable horror, the baby then died of neglect. It didn't die in Hull House, but Hull House was the only home it ever really knew.

Jean Marie Andersen's photo of a baby was taken on a tour. It could always be a result of smears and reflections, but those seldom look this humanesque, and I've been unable to reproduce it.

Monks and Girls

Two of the ghosts often reported here can't be traced to anything historical at all: the ghostly girl and the phantom monk.

Spectral monks have become a famous, and somewhat inexplicable, part of Hull House stories ever since photographs of what appeared to be ghostly monks in hooded robes coming down the staircase began to circulate in ghost circles in the 1980s. The inexplicable thing about the photos is that Hull House was never a monastery, and, in fact, never inhabited by any other groups of guys who went around dressed in hooded robes (unless the warehouse for which it was once an office was one messed-up warehouse). Reports of people seeing the monks with the naked eye are not particularly common, but they do go around; one other ghost-tour guide told me that one night his entire group saw one materialize on the staircase. This, he tells me, is the only ghost sighting he ever had on a tour.

Some speculate that these may not be monks in hooded robes, but nuns in habits dating from the time the house was occupied by the Little Sisters of the Poor. They were once described as dressing in black robes with "white handkerchiefs" on their heads, which is also interesting when one remembers the stories I got from young kids of seeing a woman with a "white thing" (bonnet) on her head.

The "little girl" sightings, though, are harder to explain. In 2006, we got photograph after photograph of what appeared to be a girl about eight to ten years old. I know of no stories of a girl haunting the place before that (in fact, it was about the *only* notably haunted place that didn't have a little girl ghost floating around), but sightings ran rampant that year, and have just recently made a modest comeback.

Multiple people who claimed to be psychics told us that it was the ghost of a girl named Rebecca (and for psychics to agree on anything about this location is pretty notable in and of itself). However, no record of a girl by that name dying in or around Hull House has ever been found. Of course, even if a girl *did* die at Hull House, one has to ask a fairly obvious question: if there's a ghostly little girl in the place, how come no one ever talked about it when Hull House was in operation? Louise de Koven Bowen said that other than the "devil baby" rumors and the woman in white in the "haunted room," she knew of no other unusual stories about the place.

False Positives

I sort of hate writing chapters like this—it's hard to explain ghost sightings away without feeling like you're spoiling everyone's fun. But one of the reasons Hull House continues to occupy such a strong part of local ghostlore is that, real ghosts or no, it's an easy place to trick yourself. On bright sunny days, no amount of stories can make the place seem all that frightening, but at night, the house and grounds can look pretty darned ominous.

There is no photography allowed inside of the museum—one should respect the museum's wishes on this matter and not ask permission to conduct paranormal investigations there (their website states that they are unable to respond to requests from paranormal groups). However, ghost-tour groups who come after hours are allowed to photograph the grounds and the windows.

The biggest generators of false positives are the windows on the front door. The staircase visible through them is one of the most famous sites in Chicago ghostlore, and a great many spooky pictures have appeared to show ghosts walking up or down it. However, the only way most people are able to photograph it is through the window in the door.

This window reflects people's faces, resulting in reflections that look pretty spooky.

Flashes and lights from the street also bounce off the glass and mix with the fingerprint smears. Between the reflections, the lights, and the smears, you can get a *lot* of pictures that look like girls in dresses, guys in hooded robes, and strange mists. To avoid these, I recommend people take pictures through the mail slot.

Photographs of things that appear to be figures in hooded robes coming down the first-floor stairs aren't unusual; at one point customers on my tours seemed to be getting them nearly every night. But one day, a particularly good one was emailed to me, and I began to analyze it on my computer. I quickly found out what the picture was: a reflection of the photographer's ear in the window. Turning up the brightness and contrast revealed the rest of his face.

Ever since then, nearly every "monk" or "hooded figure on the stairs" picture I've seen, at Hull House or anywhere else, has just looked like an ear to me—with the exception of a couple created by the fingerprint smears on the window and a few created by the reflection of the flash and the camera itself. It's amazing how much a reflection of one's ear on a clear window can look like a guy in a hooded robe!

A sample "ghost on the stairs" shot that is actually a reflection of an ear. Hector's, in this case.

In addition to the many "stairway ghosts," I've seen many photographs of feminine forms in the other windows. These, along with the "devil baby" shots that circulate online, are usually caused by lamps and other objects on display inside of the rooms. Most commonly, these pictures are taken on the south side of the building—not on the north side, where the haunted room was.

Still, not all of the pictures or everything I've seen there can be so easily explained. And just because a location generates a great many false positives doesn't mean that it *isn't* haunted. Indeed, any "real" haunted house would generate countless false positives, as every stray noise would be blamed on a ghost. Hull House may not be an "Indian burial ground," or cursed land, or the home of a ghostly devil baby, but its reputation for being haunted *does* stretch back at least 125 years.

A Nearby Ghost of Note

There was also a ghost reported *near* the spot once. In the slums behind Hull House in 1902, a remarkably screwed-up family reunion was held at the residence of one Mrs. Ward. Their house was on Polk Street, right around the corner from Hull House. Two months before, Mrs. Ward's son, Thomas, had threatened to kill her, and even fired a gun at her, hitting her in the arm. At this reunion, he was back to such tricks, beating up his mother and threatening to kill her, until his brother pulled a gun and shot him in the face. He staggered out to the back porch, where he died.

A couple of months later, his ghost began to be spotted sitting on an empty icebox on the porch, which was visible from Blue Island Avenue (which ran through the area in those days, going right behind Hull House and through the spot where the University of Illinois buildings are today). Soon, the ghost became such a common sight that crowds would gather on Blue Island Avenue to see it. By the time it hit the papers, onlookers were simply shrugging their shoulders and saying, "Tommy's on the icebox again!"

If You Go

Much of the building is open to the public; in recent years, even the second floor has been opened to visitors. The current staff is more willing to talk about ghostlore than some previous incarnations of the staff have been—like Jane Addams, they see the value in folklore. Many people who first hear about Addams through ghost stories wind up learning far more about her life and work than they ever would have otherwise.

However, the management turns down all requests from paranormal groups to run investigations there. The one time they cooperated with a TV show, they wound up regretting it when the show just retold the most ridiculous rumors about the place.

Jane Addams and many of her contemporaries were concerned that the modern world would do away with folklore and belief in fairy stories. At the very least, the continued sightings at Hull House show that they needn't have worried. Belief in ghosts survives—and sometimes even a skeptic like myself is forced to wonder if ghosts are really there, doing their part to keep folklore alive.

CHAPTER 22

Graceland Cemetery

Clark Street and Irving Park Road

Some of the people here were famous when they were alive … and some are far better known in death than they were in life.

An old superstition says that when you involuntarily shudder, it means that someone has just stepped on the ground that will one day be your grave. When I walk through Graceland Cemetery, I wonder if any step I take will make *me* shudder. I spend enough time reading about medical schools snatching bodies that I'm inclined just to cut out the middle man and donate my body right to a university, but if they have to put me somewhere, I wouldn't mind having a grave at Graceland. The company would be terrific, after all, and you're close enough to Wrigley Field to hear a baseball game now and then. Not to mention that there are several people there who were moved from City Cemetery and might be able to tell me who's in the Couch tomb (see chapter 11).

There are lots of fascinating things in Graceland, such as the grave of Augustus Dickens, Charles Dickens's no-good brother, who died in Chicago in 1866. He shares a plot with his American wife, who overdosed on morphine on Christmas Day a couple of years later.

Then there's the Getty tomb, one of the finest pieces of architecture Louis Sullivan ever designed. Sullivan himself is just across the pond in his own grave, and elsewhere in the cemetery lie such luminaries as Marshall Field, who I'd kind of enjoy slapping upside the head in the afterlife; George Pullman (ditto); and boxer Jack Johnson (who, if I were fool enough to want to hit him—not that I'd want to—would probably hit my ghost back so hard that I'd come back to life).

And there's "Eternal Silence," the monument over the final resting place of Dexter Graves and his family that is sometimes called "the Statue of Death," standing grimly against a black backdrop and appearing to stand guard over a vast empty portion of land. It's a creepy statue, even by cemetery standards; some say that if you look it in the face, you'll see your own death. (It didn't work for me.)

I did, however, once think I heard a howling sound around the inner-hill crypt of Ludwig Wolff, a plumbing-goods magnate from whose grave you're said to be able to hear howls. Some say that his grave is guarded by some sort of green-eyed supernatural beast. The howl I heard was probably either a dog from the surrounding neighborhood or one of the coyotes that frolic around in the cemetery, though. Few have taken the Wolff ghost as more than a story that came from his awesome name. Wolff himself figures in one other Chicago story: he lost a grown daughter and her three children in the Iroquois Theatre fire, and more than a thousand people came to his house for the funeral.

Eternal Silence, which is creepy even for a statue in a cemetery.

The Girl That's Never Been?

The most famous ghost story from Graceland is the tale of Inez Clarke, a girl who is said to have died when her parents locked her outside during a lightning storm; a statue of her is said to disappear and reappear during storms. Her ghost is also said to roam the grounds, playing with children and with the toys that people sometimes leave for her.

Inez's tale has long been a part of Chicago folklore, but the cemetery officials once insisted that Inez Clarke never existed. In a 2007 *Sun-Times* article, it was stated that the statue of the little girl is simply an advertisement for a monument sculptor, and that records showed that the person buried there was a child named Amos Briggs.

But as much as we snot-nosed skeptics love to see a story taken to the cleaners like that, the cemetery's claims never quite rang true. If there was no such person as Inez, why was the name "Inez" right at the base of the statue? And why did the plaque beneath say "Daughter of J. N. & M. C. Clarke" with dates of birth and death? Wouldn't setting up a statue in a space where it simply looks like a regular monument have been an odd advertising strategy? Was this something sculptors normally did? And while it was true that there was no Inez Clarke found in census records from 1880, why wasn't there at least an Amos Briggs, if he was the one buried there?

And, after all, would a mistake in the backstory really mean the ghost wasn't real to begin with?

Recent studies by author John J. Binder show that the cemetery was partly right. The correct last name of the child buried there was Briggs, but it was Inez Briggs, not Amos Briggs, who was buried nearby at the age of seven (Clarke was Inez's mother's married name). It seems that when the records for Graceland were being compiled in the 1920s, someone made a mistake. This sort of thing happens all the time; the name "Inez" does, in fact, look similar to "Amos" when written in cursive.

There's still some mystery, though; the cemetery did have on file an affidavit from Mary Clarke in which she apparently denied ever having had children besides her still-living daughter. My guess is that it was part of a probate process establishing herself as an heir or something. Did she really deny having had Inez or Inez's brother, Delbert, who is buried beside her, or were they only asking about children she'd had with her current husband?

The lightning storm story is still false, though; Inez's death certificate states that she died after a four-day bout with diphtheria. It also states that she lived at 177 Center Street (this would be the 900 block of West Carmen Avenue in the Uptown neighborhood today; her original house is long gone).

*Inez Briggs's death certificate. One can imagine how this could
have been transcribed as "Amos" when records were being copied.*

Inez Briggs

If You Go

Enter Graceland Cemetery at Clark Street, and go up "Graceland Avenue" to the Ayers monument (you can't miss it) and take a right to see Inez. Take a right upon first entering to see Eternal Silence, which is awfully hard to miss. The cemetery closes at dusk.

CHAPTER 23

Mount Carmel Cemetery

1400 S. Wolf Road, Hillside

A straight drive down Roosevelt Road will take you to this suburban cemetery. Its most famous residents, Al Capone and Julia Petta, are near the south and north gates, respectively.

One thing Chicago historians learn very quickly is that most Al Capone stories are every bit as made-up as the story about him hiring psychics. Capone is said to have owned or held parties in practically every building in town; I once had a tour customer bet me $500 that Capone used to own the building where he worked (which had not been built yet when Capone died).

In reality, Capone's reign in Chicago was a short one—he came to power around 1926, and within two years he was spending most of his time in Miami. He returned to Chicago to stand trial in 1931, then went off to jail, never to return publicly. The only property he legally owned in town was his mother's modest house on the South Side.

So when one hears that he's haunting the cemetery where he's buried, one takes it with a grain of salt, but hey—at least we know he's actually there. Many of the Capone stories concern places where he never set foot.

The 1920s was an era of massive funerals for gangsters. Bronze and silver caskets weighing over a thousand pounds, and costing tens of thousands of dollars, were standard. Flowers came by the truckload—literally. Funeral processions more than a mile long were *de rigueur*, and onlookers would crowd the streets to watch them go by. Frank Capone was given a huge funeral when he was killed in a shootout with police in 1924, and the others followed suit.

At the funeral of Mike Merlo, head of the Unione Siciliana (and peacekeeper between the gangs), there was $30,000 worth of flowers (in 1924 money) and ten thousand mourners. Dean O'Banion, the North Side boss who was shot almost immediately after Merlo died, and five thousand other people crowded the cemetery, where his $10,000 casket was buried.

The next year, when gangster Angelo Genna was killed (presumably in revenge for O'Banion's death), his own ornate casket was so heavy that it nearly broke the back porch when it was carried from the funeral. The body was taken, like those of the other gangsters of the era, to Mount Carmel Cemetery in Hillside. Genevieve Forbes-Herrick, one of the *Tribune*'s greatest crime writers, quoted an onlooker with the most memorable line as he noticed how close the recent graves were to one another. "There's Mike and Dean and Genna," he said. "When Judgment Day comes and them three graves are open, there'll be hell to pay in this cemetery."

He didn't know the half of it. In coming years, many other gangsters, including Vinnie "The Schemer" Drucci, "Machine Gun" McGurn, and a few more of the Genna brothers were buried there. Tony Lombardo, a Capone advisor who was shot right in the Loop, is there, and so is Frank Nitti, who took over for Capone when he went to prison and wound up killing himself to avoid going to jail himself. Frank Rio, Capone's bodyguard, is in a family plot. John May, a former gangster who was trying to go straight but was working on Moran trucks as a mechanic when he was killed in the St. Valentine's Day Massacre, has a modest grave there. By 1950, it was also home to its most famous resident, Al Capone himself, who is buried alongside his brothers near the south gate.

Capone is sometimes said to haunt the place. But I think that's just the sort of thing that some people *would* say. A far more famous ghost seen around the cemetery is that of Julia Buccola-Petta, known to Chicagoans as the "Italian Bride."

The Italian Bride

Julia Buccola, an Italian-born West Side girl, married Matthew Petta in 1920. They moved into a modest apartment near Western Avenue on Huron Street, only a short walk from their church.[16] Thirteen months later, Julia died at the age of twenty-nine while giving birth to their stillborn son, Filipo, on St. Patrick's Day, 1921. She was buried in her wedding dress, per an old Italian custom for women who died in childbirth (and who still fit into their dress).[17]

---

16. I'm leaving out the actual address to protect the privacy of current residents.

17. A few people I consulted confirmed that this is an Italian custom, but every single mention I could find of it in print was in a retelling of this story, which makes me wonder if the story actually created the tradition.

Her mother allegedly became plagued with dreams in which her daughter was begging to be exhumed, and six years later her mother arranged for a disinterment. Upon opening the coffin, it was found that Julia's body was perfectly preserved.

Known today as the "Italian Bride," a statue based on Julia's wedding picture was erected on her gravestone, and a picture of the exhumed corpse was added to the monument with an epitaph stating that the picture showed her six years after burial.

Photos of the dead on graves are common in the early 20th century; the "photo-ceramic" portraits were made by firing the image onto a porcelain plaque in a kiln. Taking photographs of people who had died was common in the early decades of photography, and a few such photos were probably used as tombstone portraits, but I don't know of a single other grave that shows a photograph of a body six years after burial.

People inclined to supernatural explanations sometimes consider Julia an "incorruptible," and say that her lack of decomposition after six years was a sign of holiness. Scientists argue that, while most bodies in Chicago soil decompose quickly, this sort of thing isn't exactly unheard of and can be explained in a variety of ways, most notably a condition known as "grave wax." There are also accounts of long-sealed-up bodies seeming totally unchanged until someone touches them, at which all the decay catches up to them in second. There are, in short, a lot of "X factors" in decomposition, so you really just never can tell what you're going to find when you open a coffin; no one I spoke to would offer a prediction as to what sort of shape the body could be in today. I'm more inclined toward scientific explanations myself, but that's just me. I'm in no way qualified to determine whether someone was holy.

Julia's story became a part of Chicago folklore, passed around first by word of mouth for half a century before the story began appearing in numerous books and articles around the 1970s. By then, naturally, the story had probably strayed a bit from what actually happened, and many retellings of the story get a few details wrong—most say she lived on the South Side, and some say embalming was not practiced in 1921. In reality, the West Side apartment where Julia and Matthew lived is still standing, just around the corner from both the church they attended and the funeral home where her body was prepared, both of which are still in operation.

Some suggest there was animosity between Filomena Buccola, Julia's mother, and her son-in-law Matthew; the fact that Filomena's name appears on the gravestone twice, but Julia's married name appears nowhere, does nothing to suggest otherwise. I suspected for a time that Filomena had Julia moved out of the Petta family plot or something, but none of the Petta family had died in America at the time of Julia's death.

Perhaps Filomena was angry at him for remarrying; Matthew Petta married an Iowa woman a few years after Julia's death and eventually opened a tavern near Clark and Division called Matty's Inn, which he ran until his death in 1945. Filomena's surviving great-grandchildren recently confirmed to me that she didn't approve of *any* of her children's marriages.

The closest I've heard to a primary source regarding Julia's life comes from a 1979 article, in which ghost hunter Richard Crowe quotes a woman who said she knew Julia when she was young, and believed that she would one day be declared a saint. "She died a virgin," she told Crowe. "She died on her wedding day. You have to be a virgin to be declared a saint." This, of course, doesn't stand up to known facts that Julia died in childbirth just over nine months after her wedding day.

To try to get to the root of Julia's story, I've attempted to put together more of the story of her mother's life. Filomena arrived in Chicago right at the time the "devil baby of Hull House" story was going around; it's easy to imagine that she was much like the "old world" women who went looking for it, and she may well have joined in among them. Like many of these women who clung to old ways while their family became more "Americanized," she was regarded as a bit of a terror in the family; her granddaughter Flora remembered shouting, "Shut up, Nonna!" as Filomena loudly prayed the rosary in the middle of the night.

According to the family, Filomena refused to let Julia see a doctor during her pregnancy, and was racked with guilt after her death. The nightmares began around the time she moved to Los Angeles in 1926, making the turnaround time between the nightmares and the disinterment much shorter than we've generally believed. While primary sources as to how they got permission to disinter Julia and the circumstances of the exhumation remain scarce, it clearly happened in 1927, as the photo of the reasonably well-preserved corpse is right on the gravestone with an inscription reading *Questa fotografia presa dopo 6 anni morta* ("This photograph taken six years after death").

It was Henry, Julia's brother, who paid for the exhumation and the elaborate new monument, but by most accounts he wasn't happy about the expense, which Filomena seems to have guilted him into. It caused a lot of friction in the family; for that reason, it was generally not discussed, and many details have been lost to history. Both Henry and Filomena, the most likely witnesses to the exhumation, died in the 1940s; Filomena is buried in an unmarked spot a few feet away from Julia.

Julia's ghost is sometimes said to walk the cemetery in her wedding dress; one such sighting, on Halloween in 1976, made the newspapers. According to most versions of the legend, Julia appears mostly on stormy days, wandering amongst the graves untouched by the rain or wind (for the record, the day of her death, March 17, 1921, was cloudy, but dry and warm). Some also say that you can smell a strong scent of roses around her gravesite, and some people take dirt from her grave based on a belief that it has the power to cure the sick or increase fertility. The grave itself is sometimes said to glow.

If You Go

Julia's monument is just a little to the left of the Harrison Street entrance; it's hard to miss the statue. Capone is on the other side, a bit to the right of the Roosevelt entrance. Wendy, my driver, says she sometimes sees guys peeing on his grave in the middle of the night. I *assume* they aren't the ghosts of his rivals who are buried nearby, but I have to admit it'd be good for business for me if it was.

CHAPTER 24

Some "Suggested Scares"

There are some places where there haven't been many ghosts reported, but whose history certainly makes it seem as though they *ought* to be haunted...

Cabrini-Green and Little Hell
(East of Halsted, around Division Street. "Little Hell,"
the original neighborhood on the spot, extended from
Chicago Avenue to North Avenue)

Now that the last of the Cabrini-Green housing project high-rises have been torn down, the area is ripe for some ghost hunting. None of the circulating ghost stories I've heard about Cabrini hold up well enough to research to be worth investigating, but the *true* stories about the area's history, dating back *before* it was the site of the projects, are grim enough that it seems like there *ought* to be some ghosts in the area.

Oddly, most of the real stories about the neighborhood have been ignored in favor of made-up ones. One story that circulates is that on the grounds, long ago, there was an Indian war in which the blood of hundreds of braves was spilled, and that their ghosts both haunt and curse the area. This doesn't seem to have any basis in fact; the tour guide from whom I first heard it cheerfully told me it was nonsense. One of the tribes said to have fought in the war wasn't even known to have been in the area!

The other common ghost story associated with the Cabrini-Green area is the legend of the "Candy Man." The myth goes that in the late 19th century, there was a wealthy farmer who hired a young black painter, the son of a slave, to paint a portrait of his daughter. When the painter and the daughter fell in love and she became pregnant, the father was furious, and had the young man killed. His hand was sawed off by a hired mob who chased him to the area where Cabrini-Green would one day stand, then he was covered in honey and set ablaze, causing the honey to caramelize and turning him into a "candy man" as he burned to a painful death. His ashes were scattered over Cabrini-Green, and now he returns to shed innocent blood and write quotes from *Hamlet* on bathroom walls, leaving a trail of bees in his wake.

The legend states that the Candy Man will not bother you if you're smart enough to be afraid of him, but if you're foolish enough to look in a mirror and say his name five times, he will come to kill you with the hook that replaced his sawed-off hand.

This story was presented as a regular legend well known to the people in Cabrini-Green in the first *Candy Man* movie, and even people who know that the historical tale of the guy being killed isn't real have sometimes speculated that the story began a myth that was actually told to children in the Cabrini-Green housing projects to teach them to keep their mouths shut, but even this doesn't seem to be true—not only is the myth not true, it's not even a real myth!

Willy, one of my drivers, grew up in Cabrini-Green and never heard the story until he started driving buses for ghost tours. Furthermore, the excellent 1992 film was based on a short story by Clive Barker that took place in England, not Chicago. In the sequel, the same story took place around New Orleans, for some reason. The story was not based on any real mythology.

Most of the time, when not-quite-true stories go around, it's at least an easy mistake to make, and some digging will find that the real story behind a place isn't *that* different. With Cabrini, though, the circulating stories are not only totally bogus, they're not nearly as good as the *real* history of the area.

In reality, the neighborhood bounded by Halsted, Chicago, North, and Sedgwick was, at the turn of the 20th century, a notorious Sicilian slum known as Little Hell. It had been known by that moniker since the 1870s, though parts of it back then were still part of the adjacent Irish neighborhood called Kilgubbin. "Every conceivable form of sin abounds there," wrote missionary Seth Cook Rees. "The streets are narrow, dark, filthy, and abound with dirty, ragged children." When Rees's missionary friends first set foot in the neighborhood, "a horror of darkness and spiritual depression settled down on their souls, and it seemed as if brimstone was in the air, and regiments of devils confronted them." You still meet guys like Rees—sometimes they come in from the 'burbs to drink on Rush Street and brag that they had to drive through "the real ghetto" to get there.

But anyone who lived in Little Hell would certainly have some bragging rights—murder was common there, and the murderers were almost never convicted.

Death Corner

The intersection of Oak and Milton (now Oak and Cleveland) was known as "Death Corner," and averaged about a murder a week in the 1910s. A mysterious "shotgun man" popularly blamed for most of them would hide in a nook below street level and shoot people with a sawed-off gun as they passed (in reality, he was only responsible for a small handful of the many killings there). Most of the killings were said to be the result of dealings with the Black Hand, which was a group of early extortionist gangs that terrorized Chicago before Prohibition. In Little Hell, or many other Italian and Sicilian enclaves in the city, people who came into property would get letters demanding protection money signed by "The Black Hand," and could get bombed for not meeting the demands.

At least one ghost from such a killing was reported nearly a century ago. In September 1915, Anthony Romano, a reputed member of the Black Hand, was shot six times on Oak Street, a block or two west of Death Corner. A young boy witnessed the killing but refused to talk, explaining to police that "they said they would kill me." At the inquest, when asked if she knew who killed her husband, Mrs. Mary Romano said, "Yes, every night he comes to my house."

"What does he do?" asked the coroner, who thought she was talking about the murderer.

"He walks up and down the floor and shakes the bed and wants to lie down with me. I am afraid to go out of the house and go somewhere else to sleep."

"What does he look like?"

Here Mrs. Romano got confused—she had been talking about her husband's ghost, not his murderer. "Why, [he looks like] my husband," she said. "Just like he did when he was alive!"

The case appears to have remained unsolved. Little Hell was still a notorious slum when the city decided to start razing the neighborhood and replacing it with housing projects in 1941. At the time, many of the buildings still lacked running water, and basements partitioned into multiple apartments with cardboard walls were common. Only about half the buildings had bath or shower facilities; garbage was everywhere, and the violent crime rate was still twelve times higher than the average non-slum neighborhood.

Eventually, the whole neighborhood was razed to put in the Cabrini-Green high-rises. The new buildings *were* an improvement, but soon the very name Cabrini-Green came to be synonymous with violent slums. Every residence there had hot and cold running water and no families were crammed into a single room, but high-rise public housing—which seemed like a good idea at the time—simply failed as a concept in the end.

Ghost stories from the area are fairly hard to find now, and there haven't been many ghost hunts there in years. But with such a wild history, it seems as though there *ought* to be some ghosts around here.

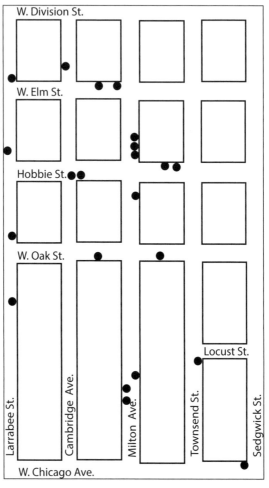

A redrawing of a newspaper diagram showing murder sites in 1916 alone actually makes "Death Corner" look relatively quiet.

With the last of the Cabrini buildings gone, there's a window of opportunity for people right now to go ghost hunting before they build a Target there (it may have been opened by the time this book comes out) and the surrounding area inevitably becomes home to more shopping centers. Will we be telling stories of a haunted Target in the future? There's already supposed to be a haunted Wal-Mart out in the 'burbs…

If You Go

Death Corner was at Oak and Milton (Milton is now known as Cleveland Avenue). It's basically a realm of deserted lots these days, and the place is ripe for some ghost hunting. The neighborhood still isn't one that I recommend wandering around alone in with too much expensive equipment (go at your own risk), but a police station is right nearby. It's currently an odd mix of empty spaces, grimy-looking liquor stores, and luxury townhouses.

Hint: Some newspapers pinpointed "Death Corner" at Oak and Cambridge, the next street to the west—in fact, just about all of the nearby corners played host to multiple killings in those days. If you don't have any luck at Oak and Cleveland, try there. Newspaper maps showing murders in the area showed dots all over the place.

CHAPTER 25

Bughouse Square

Officially known as Washington Square Park, Chicago's original "free speech park" sits just above Chicago Avenue, bounded by Clark and Dearborn on the west and east, and by Oak and Chestnut on the north and south.

"Bughouse" was once a common slang term for a mental institution, and Washington Square became known as "Bughouse Square," because it was where all the "crazy" people in town came to hang out. It's hard to imagine now, but the "Towertown" area near the Old Water Tower was once the Bohemian capital of the city: a den of commies, anarchists, radicals, and artists. Even as late as the 1950s, it was ground zero for local beatniks, who congregated nearby at Maury's Beatnik Bookstore, operated by William Lloyd Smith, who became the Beatnik Party's candidate for president in 1960.

The oldest known park in the city (or second oldest, depending on who you ask), Washington Square was once a cow pasture. It was left to the city by one Erasmus Bushnell, who supposedly said the city could have the land as a park on two conditions: the first was that a wall must be built around it (he didn't say how *high* the wall had to be, so the city got around this by putting up about four inches of limestone). The second, and best known, was that anyone who wanted to could make a speech on any subject at any time in the park.

And, up until the late 1950s, it was a very popular thing to go down to Bughouse Square, stand on a soapbox, and make a speech. On a good night, as many as three thousand people would cram into the small park to heckle the speakers. There was a colorful cast of regulars, including "Crazy Mary," "The Cosmic Kid," "One-Armed Charlie," and an assortment of hobos, lawyers, politicians, preachers, and cranks. Even now, the annual "Bughouse Square" debates bring out every conspiracy theorist and nut in the city—as well as several people with genuinely fascinating things to say.

Exploring Bughouse Square, December 2005. Photo by Jen Hathy.

Some surviving accounts show an almost carnival-like atmosphere of friendly debate between amiable weirdos and philosopher tramps, but that wasn't the tone of the place every night; the hecklers were known to get rowdy, and there were nights when things got out of hand—riots broke out from time to time, and now and then a heckler would even be killed. In 1930, a few guys were shot there, supposedly on Al Capone's orders, and one of them was killed. There was also a suicide there in 1896; a man with a tattoo reading "R.N." was found dead of a self-inflicted gunshot wound on a bench near the fountain.

It's also not impossible that a few bodies are buried beneath the park; it's right in between the original cemetery at Chicago Avenue and the City Cemetery, which stood where Lincoln Park is now—and for city parks to be used as burial places in times of disasters or epidemics is hardly unheard of. Workers in New York's Washington Square found a mysterious domed brick crypt containing twenty skeletons buried beneath the park in 1965; it was thought to house plague victims from the late 18th century. Bodies have certainly been found near Bughouse, if not actually right in it.

It was also sort of a tradition for regular speakers to have their funerals in the park. When "The Cosmic Kid" died in 1949, he was given a funeral in the park by the Chicago Druidical Society, who gave him the nearest approximation they could of a "Druidical" funeral ceremony. Historians really have very little idea of what the Druids actually did or believed (most info we have comes from really unreliable sources), but a newspaper photo of the funeral shows just about what you'd imagine: guys in white robes accompanied the coffin around the park with torches. As far as I can tell, this is the only thing the Chicago Druidical Society ever did; it seems to have been composed mainly of the Kid's fellow soap-boxers, and I'd brush it off as a joke if the surviving photos didn't make it look as though they'd spent decent money on the robes.

There's also a darker side to the park's more recent history. In the late 1970s, when the park was mostly a cruising ground for people coming out of the gay bars that lined Clark Street in those days, serial killer John Wayne Gacy would hang around dressed as a cop, threatening to arrest people if they didn't perform certain favors for him in the bushes. Whether he truly picked up any victims in the park is not known, but it's certainly not impossible. He told assistant state's attorney Lawrence Finder that the Bughouse Square area was his main "cruising ground," and it's generally thought that a few victims came from there.

So, with these stories, it's possible that there could be a ghost or two roaming about the place. It's not really in this volume as a "haunted location" so much as a "suggested investigation spot." All I can really say to back up any ghost stories is that I *did* once get an audio recording there; early in my career as a Chicago ghost hunter, I took a few microphones out there, and one of them picked up a string of swear words ending in the word *fascist*, which is a pretty good example of what a Bughouse Square heckler would have sounded like. Perhaps it was just someone nearby that I didn't notice at the time, but this "phantom foulmouth" is perhaps my favorite ghost in the city.

If You Go

Nestled in the heart of the Gold Coast, albeit alarmingly close to the drunken revelers of Rush Street and the "Viagra Triangle," the neighborhood around the park now is an odd mix of the very rich and the very drunk. However, the park is a few blocks out of the way of most tourist attractions and bars, so it's usually fairly quiet and really quite pleasant at night.

CHAPTER 26

Camp Douglas

*This Civil War prison stood between 31st and 34th Streets,
and stretched a few blocks west of Cottage Grove Avenue.
Every single other Civil War prison site is supposed to be
haunted; why shouldn't ours be?*

I've run Civil War tours in the city from time to time. One wouldn't think it would be possible to do tours like that in a city that was far away from any Civil War battle, or in a city where practically no Civil War–era building survived a fire that took place six years after the war ended, but there's really more Civil War history in town than you'd think.

For instance, the "Republican Wigwam" where Abraham Lincoln was nominated for president in 1860 stood near Wacker and Lake. Nearby, on the other side of the "Alley of Death and Mutilation" from the Iroquois Theatre site, stood the Tremont House hotel, where both Abraham Lincoln and John Wilkes Booth stayed while in Chicago;

Lincoln gave a version of his "House Divided" speech from the balcony. A short hike away from this was the McVicker's Theatre, where Booth was the hit of 1862.

Around Illinois and Dearborn, where the fire station (and former gallows site) is now, there was once a market square where Senator Stephen A. Douglas came to give a speech promoting the Kansas-Nebraska Act, which would have allowed slavery to spread out of the South. It started a mini-riot.

Down south thirty blocks or so is the monument to Douglas, which features a statue of him on top of a huge pillar. At the bottom of the pillar, you can walk right into the tomb where his sarcophagus sits. Last time I was there, they had brochures set up *on* the sarcophagus, which I thought was wonderfully tacky.

A bust (and brochures) top the sarcophagus in Senator Douglas's crypt, which is right near the site of the prison camp that bore his name.

Just south of that monument, on land the senator donated to the war effort, stood Camp Douglas. The "camp" began life as a training camp for Union troops (Chicago supplied a massive number of soldiers for the Union), but it soon become a jail for Confederate prisoners of war. About 15,000 prisoners were held there over the course of the war, and about a third of those men would die there. Most of the bodies were taken to the old City Cemetery at Lincoln Park (see chapter 11), but many others seem to have been buried on the grounds. Some are probably still there.

Stories of prisoners being tortured there are fairly common, as they are at any Civil War prison site. Smallpox ravaged the camp occasionally. Starvation and cold weather were constant dangers. And, through it all, the young daughters of Colonel B. J. Sweet, the guy in charge, would wander cheerfully around, singing, "Are you all dead yet?" to the tune of the bugler's sick call. They must have been delightful children.

Much of the grounds is now just empty fields, though there are a few high-rise apartment buildings on the grounds as well. There have recently been some archaeological digs on the grounds; workers have just uncovered some original foundations of one of the buildings.

Reports of ghosts in the Camp Douglas area have trickled in from time to time. One woman who came to one of my library talks told me that she'd always been told to avoid the area around 33rd Street as a child because there were Civil War ghosts there.

My own crew went out there one night, and at one point thought we heard a person shouting at us across the field. When we looked back, we saw nothing. The voice wasn't audible on our recording, and the investigation turned out to be otherwise futile, but recently other groups have been making far more ambitious investigations here, and it may be that Camp Douglas will one day be counted among the most notable haunted spots in town.

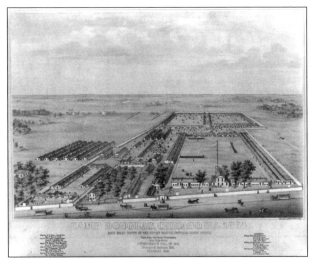

Camp Douglas, where roughly five thousand prisoners of war perished.

After all, it's hard to imagine that Camp Douglas *isn't* haunted. Who ever heard of a Civil War graveyard, prison, battle site, or hospital that wasn't supposed to be haunted? Like abandoned asylums and prisons, Civil War sites are practically *always* said to be home to all kinds of ghosts.

Another Nearby Mystery

The Winchester Mystery House—where Sarah Winchester let the spirits of men killed by Winchester rifles dictate the construction of a wild and crazy mansion—is one of the San Francisco Bay Area's biggest tourist attractions these days.

The mansion features doors to nowhere, stairways that lead to walls, secret passages, and blind hallways galore.

Once upon a time, we had similar house in Chicago. In the Civil War days, the *Chicago Times* was a phenomenally racist newspaper that wrote some of the most colorful anti-Lincoln and pro-slavery articles of the era. The publisher, Wilbur F. Storey, is still vaguely remembered in Civil War circles for his response to the Gettysburg Address, which he described as "silly, flat, dishwatery utterances."

Storey may not have been completely sane from the get-go, but he lost much of whatever sanity he had toward the end of his life, when he let the voices in his head (mainly one that he called "Little Squaw" and who called him "White Chief") tell him how to squander his personal fortune building a tremendous white marble mansion at 43rd Street and Vincennes Avenue.

By most accounts, the inside of "Storey Castle" (also known as "Storey's Folly") was a massive maze that may have even rivaled the Winchester House for trap doors and blind alleys. In one of his more lucid moments, while being taken out for exercise by an aide, Storey is said to have gazed long and hard at the unfinished building and said, "I wonder what damned fool is putting that up?"

The building was unfinished at the time of Storey's death, and no photograph is known to exist—just a couple of line drawings from newspapers—but it seems to have loomed large in the imaginations of children who grew up while it was standing. The last bits weren't removed from the grounds until 1906, and some of the marble may still be visible in the Bronzeville neighborhood, since the materials were reused in new houses nearby. One paper said there were enough materials to furnish housing for fifty new houses that could each hold a family of five, including more than a million bricks. An 1892 newspaper from Kalamazoo stated that neighbors had seen Storey's ghost walking around the vicinity.

A surviving image of the long-lost "Storey Castle."

If You Go

Most of the grounds are accessible for walking around; just don't make too much noise and pester the people in the high-rises nearby. Some say the neighborhood isn't great, but I've never had an issue there. Some people say that about *every* neighborhood that isn't the Magnificent Mile.

CHAPTER 27

Other Notable Haunts

No one can possibly put out a complete book of Chicago ghost stories—nearly every old building seems to have a ghost story attached to it. Here are some notable ones that I know about but haven't explored in too much depth (and a few that I've explored and investigated without enough success to warrant longer entries).

The Hotel Florence

11111 S. Forrestville Avenue

This old hotel sits in the neighborhood of Pullman, once a town itself that George Pullman built for his employees, and which he ruled with an iron fist. There were lots of violent labor strikes in the Pullman era, and old man Pullman himself was buried in a secure crypt surrounded by tons of cement to keep his body safe from vandals (see also the section on the "Headless Horseman of 49th Street" in this chapter).

The finest building in Pullman was the Hotel Florence, the only place in the area that served liquor (though Pullman workers couldn't drink there—only Mr. Pullman and his guests could). There was one nasty crime in which a maid had her eyes shot out by her estranged husband (though she lived).

In recent years, reports have come in that some workers occasionally assigned to or around the building (delivery workers, etc.) swear that it's haunted.

I first heard reports while the building was undergoing renovation; ghost hunters don't agree on much, but many note that ghost reports tend to increase during renovations.

The Hotel Florence as it appeared in the 1970s, when it was photographed for the National Register of Historic Places. Not many particularly gruesome deaths can be traced to it, but it sure looks haunted.

The Biograph Theater and Dillinger's Alley
2433 N. Lincoln Avenue

John Dillinger saw his last movie, *Manhattan Melodrama*, in 1934 at the Biograph Theater, which still stands. On his way out, he was pursued by FBI agents who shot him to death in the nearby alley, which is now a common attraction of Chicago ghost tours. Rumors have long held that you can sometimes see a glowing blue figure—the ghost of Dillinger—running down the alley. I've never met anyone who actually saw this, though, and have never been all that impressed with the alley as a haunted spot. I still take tour groups there now and then, though, so perhaps something will happen to change my mind one day.

Holy Family Cathedral
1080 W. Roosevelt Road

Father Damen is sometimes said to haunt this church, as well as the adjacent St. Ignatius school. There are also stories of a priest being led to give last rites to a dying woman by the ghosts of her sons, who are memorialized with a couple of statues inside of the cathedral. Also, the church has one impressive collection of holy relics, if you're into that sort of thing.

The Drake Hotel
140 E. Walton Street

The Drake doesn't seem to be as comfortable with publicizing its ghost stories as some hotels are, but you can get some interesting stories if you catch the security guards at just the right time. Stories go around about a Woman in Red said to be the ghost of a woman who jumped to her death there on New Year's Eve in 1920. I couldn't find a historical story to back it up, though there were a few suicides there over the years, and my team's investigation determined that it *could* have been covered up. The hotel was advertising itself as the finest in the world and certainly wouldn't have wanted the story to get out. Many of the windows would have led the woman to fall not on the sidewalk, but on a setback a few stories up, from which a body could conceivably have been removed without attracting the attentions of the press. Still, though every employee knows the story of the Woman in Red, I've never found one who could relate a firsthand account.

There's also a story about Woman in Black. There is a historical story about such a woman there, but she was the murder*er*, not the murder*ee*. In 1944 Adele Born Williams, a socialite, was shot to death in her suite; she lived long enough to say that the killer was an old woman in a black fur coat who shot her with an antique pistol. The case was one of the most tantalizing of the year, and it was never solved.

Employees sometimes speak of the "Captain's Quarters," a little nook in the hotel's famous restaurant, the Cape Cod Room, as being spooky. And it *is* spooky, but it's one of those places that would be spooky no matter where it was. It could be in the middle of Disney World and it would still be spooky (indeed, some of the art on the walls reminds me of a painting in the Haunted Mansion).

The Field Museum

In the 1930s, a security guard heard a scream coming from the Egyptian wing, and found one of the mummies lying face down. Henry Field, an anthropologist and nephew of Marshall Field himself, investigated, and found that nothing could have shaken the building enough to knock the mummy over, and that no human could have gotten into the sealed case (there were poisons floating around inside of it to protect the mummies). Exactly which mummy it was is now a mystery—it's usually said to be Harwa, who in life was the Doorkeeper of the Temple of Amun, but Field described the mummy as having a "naked withered body," and Harwa is covered up like a decent and respectable mummy. Field called it "just one more example of things we cannot explain."

The Dybbuk of Bunker Street

Bunker Street hasn't existed since the 1920s; it's now Grenshaw Street, which shows up occasionally, a block or so at a time, at the 1100 South portion of the grid in the southern portion of the Loop (one block north of Roosevelt Road), and stretched from the Loop to the Near West Side around an area that was then called "Satan's Mile."

In 1902, an outbreak of typhoid fever in the crowded neighborhood was blamed on a "dybbuk," a demon-like spirit in Jewish folklore. Even after being told about how crowded conditions and overflowing toilets could spread disease, old women in the neighborhood continued to insist that the sickness was caused by a dybbuk, which, they said, a rabbi could expel from the body of a righteous person, but could not be exorcised from a sinner.

Surviving descriptions of the area around Bunker and Halsted Streets do make it seem as though the place was ripe for typhoid. A witness who spoke to the Federal Writers' Project about the dybbuk in 1939 said that there were six families living in her house, which was built to hold only one, and that all the families, some with as many as eight children, shared one single toilet at the end of a hall.

Still, though typhoid was also common in the Irish neighborhoods, the old women insisted that whenever a Jew on Bunker Street became sick, or when a child went astray and was sent to reform school, that the dybbuk had gotten into them. Even when told that the sickness was spread by flies, they simply explained that a dybbuk could get into both the smallest and largest things, and must have gotten into the flies.

The story was said to have died out after a Jewish girl married an Irish boy and neither of them were killed off by the dybbuk (or the devil, as the Irish neighbors expected), but it remained a topic of conversation. Hilda, the woman who told the story, joined a gang as a teenager and ended up spending years in prison before tiring of the life and opening a cigar shop on the South Side. "Just the other day," she said, "an old neighbor came into the store. What do you think we talked about? The dybbuk of Bunker Street!"

Folklore says that uttering something blasphemous—such as "I would rather have the next baby be a devil than another girl"—can summon a dybbuk. Given Bunker Street's proximity to the Hull House neighborhood, it's to be assumed that many of the women who spoke of the dybbuk in 1902 were among the same women who spoke of the devil baby a decade later.

The Old Water Tower
806 N. Michigan Avenue

Some say that the Water Tower is haunted by the ghost of a guy who hanged himself inside of it during the Great Fire; stories go around that people have seen his silhouette swinging back and forth in the windows. I've never been able to see much of *anything* through those windows. That it was built over an abandoned graveyard probably shouldn't be ignored.

Water Tower Place
835 N. Michigan Avenue

Many employees at the shopping mall near the Water Tower say that they've seen a gray, ghostly man whose most memorable feature is his black shoes.

Old Lady Tillie Klimek's House
900 block of N. Winchester Avenue[18]

Tillie Klimek's full name by the time of her 1923 trial was Otillie Grubrek-Mitzkiewicz-Ruskowski-Kupszyk-Klimek. While only convicted of one murder, she seems to have been very much in the habit of poisoning men that she married (and possibly some other family members and neighbors as well), and was even known to sit at their deathbeds making fun of them. She lived in several houses in the Ukrainian Village, a few of which are still standing. Her old house near Winchester and Augusta has been rumored to be haunted—I received several emails from people associated with the building after blogging about it—but there have been no concrete sightings yet that I know of.

The Stockyards
Exchange Avenue and Peoria Street

I swear that sometimes you can still smell the old stockyards in the area around the gate. When the stockyards were

---

18. Again, the actual address is known, but in order to protect the privacy of the current residents, I'm not putting it in the book.

in operation, the officers at the stockyards' police station, which stood at 4762 S. Halsted (in post-1909 numbering), told stories about a ghostly man in a flowing white beard who would show up at the door during snowstorms. It is very difficult not to make a crack about Santa Claus here, but police believed it to be the ghost of an old soldier who had trekked through the snow to the police station one night around 1902, asking for shelter from the storm. He died in the station overnight.

As was done with the ghosts who appeared in the snow in Lincoln Park, some suggested that this was just an optical illusion formed by the snow swirling in the wind. This seems like a responsible way to look at things, but next time it's snowing, open your door and see if you can possibly imagine mistaking the swirling snow for a man in a white beard.

Many were the deaths at the stockyards—workers occasionally died from the abominable conditions in the slaughterhouses; streetcars, trains, and trolleys seemed to collide or explode near the gates with alarming regularity; all sorts of riots took place in the yards; and a great many killers were brought into the stockyards' police station for booking at one time or another. There were a number of deadly fires there, including one in 1910 that claimed the lives of twenty-one firefighters. Just behind the still-standing gates now sits a monument listing the names of all firefighters killed on duty in Chicago.

Among the names is that of Francis Leavy, who became the subject of a Chicago ghost story himself; the morning he was killed, he is said to have rested his hand against a window at the fire station at 13th and Oakley and told colleagues that it would be his last day with the fire department. That very day, a blaze at Curran Hall killed Leavy, along with seven others. His handprint was still visible on the window the next day, and could not be washed off. According to legend, the handprint remained on the spot for twenty years, until the window was broken by a paperboy throwing a newspaper through it on the anniversary of the fire. Some say that a photograph of the handprint on the window was published in a firefighter's newsletter some years ago, but no photo of it is currently in circulation.

The stockyards area continues to be an area that turns up in "news of the weird" columns occasionally—recently, an alligator was found in "Bubbly Creek," the polluted creek that ran through the grounds.

An abandoned fire station on the stockyards grounds. Twenty-one men stationed here perished in a 1910 blaze. Perhaps the ghost with the white beard still wanders the stockyards on snowy nights, looking for a new place, since the stockyards' police station was discontinued in 1961.

Carl Wanderer Murder Site
4732 N. Campbell Avenue

Carl Wanderer, sometimes suspected to haunt the site where he was hanged, is also said to have created a couple of ghosts when he shot his wife and the mysterious drifter outside of the house; rumor has it that screams have been heard here (see chapter 2 for more on Wanderer).

Screaming Lizzie
5100 N. Lincoln Avenue

Here on the Northwest Side, one Lizzie Kausehull was killed by Edward Rodhaubt. Edward had been stalking Lizzie, following her home from the streetcar stop daily, pestering her to marry him. On November 18, 1905, he ran up to her at this spot and stabbed her four times before shooting himself in the head. Some say screams are heard here on full moons.

Mrs. Murphy and Sons Irish Bistro
3905 N. Lincoln Avenue

A fine restaurant and pub built into the old Burkhard Undertaking parlor, about which some pretty grisly rumors have swirled. Neighborhood gossip told of corpses being violated, and of mobsters "double dipping" by burying second bodies in coffins. None of this is definitively known to be true, but we do know that the corpses of Lizzie Kausehull ("Screaming Lizzie," see previous paragraph) and her killer, Edward Rodhaubt, were taken here in 1905.

The Headless Horseman of 49th Street

W. 49th Street and S. Loomis Street

It's occasionally said that the railroad tracks here are haunted by the headless ghost of a cavalryman who was killed during the Pullman Strikes in 1894. No such beheading seems to have taken place, though 49th and Loomis *was* the site of a bloody battle in July of that year, as soldiers began to fire on striking workers. Striking workers had been making plans to disrupt rail service to protest George Pullman's treatment of them; soldiers were given orders to fire on any man seen tampering with railroad property, and the troops were told to shoot to kill. Several workers, and at least one onlooker, were killed—some by gunshots, some by bayonet.

The railroad tracks on 49th Street. The story may not completely hold up, but if I were a headless horseman, this is just where I'd ride.

However, though newspapers and police memoirs detailed all of the casualties, no mention was made of anyone being beheaded, and the tracks currently on the site aren't exactly the same ones that stood in 1894; they were grade level at the time, and were elevated to their current height a few years later. Still, the fact that a backstory isn't quite right doesn't always mean that the ghost isn't real—there *were* plenty of accidents on those tracks over the years—and the place sure *looks* like the sort of place where a headless horseman would show up.

Germania Place

1538 N. Clark Street

Situated right near Lincoln Park, within sight of the Couch tomb, Germania Place is an 1888 ballroom that was once home to the choir who sang at Abraham Lincoln's Chicago funeral. A mysterious man's silhouette has been seen around the place. Cooks and chefs there are said to believe that this ballroom is haunted.

"Saint Julian's Hospital"

Several employees of the hospital (who, for obvious reasons, insist on anonymity) tell me that one particular wing, which was once a pediatric ward, is haunted, like so many other places, by the ghost of a little girl.

It seems that whenever a patient reports that there's a little girl in their room, everyone in the ward knows that person is going to die that day. Nurses seem fairly casual about this. "We'll hear them saying, 'Who's that little girl?'" one told me, "and we'll say, 'Uh oh, it looks like Mr. Jones is going to die tonight.'"

Those of you who went to look this place up without reading this paragraph have no doubt noticed that there is no Saint Julian's Hospital in Chicago. But I am strictly, strictly, *strictly* not allowed to put the actual name of this hospital in a book. I tried to come up with a more generic name, like St. James or one of the other saints, but it seems that half the saints in the world have an actual hospital bearing their name somewhere in Chicagoland, except for Saint Julian, whom I always thought was neat because he's simultaneously the patron saint of wandering musicians, murderers, and clowns.

Bibliography

Personal Correspondence

Ursula Bielski has said many times that simply talking to people is a better way to track ghosts than any piece of equipment on the market, and I agree. One firsthand account of seeing a ghost in the alley behind the Oriental Theatre is worth a million EMF-meter readings to me.

Many firsthand witnesses declined to be named, for obvious reasons, but this work has been greatly enriched by my talks with the many historians, writers, witnesses, scholars, and ghost hunters with whom I've had the privilege of corresponding, including, but not limited to:

Jean Marie Andersen, Pamela Bannos, Ursula Bielski, James C., Circuit Court of Cook County Archives, Congress Hotel staff, Dave Cowan, Pete Crapia, Drake Hotel staff, Jen Hathy, Richard Herrera, Rory Hood, Judy Huff-Felz, Ray Johnson, Lisa Junkin, Dale Kaczmarek, Seth Kleinschrodt, Stephanie Kuehnert, Terry Larkin, Patricia Brougham

Linkowsi, Robert Loerzel, Dane Ladwig, Lexie Manke, El-
liott Mason, Jeff Mudgett, "Resurrection Nelson," the Newberry Library, Daniel Pinkwater, Erin Pieschke, Pilgrim
Operations Inc., Rago Brothers Funeral Home, Hector
Reyes, Ken Scholes, Susan Sherman, Frank Skony, John Stephenson, Troy Taylor, Harold Washington Library, Wendy
Weaver, Willy Williams, and Jason Wisser.

Records
Criminal Court
Stone v. People
Hoch v. People
Cardinella v. People
Quinlan v. Badenoch
Commonwealth v. Holmes

Miscellaneous
Caroline E. Couch (probate files)
Sanborn Fire Insurance maps
And countless census forms, marriage records, death certifi-
    cates, draft cards, and other such public records

Web
Bannos, Pamela. *Hidden Truths: The Chicago City Cemetery
    and Lincoln Park*. http://hiddentruths.northwestern.edu.

Books and Articles
Addams, Jane. *The Long Road of Woman's Memory*. Chicago:
    Macmillan, 1917.

———. *Twenty Years at Hull-House.* Chicago: Macmillan, 1911.

———. "Why the Ward Boss Rules." *The Outlook*, April 2, 1898.

Andreas, A. T. *History of Chicago, Volume 1.* Chicago: A. T. Andreas, 1886.

Asbury, Herbert. *Gem of the Prairie.* New York: Knopf, 1940.

Beardsley, Richard, and Rosalie Hankey. "The Vanishing Hitchhiker." *California Folklore Quarterly*, vol. 1, no. 4 (October 1942): 303–35.

Bell, Michael E. *Food for the Dead: On the Trail of New England's Vampires.* New York: Carroll & Graf, 2001.

Bernstein, Arnie. *The Hoofs and Guns of the Storm.* Chicago: Lake Claremont Press, 2003.

Bielski, Ursula. *Chicago Haunts: Ghostly Lore of the Windy City.* Chicago: Lake Claremont Press, 1998.

Bielski, Ursula, and Matt Hucke. *Graveyards of Chicago.* Chicago: Lake Claremont Press, 1998.

Bowen, Louise de Koven. *Open Windows: Stories of People and Places* Chicago: R. F. Seymour, 1946.

Corbitt, Robert. *The Holmes Castle.* Chicago: Corbitt and Morrison, 1895.

Crowe, Richard T. *Chicago's Street Guide to the Supernatural.* Oak Park, IL: Carolando Press, 2000.

Eig, Jonathan. *Get Capone: The Secret Plot That Captured America's Most Wanted Gangster.* New York: Simon & Schuster, 2010.

Everett, Marshall. *The Great Chicago Theater Disaster*. New York: Publishers Union of America, 1904.

Field, Henry. *The Track of Man: Adventures of an Anthropologist*. London: Peter Davies, 1955.

Gale, Edwin. *Reminisces of Early Chicago and Vicinity*. Chicago: Lakeside Press, 1912.

Henderson, Harold. "Grave Mistake: How Did the Old County Cemetery Get in the Way of Ridgemoor Estates?" *Chicago Reader*, September 21, 1989.

Hull, Charles J. *Reflections of a Busy Life*. Chicago: Knight and Leonard, 1881.[19]

Kaczmarek, Dale. *Windy City Ghosts*. Alton, IL: Whitechapel Productions Press, 2000.

Johnson, Raymond. *Chicago's Haunt Detective*. Atglen, PA: Schiffer Publishing, 2011.

Larson, Erik. *The Devil in the White City*. New York: Crown Publishers, 2003.

LaVey, Anton. *The Devil's Notebook*. Port Townsend, WA: Feral House, 1991.

Loerzel, Robert. *Alchemy of Bones: Chicago's Luetgert Murder Case of 1897*. Urbana: University of Illinois Press, 2003.

Polacheck, Hilda. Interview with Federal Writers' Project, July 6, 1939.

Selzer, Adam. *Devil Babies* (e-book). Woodbury, MN: Llewellyn, 2012.

---

19. This book is something of an oddity; publishers list the date as 1881, but the copy available from the Newberry Library, one of only a few in circulation, contains diary entries from some years after that.

———. *Inside the Murder Castle* (e-book). Woodbury, MN: Llewellyn, 2012.

———. *The Resurrection Mary Files* (e-book). Woodbury, MN: Llewellyn, 2012.

———. *Three Terrifying Tales from Chicago* (e-book). Woodbury, MN: Llewellyn, 2012.

———. *Your Neighborhood Gives Me the Creeps*. Woodbury, MN: Llewellyn, 2009.

Terkel, Studs. *Touch and Go: A Memoir*. New York: The New Press, 2007.

Williams, Mentor. "John Kinzie's Narrative of the Fort Dearborn Massacre." *Journal of the Illinois State Historical Society*, vol. 46 (Winter 1953).

Wooldridge, Clifton. *Hands Up! In the World of Crime: or, 12 Years a Detective*. Chicago: Thompson & Thomas, 1901.

Much of my research is done in newspaper archives; to list every article I perused in the course of research would necessitate a bibliography as long as this book. Here are some of the most useful articles, listed in chronological order:

"Border Ruffian Sexton Robbing Graves," *Chicago Tribune*, November 9, 1857.

"Splendid Vault," *Chicago Tribune*, August 14, 1858.

"The Spirit of the Jail," *Chicago Tribune*, December 13, 1867.

"Body Snatching: Thrilling Adventure with Resurrectionist at the Pauper Burying Ground," *Chicago Tribune*, February 8, 1870.

"A Ghastly Array," *Chicago Tribune*, February 28, 1875.

"Talking with a Professional Subject Gatherer," *Chicago Tribune*, June 23, 1878.

"A Notable Charity: The Home for the Aged Poor as Managed by the Little Sisters," *Chicago Tribune*, July 6, 1879.

"… To Eternity," *Chicago Tribune*, November 12, 1887.

"Vampire of Lakeview," *Chicago Tribune*, November 4, 1888.

"Miss Culver's Fortune," *Chicago Tribune*, February 21, 1889.

"Hid in Secret Room," *Chicago Tribune*, March 31 1893.

"Is a Day of Blood: Soldiers Shoot Down Rioters in Many Railroad Yards," *Chicago Tribune*, July 8, 1894.

"Honor Their Dead,"*Chicago Tribune*, May 26, 1895.

"Connor's Story Told: What He Knows of Holmes and His Crimes," *Chicago Daily Inter-Ocean*, July 26, 1895.

"Castle Is a Tomb," *Chicago Tribune*, July 28, 1895.

"Not in the Castle: Anna Williams Probably Killed on North Side," *Chicago Daily Inter-Ocean*, July 28, 1895.

"More About Holmes: Another 'Castle' Explored," *Chicago Record*, August 22, 1895.

"Another Holmes Building Found," *New York Times*, August 23, 1895.

"Holmes' Evil Eye," *New York World*, April 19, 1896.

"Ghost Didn't Walk," *Chicago Daily Inter-Ocean*, May 9, 1896.

"Agatha Tosch Testifies," *Chicago Tribune*, September 1, 1897.

"Bury Free of Cost," *Chicago Tribune*, September 12, 1897.

"Spooks at Sag Bridge," *Chicago Tribune*, September 20, 1897.

"Skeletons of Nine Indians: They Were Dug Up at Sag Bridge, Ill.—The People See Ghosts," *New York Times*, December 3, 1897.

"Visited By Ghosts," *Chicago Tribune*, February 13, 1898.

"North Clark Street's Fight Against Vice," *Chicago Tribune*, September 4, 1898.

"Captain Ostheim, Officer Who Shot Himself," *Chicago Tribune*, April 10, 1900.

"Ghosts Dwell in Chicago," *Chicago Tribune*, January 27, 1901.

"Ghost of Mrs. Luetgert," *Des Moines Daily News*, April 4, 1901.

"Chicago's Ghost Castle," *The Massillon Independent* (Massillon, Ohio), October 3, 1902.

"Crowd Excited by Alleged Ghost of Murdered Man," *Chicago Tribune*, December 1, 1902.

"571 Dead Bodies Found in Ruins," *Chicago Tribune*, December 31, 1903.

"In the Alley of Death and Mutilation: Jumping from the Fire Escapes to Escape the Flames," *Chicago Tribune*, December 31, 1903.

"Curtain Bought Because Cheap," *Chicago Tribune*, January 2, 1904.

"Ghouls Reaped a Harvest," *New York Times*, January 3, 1904.

"Hand of Ghoul Found in Debris of Iroquois Theatre," *San Jose Evening News*, January 14, 1904.

"Is the County Jail Haunted?" *Chicago Tribune*, October 21, 1906.

"The Haunted Police Stations of Chicago," *Chicago Tribune*, May 5, 1907.

"How to See Ghosts," *Chicago Tribune*, June 2, 1907.

"Suicide Ends Long Debauch: Roy Gormley Shoots Himself," *Chicago Tribune*, June 9, 1908.

"100 Black Hand Brigands and 100,000 Italians Sneer at the Police," *Chicago Tribune*, March 6, 1910.

"To Open Couch Tomb," *Chicago Examiner*, May 5, 1911.

"Policeman Guards Sealed Couch Tomb," *Chicago Examiner*, May 6, 1911.

"Chicago Mystified By 'Devil Child,'" *Trenton Evening Times*, October 31, 1913.

"'Who Are You?' Thousands Ask at Huge Morgue," *Chicago Tribune*, July 26, 1915.

"Bells Toll All Day at Rites over Boat Dead," *Chicago Tribune*, July 29, 1915.

"Woman Says Murdered Husband Haunts Her," *Chicago Tribune*, September 30, 1915.

"Ghost Ship and the Solitary Mortal Who Inhabits It," *Chicago Daily News*, November 23, 1915. (Article about the *Eastland*.)

"Wanderer Dies Scorning Plea for Confession: Triple Slayer Goes to His Death Singing," *Chicago Tribune*, October 1, 1921.

"Chicago Ne'er Had a Funeral Like Genna's," *Chicago Tribune*, May 30, 1925.

"Opera Singer Dies as Crowd Awaits Him," *Chicago Tribune*, December 1, 1925.

"Girl Killed, 5 Hurt as Auto Falls in a Ditch," *Chicago Tribune*, July 21, 1927. (Article about Anna Norkus.)

"In the Wake of the News," *Chicago Tribune*, May 21, 1932. (A ghost at Couch tomb.)

"Killed in Crash," *Chicago Tribune*, March 12, 1934. (Article about Mary Bregovy.)

"Ghostly Hitch Hiker Blamed for Crash," *Salt Lake Tribune*, May 28, 1935. (This is an early Resurrection Mary account.)

"Drama in the Death House," *Chicago Tribune*, December 13, 1936. (Article about Johann Hoch.)

"Plunge Kills Mother, Two Boys," *Chicago Tribune*, August 4, 1939. (Article about the Langer family.)

"3 Chicago Deaths Blamed on Nazis," *New York Times*, August 5, 1939. (Another article about the Langers.)

"What Happened to Haunted Houses?" *Chicago Tribune*, April 7, 1957.

"Hitchhiking Hattie, Girl Ghost," *Cedar Rapids Gazette*, May 10, 1959.

"Police Probe Desecration of Cemetery," *Chicago Tribune*, April 19, 1965. (Bachelor's Grove article.)

"7 Seized in Grave Digging," *Chicago Tribune*, September 14, 1973. (Bachelor's Grove article.)

"Richard Crowe and His Favorite Chicago Haunts," *Daily Northwestern*, March 6, 1978.

"Cryptic Rider Leaves Taxi Driver with the Willies," *Chicago Tribune* (suburban pullout), January 1979.

"Legend Makes an Appearance," *The Times* (suburban weekly), September 13, 1980.

"Meet the Folks on Archer: The Dead Ones," *Chicago Tribune* (Weekend Tempo), October 29, 1982.

"Ghost Hunter Goes for Bust in the Spirit of a True Professional," *The Oregonian* (Portland), September 12, 1984.

"NU Grad's Tour Shows Chicago's Colorful, Bizarre Past," *Daily Northwestern*, October 8, 1985.

"Tavern Owner Held in Wife's Ax Killing" *Chicago Tribune*, April 10, 1986.

"Do You Believe in Ghosts?" *La Grange Suburban Life Citizen*, October 31, 1990.

Bukowski, Doug. "Chicago's Other U-Boat," *Chicago Tribune*, January 28, 1998.

Konkol, Mark. "Ghost Busted?" *Chicago Sun-Times*, October 26, 2007. (Article about Inez Clarke/Briggs.)

———. "Ghost Story Back from the Dead," *Chicago Sun-Times*, October 30, 2009. (Article about Inez Clarke/Briggs.)

Photo Credits

Louisa Luetgert: public domain . . . 94

Florentine Room shadow: photo by John Stephenson . . . 107

Lincoln funeral train: available from the Library of
    Congress . . . 114

Procession at Old Courthouse during Lincoln's funeral:
    available from the Library of Congress . . . 115

Mask at Old Town Tatu: photo taken by the author . . . 133

Tomb of Ira Couch in Lincoln Park: photo taken by the
    author . . . 141

Inside the tomb of Ira Couch: photo taken by the
    author . . . 143

Johann Hoch's wives: available from the Library of
    Congress . . . 223

Snowflake at Dunning: photo taken by the author . . . 230

Bachelor's Grove: photo taken by the author . . . 236

"Infant daughter" grave: photo taken by the author . . . 242

Ghost-woman on grave: by permission of Judy
    Huff-Felz . . . 244

Scan of Judy's copy of the famous grave shot: by permis-
    sion of Judy Huff-Felz . . . 245

The author on the gravesite: photo taken by
    Jen Hathy . . . 247

Hull House exterior: photo taken by the author . . . 251

Baby ghost at Hull House: photo taken by Jean Marie
    Andersen . . . 272

Stairs at Hull House: photo taken by the author . . . 276

Eternal Silence: photo taken by the author . . . 281

To Write to the Author

If you wish to contact the author or would like more information about this book, please write to the author in care of Llewellyn Worldwide Ltd. and we will forward your request. Both the author and publisher appreciate hearing from you and learning of your enjoyment of this book and how it has helped you. Llewellyn Worldwide Ltd. cannot guarantee that every letter written to the author can be answered, but all will be forwarded. Please write to:

Adam Selzer
℅ Llewellyn Worldwide
2143 Wooddale Drive
Woodbury, MN 55125-2989

Please enclose a self-addressed stamped envelope for reply,
or $1.00 to cover costs. If outside the USA, enclose
an international postal reply coupon.

GET MORE AT **LLEWELLYN.COM**

Visit us online to browse hundreds of our books and decks, plus sign up to receive our e-newsletters and exclusive online offers.

- **Free tarot readings • Spell-a-Day • Moon phases**
- **Recipes, spells, and tips • Blogs • Encyclopedia**
- **Author interviews, articles, and upcoming events**

GET SOCIAL WITH **LLEWELLYN**

Find us on
Facebook
www.Facebook.com/LlewellynBooks

Follow us on

www.Twitter.com/Llewellynbooks

GET BOOKS AT **LLEWELLYN**

LLEWELLYN ORDERING INFORMATION

Order online: Visit our website at www.llewellyn.com to select your books and place an order on our secure server.

Order by phone:
- Call toll free within the U.S. at 1-877-NEW-WRLD (1-877-639-9753)
- Call toll free within Canada at 1-866-NEW-WRLD (1-866-639-9753)
- We accept VISA, MasterCard, and American Express

Order by mail:
Send the full price of your order (MN residents add 6.875% sales tax) in U.S. funds, plus postage and handling to: Llewellyn Worldwide, 2143 Wooddale Drive Woodbury, MN 55125-2989

STAGE AND HANDLING
ANDARD (U.S. & Canada):
ase allow 12 business days)
5.00 and under, add $4.00.
5.01 and over, FREE SHIPPING.

TERNATIONAL ORDERS (airmail only):
.00 for one book, plus $3.00 for
h additional book.

t us online for more shipping options.
es subject to change.

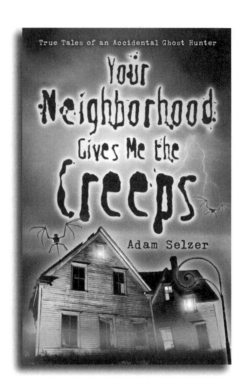

True Tales of an Accidental Ghost Hunter

Your Neighborhood Gives Me the Creeps

Adam Selzer

Your Neighborhood Gives Me the Creeps
True Tales of an Accidental Ghost Hunter
ADAM SELZER

Getting pushed down the stairs by unseen hands? An old spirit hag sitting on your chest, holding you down? Strange glowing ectoplasm escaping from a grave? Don't believe everything you hear . . . but then again, some things can't just be brushed off.

Come aboard the ghost bus and get a glimpse of Chicago's ghostly goings-on. With a healthy dose of skepticism, professional ghostbuster Adam Selzer takes you on a tour of his famously spooky town and the realm of the weird. Tag along with your tour guide Selzer, as well as bus driver and improv comic Hector, psychic detective Ken, and prolific author Troy Taylor, as they uncover cool evidence of the supernatural. Entertaining and thought-provoking, this book will make believers and skeptics alike want to tromp through their local cemetery to see if it's really haunted (or just dark and creepy).

978-0-7387-1557-5, 288 pp., 5³⁄₁₆ x 8   **$15.95**

RICHARD SOUTHALL

HAUNTED

ROUTE 66

GHOSTS OF AMERICA'S LEGENDARY HIGHWAY

Haunted Route 66
Ghosts of America's Legendary Highway
RICHARD SOUTHALL

Pack the bags, hop in the car, and head west on a haunted journey of spine-tingling history and paranormal activity along legendary Route 66! This travel companion brings you from Chicago to Santa Monica, California, investigating over one hundred ghostly hotspots filled with fascinating facts and lingering spirits.

From amateur and professional ghost hunters to nostalgic fans, everyone can take their own haunted adventure on Route 66. Discover the famous highway through historic locations and gripping ghost stories about Al Capone and the gang wars of Chicago, Charlie Chaplin and the Venice Beach boardwalk in Los Angeles, and much more. This one-of-a-kind collection, with chapters organized by state, paves the way for your grand tour.

978-0-7387-2636-6, 240 pp., 6 x 9   **$15.99**